Integrating Socio-Legal Studies into the Law Curriculum

Palgrave Macmillan Socio-Legal Studies

Series Editor

David Cowan, Professor of Law and Policy, University of Bristol, UK

Editorial Board

Dame Hazel Genn, Professor of Socio-Legal Studies, University College London, UK

Fiona Haines, Associate Professor, School of Social and Political Science, University of Melbourne, Australia

Herbert Kritzer, Professor of Law and Public Policy, University of Minnesota, USA

Linda Mulcahy, Professor of Law, London School of Economics and Political Science, UK

Carl Stychin, Professor of Law and Social Theory, University of Reading, UK

Mariana Valverde, Professor of Criminology, University of Toronto, USA

Sally Wheeler, Professor of Law, Queen's University Belfast, UK

Integrating Socio-Legal Studies into the Law Curriculum

Edited by

Caroline Hunter
University of York, UK

palgrave
macmillan

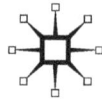
First published 2012 by
PALGRAVE MACMILLAN

Palgrave Macmillan in the UK is an imprint of Macmillan Publishers Limited,
registered in England, company number 785998, of Houndmills, Basingstoke,
Hampshire RG21 6XS.

Palgrave Macmillan in the US is a division of St Martin's Press LLC,
175 Fifth Avenue, New York, NY 10010.

Palgrave Macmillan is the global academic imprint of the above companies
and has companies and representatives throughout the world.

Palgrave® and Macmillan® are registered trademarks in the United States,
the United Kingdom, Europe and other countries.

ISBN 978-0-230-30448-2   ISBN 978-1-137-01603-4 (eBook)
DOI 10.1007/978-1-137-01603-4

This book is printed on paper suitable for recycling and made from fully
managed and sustained forest sources. Logging, pulping and manufacturing
processes are expected to conform to the environmental regulations of the
country of origin.

A catalogue record for this book is available from the British Library.

A catalog record for this book is available from the Library of Congress.

10 9 8 7 6 5 4 3 2 1
21 20 19 18 17 16 15 14 13 12

Contents

Part II Socio-Legal Studies in the Foundation Subjects

Acknowledgments

We would like to thank the Nuffield Foundation for their support for this book. The Nuffield Foundation is an endowed charitable trust that aims to improve social well-being in the widest sense. It funds research and innovation in education and social policy and also works to build capacity in education, science and social science research. The Nuffield Foundation has funded the survey and workshop that led to this book and has contributed generously towards the costs of the book itself, but the views expressed are those of the authors and not necessarily those of the Foundation. More information is available at www.nuffieldfoundation.org.

The workshop was also supported by the United Kingdom Centre for Legal Education (UKCLE), which sadly closed in July 2011.

Our thanks go out to all those who took part in both the survey and, in particular, in the workshop.

Contributors

Rosemary Auchmuty is Professor of Law at the University of Reading, where she teaches Land Law and Equity and Trusts. She also teaches English Land Law and Equity and Trusts to French undergraduates at the Université Paris-Ouest, Nanterre Le Defense. Her research interests, apart from property law, include gender, sexuality, legal history and popular culture.

Sarah Blandy is Reader in Property Law at the University of Leeds, where she teaches Equity and Trusts as well as the Advanced Legal Research and Law Reform module. She has conducted empirical socio-legal research into a range of housing-related issues, including gated communities, housing possession cases and most recently a qualitative study of residents' experiences of sharing space in multi-occupied housing.

David Cowan is Professor of Law and Policy at the University of Bristol. He is also the editor of the Palgrave Macmillan Socio-Legal Studies series.

Karen Devine is a Lecturer in Law at Kent Law School, University of Kent, where she teaches on undergraduate modules in both Obligations and Medical Law. Her research interests lie in medical negligence, in particular the relationship between legal obligations and bodily integrity, and the role of informed consent. Her PhD examined the legal implications of umbilical-cord blood stem cell collection, including an empirical study within the National Health Service (NHS) on the use of third parties in the procurement of the cells.

Simon Halliday is a Professor of Law at the University of York and a Conjoint Professor of Law at the University of New South Wales, Australia. He teaches Public Law at the University of York. His research examines the significance of law for public administration. He is the author of *The Appeal of Internal Review* (with D Cowan, 2003 Oxford: Hart Publishing) and *Judicial Review and Compliance with Administrative Law* (2004 Oxford: Hart Publishing). He is editor of *Human Rights Brought Home: Socio-Legal Perspectives on Human Rights in the National Context* (with P Schmidt, 2004 Oxford: Hart Publishing) and *Conducting Law and Society Research: Reflections on Methods and Practices* (with P Schmidt, 2009 Cambridge: Cambridge University Press).

Caroline Hunter is Professor of Law at York Law School, University of York, where she teaches on undergraduate modules in both Property and Public Law. Her research interests lie in housing law and she has conducted a number of externally funded empirical studies on housing possession cases, the governance of anti-social behaviour and the treatment of homeless applicants.

Morag McDermont is a Senior Lecturer in the Law School at Bristol University where she teaches Socio-Legal Studies and Public Law. Her research interests include: the application of social theory, in particular governmentality perspectives, to socio-legal inquiry; social housing and the third sector; administrative law. She has recently been awarded a four-year grant by the European Research Council for a programme of work: 'New sites of legal consciousness: a case study of UK advice agencies'.

Bronwen Morgan is Professor of Socio-Legal Studies at the University of Bristol and teaches Jurisprudence, Public Law and Socio-Legal Studies to undergraduates as well as Socio-Legal Studies to postgraduates. Her research interests focus on regulation and global governance, and she has conducted externally funded empirical research on bureaucratic regulatory reform in Australia and international comparative research on the governance of access to water. Her current research focuses on community-based responses to climate change, and the rise of the regulatory state in the developing world.

Linda Mulcahy is a Professor in the Law Department at the London School of Economics where she teaches Alternative Dispute Resolution and the Law of Contract Law. Her research focuses on disputes and their resolution but she has a long-term interest in obligations. She has received a number of grants in support of empirical projects that have looked at disputes between doctors and patients, car manufacturers and dealers, neighbours and mediation of medical negligence claims and judicial review actions. A former chair of the UK Socio-Legal Studies Association and current editor of *Social and Legal Studies*, Linda brings a strong interdisciplinary flavour to her work.

Charlotte O'Brien is a Lecturer at York Law School, University of York, where she teaches EU Law and Public Law. She also teaches in the Law Clinic module. Her research interests include the realization of EU rights in the UK (particularly free movement and social security cases), access to administrative justice, equality law and principles, migration, citizenship and human rights.

Penelope Russell is a Lecturer at the School of Law, University of Sheffield, where she teaches the undergraduate module of Family Law. She supervises postgraduate dissertations and also carries out her own research projects, which are empirical and in the field of family law.

Peter Vincent-Jones is Professor of Law at the School of Law, University of Leeds. His main teaching and research interests are in contract and public law, regulation, and socio-legal studies. He has published widely on the privatization and contractualization of public services in the UK and Europe, and has been Principal Investigator for research projects funded by the Economic and Social Research Council, the NHS Service and Delivery Organisation, and the European Commission.

Matthew Weait is Professor of Law and Policy and Pro-Vice-Master (Academic Partnerships) at Birkbeck College, University of London. His core teaching is in the areas of legal methods and legal skills, and he also convenes a module on legal life writing. Matthew's research centres on the impact of law on people living with HIV. A commitment to using research and scholarship in the service of legal change has involved him in consultancy work for UNAIDS, HIV Europe and the World Health Organization, and membership of the Technical Advisory Group for the UN Development Programme-led Global Commission on HIV and the Law.

Sally Wheeler is a Professor of Law at Queen's University Belfast. She teaches on undergraduate modules in Obligations and Company Law and on Corporate Governance modules at postgraduate level. Her research interest lies in the area of corporations.

1

Introduction: Themes, Challenges and Overcoming Barriers

Caroline Hunter

The Nuffield Inquiry on Empirical Legal Research, *Law in the Real World: Improving our Understanding of How Law Works*, published in November 2006, identified a national lack of capacity in empirical legal research. A number of reasons were canvassed for this, including the historical domination of law schools by theoretical and doctrinal-based research and the constraints of the professionally influenced curriculum. Thus:

> Lacking a broad perspective on legal inquiry and constrained by a lack of skills and familiarity with empirical research, when law graduates who do consider an academic career choose postgraduate courses and topics for doctoral research, they naturally gravitate towards doctrinal topics and issues in law. (Nuffield Inquiry, 2006, para. 87)

The report concluded that there was a need to support initiatives to address the needs of potential legal empirical researchers at all stages of their careers, including at the undergraduate level.

In fact, there is little data about the extent of the use of empirical research in the undergraduate law curriculum. In order to try and fill in some of this lack of information the Nuffield Foundation funded a small research project comprising an online questionnaire and one-day seminar. The questionnaire sought to gather data on:

1 whether undergraduates are being taught skills that would enable them to either carry out or critique empirical work;
2 whether they are actually carrying out empirical projects of their own;
3 whether empirical work figured in other ways in teaching and assessment.

The survey was not intended to map where empirical research is and is not being used, but rather to engage with those who have included it in the curriculum in order to be able to identify the range of practice. Thence, the intention was to disseminate examples of interesting and innovative practices to others who may be interested in incorporating empirical research into their teaching.

The questionnaire was available online between January and May 2009. Invitations to take part (and reminders) were sent out through the Socio-Legal Studies Association, the Society of Legal Scholars and the Association of Law Teachers. Twenty-seven responses to the questionnaire were received, although three of these simply declared that there were no relevant modules at the particular institution. Seventeen different law schools were represented. As mentioned, the questionnaire was primarily intended to identify a range of practice rather than engage in a mapping exercise. Indeed, as some responses were specifically solicited, it can in no way be thought of as representative.

While it unearthed some interesting modules and practices, some of which were discussed in the subsequent seminar and in this volume, there did not seem to be a plethora of examples. Indeed, it seemed to point (if no more) towards the same conclusion as Bradney (2010, p. 1028) that there is little teaching of empirical legal research in UK law schools.

The second part of the project, the seminar[1] was held in July 2009 at the University of York. It provided an opportunity to discuss further some of the issues around the teaching of empirical legal research. Some of the discussions from the seminar are reflected in the chapters in this book, which seeks to take that approach forward, but situate it in the wider context of socio-legal studies, rather than focusing purely on empirical legal research.

The dichotomy between doctrinal law and other approaches to understanding law is perhaps not as stark as it once was. The chapters in this volume indicate the varied extent to which a socio-legal approach is already ingrained in the teaching of different parts of the law curriculum. Thus, Simon Halliday in his review of public law states 'a principal contention of this chapter is that many aspects of what could easily be called a "socio-legal" approach have long been integrated into the study of public law in the UK' (p. 143). Others, however, point to teaching traditions (e.g. in property and trusts and European Union (EU)) where a black-letter approach still tends to dominate.

That tradition nonetheless would seem to be on the decline in UK law schools. Cownie (2004) has noted that UK legal academics are as likely as not to consider themselves as socio-legal in their *approach*. What such approaches mean in practice may, of course, be very variable. Definitions of the socio-legal can be hard to pin down. The oft-cited Economic and Social Research Council (ESRC) definition of socio-legal studies (ESRC, 1994) provides as good

---

1 Supported by the UK Centre for Legal Education (UKCLE).

a starting point as any: 'an *approach* to law' which 'covers the theoretical and empirical analysis of law as a social phenomenon' (emphasis in original). An even more inclusive view can be seen in the current strap-line of the Socio-Legal Studies Association: 'Where law meets the social sciences and humanities'. The breadth of such an approach is reflected in the approaches in this volume. Thus, there is an interest in law as 'text' seen in Matthew Weait's discussion of transcripts from criminal trials, in Rosemary Auchmuty's discussion of the importance of history in teaching property and equity, and in Karen Devine's approach to tort cases as stories.

The chapters in this book make the case for the inclusion of a broad approach to the socio-legal and its incorporation into the undergraduate curriculum. However, such an approach does not mean that empirical legal research will necessarily be encompassed within it. Indeed, Cownie (2004, p. 57) suggests that a number of academic lawyers who describe themselves as black letter do so because they associate socio-legal approaches with carrying out empirical research. Of course, the two are not necessarily coterminus, in that a socio-legal approach to law does not have to be empirical. Although the Nuffield Inquiry (2006, para. 183) concluded that:

> it is important now to reframe the issue as one of capacity to carry out empirical research, not as one of 'socio-legal studies'. What is missing is not text-based studies that allude to law's social context, but studies of how legal processes, outcomes or structures actually are in the 'real world',

the approach taken in this book is that the two cannot be disaggregated. Thus, in order to understand what can be gained from an empirical study, students must be able to situate this in the broader theoretical frames of socio-legal studies. Empirical legal research cannot sit in a vacuum, it will proceed out of a socio-legal approach to teaching. Thus, in this volume we have not sought to isolate it, but rather to examine how, in a socio-legal approach to teaching, learning about empirical legal research may also emerge.

What is meant by empirical legal studies is, like the definition of socio-legal studies, open to debate. The Nuffield Inquiry provided a short definition which defined empirical legal research as: 'the study through direct methods of the operation and impact of law and legal processes in society, with a particular emphasis on non-criminal law and processes'.[2] Cane and Kritzer (2010) note how a lively interest in empirical legal research has emerged, particularly over the last 20 years or so, in both the USA and the UK. While the empirical legal studies movement in the US has had more of a focus on quantitative research, Cane and Kritzer (2010, p. 1) refer to a 'healthy

---

2 This was adapted from Baldwin and Davis (2003).

pluralism of empirical approaches to the study of law and legal phenomena'. This includes both quantitative and qualitative social science.

In this volume we have also taken a broad pluralistic approach. Examples and suggestions include the analysis of trial documents, the collection of quantitative data, and reference to a wide range of very diverse existing empirical studies.

Scope

The book is divided into two parts. In the first part we consider the practices in three particular modules in Bristol, Leeds and Sheffield Universities. The first two are examples of standalone modules that seek to address socio-legal studies and include a specific engagement with empirical legal research. The third provides a discussion of an assessment method that requires students to engage in such research. All three chapters provide practical examples of how such modules/assessments may be devised, while also reflecting on the problems and limitations they present.

The second part concentrates on what are referred to as the qualifying law degree (QLD) subjects. This focus comes out of the importance of such modules to the undergraduate curriculum, and the disappointment that the initial survey found only one respondent who indicated that empirical research was used in a core QLD module (property). In addition, none of the modules mentioned in the survey were taught in the first year of the under-graduate degree – where QLD subjects predominate.

It is worth considering further what can be offered by each of these approaches – the standalone module and incorporation into the QLD subjects – and their limitations.

Standalone modules and dissertations

The questionnaire elicited details of a number of standalone modules specifically addressing the sociology of law or socio-legal studies. At the seminar, a discussion of the types of sociology of law modules that are offered suggested that these may not include a large element of empirical work, but tended to be more theoretically based.

Another form of standalone module that did not have a specific subject content was the 'law-in-action' type module. Two were mentioned in responses to the questionnaire as including an empirical element. Such modules involved students working with community and other groups, often including some form of action research. It was noted in a response to the questionnaire that in the module at Keele, which was only in its first year, 'empirical evidence was drawn on regularly by the students in preparing their research projects'.

The two chapters in Part I focusing on standalone modules both describe examples of socio-legal modules that address empirical legal research. They provide a contrast: one (Leeds) is a compulsory module to all second-year students and the other (Bristol) is an optional module for third-year students. In Leeds, the module developed out of a need to prepare students for their compulsory third-year dissertation. Peter Vincent-Jones and Sarah Blandy describe how the module has evolved over a ten-year period, away from what might be recognized as a traditional social science 'methods' module (taught by staff from outside the law school) to one designed to equip 'students with critical skills necessary to evaluate the arguments of academic writers, drawing on qualitative/quantitative research, in specific journal articles selected as case studies in the use of socio-legal research methods' (p. 48). This 'critical consumer' approach enables students to critically use existing empirical studies in their final-year dissertations. Vincent-Jones and Blandy note that:

> Although the majority of law students at Leeds continue to base their final-year dissertations on what might be described as 'doctrinal' subject matter, a significant minority choose topics which require at least some discussion of 'law in society', and a number of dissertations are genuinely socio-legal. (pp. 50–1)

The dissertation, it could be argued, provides a real opportunity for students to take a socio-legal approach and even to undertake some empirical research. Nonetheless, the seminar discussion provoked quite a debate on the 'problem' of empirically based dissertations, no doubt reflected even in the discouragement at Leeds of students undertaking their own empirical studies. Reflecting on her experience at Westminster University, at the seminar Sylvie Bacquet concluded that there were a number of problems in students undertaking empirically based dissertations. First is the absence of suitably trained supervisors and the clear reluctance of some academics to engage in empirical research. Second, there are often ethical constraints. Finally, undergraduate researchers often have problems of credibility in accessing data subjects. As well as these barriers that presented themselves to students, there could also be problems for students who were unable to assess whether empirical research was suitable to their project or who made unrealistic assumptions about the scope of empirical projects they could undertake (e.g. planning to interview victims of honour crimes).

A number of these problems were also reflected in a comment made in response to the questionnaire from an academic at a different institution:

> Empirical research is not encouraged but allowed for purposes of completing a final year dissertation where such enquiry is

considered essential to achieve its objective, and where safeguards are adhered to. These safeguards take the form of an individual training session with empirically trained law staff to discuss whether empirical research would be appropriate and feasible in the time frame, what research design might be suitable, any ethical aspects and research methods that would be appropriate (from a limited range allowed). Approval in Principle is required before students may approach potential participants or gatekeeping organisations. Completion and approval of a School Research Ethics application is also necessary along with a further session with empirically trained law staff prior to interview schedules or survey questionnaires being used. Few undergraduates have availed themselves of this opportunity since this system was introduced because few resources are allocated to it, and all but the very keen are [un]likely to opt for our fairly complicated procedure, but the Research Ethics Committee currently feels we should not remove this possibility for determined students so we are retaining the present system.

At the seminar, a number of practical responses to these problems were offered. First, it was suggested that staff might like to be more proactive in indicating areas where they would be prepared to supervise empirical dissertations. Second, it was pointed out that the British Library contains a number of resources that could be used for analysis, such as the 'legal lives' oral history project. Finally, we were reminded that at an undergraduate level it is often the 'doing' rather than the final product that is the most important learning outcome from a dissertation. Small projects based on qualitative interview data may not be generalizable but may provide the student with an invaluable experience and sufficient data for an undergraduate dissertation.

While the focus in the Leeds module is on substantive areas of law, which the students will already have encountered as preparation for their dissertation, the Bristol module has a different approach and purpose. The Bristol module is intended as an option for final-year students who are looking to engage with law 'from the outside' through a social science lens. Morag McDermont, Bronwen Morgan and David Cowan describe how they seek to combine a range of theoretical approaches with different (empirical) methodological approaches, such as feminist research methods and legal consciousness. The chapter reports the enthusiasm of students for the module, but also the disappointment that this has not led to a greater number of students feeding into the MSc programme in Socio-legal Studies.

Both the Leeds and Bristol modules provide a basis for reflecting on how a greater engagement with empirical legal research can be brought into the curriculum through dedicated modules.

Qualifying law degree

While the standalone modules provide one way of introducing socio-legal studies into the curriculum and offering an engagement with empirical legal research, they are likely to be offered in the second and third years of study, when students may already have become fixed in their views as to what is required in the study of law. It is thus important that a socio-legal approach permeates not just such standalone modules but all elements of the degree programme and in particular the QLD compulsory modules.

All QLDs (in essence all law degrees in England and Wales) are required to comply with the *Joint Statement Issued by the Law Society and the General Council of the Bar on the Completion of the Initial or Academic Stage of Training by Obtaining an Undergraduate Degree* (Law Society and General Council of the Bar, 1999). Schedule 2 of that document sets out the 'Foundations of legal knowledge', which comprise seven legal areas that must be covered in a QLD. The chapters in Part II of this book reflect these, although different law schools may divide them up in slightly different ways.

It has been noted (see Charlotte O'Brien's chapter, quoting Ball and Dadomo, 2010) how the constraints of the *Joint Statement* can be used as a reason (or perhaps excuse) for keeping to a more traditional doctrinal approach to the qualifying subjects. However, the statement provides no real prescription at all as to the content of any QLD module. The schedule simply requires that 'the key elements and general principles' are taught. Whether because of the perceived requirement to comply with some mythical prescription or not, as Charlotte O'Brien in her chapter on EU law further notes, there is a danger in the curriculum of feeling the need to 'teach everything' (p. 185) and this can be true in other subject areas as well. Such an approach can lead to there being little room in the curriculum for anything but (an ever-expanding) amount of doctrinal law. The chapters in Part II reflect an approach that, hopefully, steps back from this and encourages those designing foundation modules to find room for key socio-legal questions about, for example, the reach and effect of the key elements and general principles as well as their doctrinal content.

The chapters all represent the authors' own take on the particular subject and are not intended in any way as prescriptive. Rather, we hope they will provide a stimulus to the pedagogic imagination. The chapters take different approaches, with some offering more advice on day-to-day classroom activities and assessments than others. Those on public law, property and equity and EU law give an overview of the subject and look at how taking a thematic approach to teaching can allow socio-legal issues to emerge (something I shall return to below). Karen Devine focuses on the particular approach to teaching obligations, and in particular tort, at Kent Law School. Matthew Weait and

Linda Mulcahy and Sally Wheeler in the chapters on crime and contract start from a narrower point. Both take an individual case (in crime, a trial transcript; in contract, a decision that went on appeal from the Technology and Construction Court through the Court of Appeal to the Supreme Court) as their starting point.

The Nuffield Inquiry focused primarily on empirical legal research in civil rather than criminal justice. In criminal law, as Matthew Weait points out, there is a debate as to how far the existing myriad of criminal justice and criminological literature (empirical and otherwise) can be said to be socio-legal (there is always a question as to how far there is an overlap between criminologists and socio-legal scholars). Rather than provide a survey of that literature, he focuses on 'the legal and pedagogical expertise of those who typically teach criminal law, and of the expectations and interests of those who are studying it' and suggests 'one specific way in which we might bring the lived experience of criminal law into the classroom' through the use of trial transcripts (pp. 161–2). He suggests that:

> active engagement with the trial provides those teaching and studying criminal law in the undergraduate curriculum with the opportunity not only to gain a richer understanding of the law in action (a central concern of socio-legal studies) but also of the appellate cases which constitute its core. (p. 163)

A similar approach, which can open up questions about the way in which the higher courts 'construct' cases, can also be seen in Linda Mulcahy and Sally Wheeler's chapter on contract law. Their focus on the decisions in a single case in the three courts in which it appeared provides a way of opening up a 'context-based study'. The case not only offers the opportunity to look at the operation of a contract in the 'real world', but also how and why the litigation proceeded (and thus a potential case study of the effect of the Woolf reforms) and an opportunity to reflect on how the higher courts construct the story. Indeed, this focus on legal story-telling emerges across a number of the chapters in this volume.

Assessment

As Penelope Russell points out in her chapter in Part I, assessment has long been recognized as having an enormous impact on student learning (Rowntree, 1987; Boud, 1995). If socio-legal studies is to become integral to the undergraduate curriculum it must not be an add-on which students can take or leave, but must be included as a central part of what is assessed. It is perhaps trite to point out that learning outcomes, content and teaching method need to be aligned with any assessment (Biggs, 1996, 'constructive alignment'), but it is undoubtedly the case that students will not value any content that is not aligned with the assessment. The questionnaire did not elicit many responses that pointed to specific engagement with empirical research through assessment, at best it seems to arise through essay titles that require consideration of existing empirical evidence.

This is perhaps not so surprising. As Charlotte O'Brien points out, Ball and Dadomo's (2010) survey of EU law teaching reveals a very conservative approach to assessment forms. As she puts it in relation to EU teaching:

> [W]e should think about whether the exams and essays we set measure the things we wish students to learn – the ability to think creatively about social implications of aspects of EU law, to reflect on the impact of topical developments, and to spot and back up EU legal argument. (p. 187)

For EU, we could substitute any of the QLD subjects. During the seminar it was pointed out that law students are particularly assessment-focused, and therefore generally resistant to innovation in this area, thus perhaps reinforcing conservative assessment strategies. Including socio-legal elements of the curriculum may mean, however, opening up students to a more varied diet of assessment than is currently the case. As is stressed in the chapters that follow, where innovation is used it will be important to prepare the students and embed the assessment in the learning.

A number of different forms of assessment were mentioned in the survey and seminar responses, which may lend themselves to critical engagement with empirical research, for example, writing a memo to different policy organizations in an EU module, giving the option of doing a poster presentation, using reflective diaries. Other suggestions emerge in various chapters in this volume, including contract-drafting, content analysis (of judgments or academic journal articles), judgment-writing, use of news reports. While these may not all require the classic collection and analysis of empirical data, they do all open students up to a broader range of assessment types (thus ensuring that students do not see anything outside a narrow range of problem and essay-type assessments as unusual and something to be afraid of) and may incorporate some reflection on empirical research.

The assessment in the Leeds module described in Peter Vincent-Jones and Sarah Blandy's chapter requires such reflection explicitly, while the preparation of the research proposal required in Bristol and described in Morag McDermont, Bronwen Morgan and David Cowan's chapter requires consideration and justification of the research method to be used for the project. Interestingly, this has now become the second piece of assessment for the module rather than the first, because '[t]his was the piece of coursework that caused students most anxiety. In feedback, several said it was unlike anything else they had been asked to do as a law student.' (p. 31)

Penelope Russell's chapter provides a particular example of asking students to directly undertake empirical research. There are, as she points out limitations to what the students undertake at Sheffield. Important parts of the process of empirical research – in particular the study design – are not required of the students. Nonetheless it provides an important example of innovation that has also been used at other universities. She also describes the anxiety felt by students but sets out the steps that can be taken to allay any fears.

Issues emerging

A number of issues emerge from the discussions at the seminar and the chapters in this volume on which it is worth reflecting further.

Module content: relevance, themes and history

In mapping an approach to take to their subject, the authors of the chapters on property and equity, public law, tort and EU law all, to a greater or lesser extent, touch on three important elements in giving it a socio-legal quality: the importance of contemporary relevance and, at the same time, history and the use of cross-cutting themes.

The use of current issues can provide a way in to students and, importantly from a socio-legal perspective, provide real-world examples with all their necessary messiness, which may be missing from constructed legal problems or indeed the construct that is placed on legal facts by the higher courts. Karen Devine shows how it is possible to use issues in popular culture that are likely to be familiar to students (the treatment of Susan Boyle in *Britain's Got Talent*, the royal wedding of Prince William and Kate Middleton) to unpack the socio-legal elements and practice of tort law in the real world.

As Simon Halliday points out, history, on the other hand, provides a form of empirical research of the past (Trevor-Roper, 1969). Understanding history adds much to students' understanding of public law and property law. Indeed, for Rosemary Auchmuty, a questioning historical approach opens the way to students valuing non-legal sources and for understanding doctrinal sources for what they are: 'historical documents, products of a particular social context and an individual author or group of authors with an intended goal and audience'(p. 76).

The use of cross-cutting themes also opens up the socio-legal imagination. Rosemary Auchmuty suggests that with a thematic approach 'socio-legal concerns are seen to be pervasive, and property law assumes a coherence that binds together what might otherwise appear to be a collection of disparate subjects' (p. 82). Simon Halliday and Charlotte O'Brien make similar points in relation respectively to public law and EU law. Indeed, some of the same themes emerge across these modules: gender, culture, legitimacy, and distinctions between commercial and private interests. Such thematic approaches will, it seems, enable links to be made not just within modules but also across them.

Research-led teaching

There is some debate about the meaning of 'research-led teaching' (Zamorski, 2002; Healey, 2005). It can cover both placing the students as an audience for teachers' own research and engaging students directly in research activity (Zamorski, 2002, p. 415). In relation to the former, it is perhaps unsurprising that what emerges from the chapters in this volume is how the approaches taken enable academics to include their research in their teaching. More innovative methods of teaching (as discussed by Charlotte O'Brien and Karen Devine) may lend themselves more easily to this, because problems (used in York Law School for problem-based learning) or case classes and special studies (used in Kent Law School) can be centred on the particular research interests of staff. Both enable students to actively engage with the research interests of the staff involved.

The type of assessment discussed by Penelope Russell enables students to engage directly in research, which, as noted, may be aggregated to form data which can be used in published research.

The limitations of the textbook

Two different textbook issues emerge from the various chapters. The first relates to those textbooks in the QLD subjects. As Bradney (2010, p. 1028) points out, empirical legal research is largely missing from textbooks, even where such research has been carried out. Although the authors in this volume point out some notable exceptions, they conclude that in the majority of QLD subjects the textbooks available are a constraint to a socio-legal approach to teaching. As Rosemary Auchmuty puts it:

> How are we to persuade students that the textbook account is inadequate? The textbook is *the* Authority in many of our classrooms; for most students, what appears in a book published by Oxford University Press *must* be more reliable than something said by their obviously biased lecturer in class. (p. 77)

The second is a lack of socio-legal methods textbooks available for use with students. Both chapters on standalone modules point to the lack of a suitable textbook on socio-legal studies. Peter Vincent-Jones and Sarah Blandy refer their students to a number of non-law-specific social-science methods texts. This situation may, however, be eased by a number of new publishing initiatives, including the series in which this volume appears.

Ethical issues

The undertaking of empirical legal research undoubtedly requires students to have an understanding of the ethical issues of research. Indeed, even if not undertaking their own empirical research, it is something that students should understand in taking a critical approach to all research. In another context – that of professional practice of lawyers – ethics is also an important subject to which students may be introduced at an undergraduate level. The questionnaire indicated ethics being taught across eight different modules, primarily in dissertation-training or methods modules, but there were also three responses that indicated that, even within a methods module, no ethics were being taught. In leading the discussion on this at the seminar, Julian Webb suggested that ethics was 'Cinderella's Cinderella subject'.

There were a number of potential reasons for this:

- the doctrinal bias of the undergraduate curriculum;
- the emphasis on research-informed teaching *not* research-based learning and teaching;
- a lack of awareness of/ambivalence towards socio-legal research ethics;
- resource issues driven by the 'massification' of law schools, including the move to optional dissertations;
- a lack of appropriate texts and materials;
- the chilling effect of university research ethics committee procedures.

This last point provoked some discussion of the very varied practices between different institutions, and the overemphasis on some of the science-based model of ethics approval. It was felt, however, that there are ways to introduce and engage students in ethical issues. These included making students more reflective of their own and their lecturers' practices in class, for example, considering how asking different questions of students about personal experiences would make them feel, writing rules for class discussions about matters that might raise sensitive issues, asking students to right rules about how to be respectful and confidential. This then has the potential to widen to debates about research practices that may be unethical.

The Socio-Legal Studies module at Bristol, described by Morag McDermont, Bronwen Morgan and David Cowan in their chapter, includes a focus on research ethics. They seek to ensure that their students:

> understand ethical compliance as something much broader and more important than researchers merely protecting themselves against either claims of unethical behaviour or the risk of withdrawal of funding from institutions that do not have ethical review procedures in place. (p. 28)

The seminar is 'intended to develop critical thinking about the role research ethics can, should and does play in shaping research into the law and powerful legal actors' p. 28). They suggest that this is an area where there is much useful literature. Indeed, at the seminar, Julian Webb pointed to a useful article written by Mark Israel and Ian Hay of Flinders University, Adelaide, 'Good ethical practice in empirical research in law'.[3]

Conclusion

Bradney (2010) has suggested that (good) empirical legal research ought to be part of the law school curriculum, but that:

> Empirical legal studies can only be properly incorporated into the law school curriculum if students not only use and understand such studies but also understand the methods used and the theories on which they are based. (2010, p. 1036)

Fulfilling such a requirement is, as he points out, difficult because of the already full curriculum requirements of the profession. He suggests that it is not enough for students to have an introduction to such methods: 'Regular and frequent practice is necessary before students will become accomplished in the application of the knowledge that they will have acquired on such a course.' (2010, p. 1039)

This seems to me to be the counsel of perfection. Many students in social science courses, such as sociology and social policy, do not undertake methods courses until their second year and do not undertake all but the smallest amount of direct empirical research themselves (probably in some small-scale qualitatively based dissertation). This does not prevent them being introduced to a range of empirical research across their courses.

As Peter Vincent-Jones and Sarah Blandy argue, it is possible for law students to become critical consumers of empirical legal research. To do this, I would argue that socio-legal ideas must permeate the curriculum and there must be some explicit introduction not only to socio-legal theories but also empirical methods. The chapters in this volume illustrate how it can be done.

A number of barriers to opening up the curriculum to expose students to empirical research were revealed through the questionnaire and seminar. First, there is certainly some resistance from faculty members who do not see the relevance of such research to the undergraduate law curriculum. At present, where exposure does occur, it tends to be in modules outside

---

3 Available on the UKCLE website: https://webmail.york.ac.uk/session/cmh516/NOSEQ/ rawdisplay/561/21975/2/application%2fmsword/www.ukcle.ac.uk/research/ethics/index. html.

the QLD and in second and third-year modules. Inclusion in QLD modules seems unlikely while the core textbooks, which are relied on for teaching, do not include this material. Even if textbooks do not change, moving away from a reliance on them creates that crucial space to broaden the discussion.

Second, when students do not encounter these ideas in their first year or in QLD modules, it is likely to lead to at least anxiety if not resistance from students when they are asked to encounter novel ways of thinking and, particularly, of assessment. Engagement with the law from a socio-legal viewpoint needs to start in the first year, so that students become critical consumers of socio-legal research (including empirical research) from the beginning of their degree. Given the assessment focus of students, their concerns when encountering new forms of assessment need to be addressed, both through widening the forms of assessment they encounter throughout their degrees and by ensuring that the assessment is embedded within the module, so that the students are supported in producing the assessment.

As Cownie (2004, p. 60) points out, students have a more vocational approach to their studies than legal academics. They often need convincing about why what they are taught is relevant, particularly to their (hoped for) future careers as practising lawyers. Links can readily be made between empirical research and the real practice of law. As Karen Devine notes, the special studies as Kent Law School enable some staff to draw on their past experiences in practice, yet in an area where they can also draw on empirical studies. Further, those who have only encountered tort law as a doctrinal subject will find that practice is far more concerned with issues such as negotiation and bargaining, about which there is a wealth of empirical evidence. Indeed, knowledge of this literature might be a far better preparation for practice.

This volume focuses on opportunities within the existing curriculum; it should also be noted that there may be other extra-curricular activities in which students can be encouraged to engage in empirical research. Leanne Smith from Cardiff University responded to the questionnaire by sending details of a project she ran with five undergraduate students funded by a university research opportunities for undergraduates fund. The small empirical project investigated the attitudes of lawyers to the enforcement of contact between children and non-resident parents. The data were collected over two weeks through an online questionnaire and elicited 91 responses. The students wrote up the results, which have been published (Dyer et al., 2006).

Participants at the seminar noted that many universities have similar schemes that enable undergraduates to be engaged in research, and that this could be a fruitful way to develop an interest in empirical research amongst undergraduates.

While it is unlikely that in the undergraduate law curriculum there will be room for detailed training in empirical methods, there is certainly room for critical exposure. That exposure should start in the first year in order that students see it as the norm to become critical consumers of empirical research about law throughout their degree. Hopefully, the chapters in this volume will provide some inspiration for this. For those who then wish to take this further, the examples provided indicate what can be done to foster and encourage students to engage with and in empirical research.

References

Baldwin, J and G Davis (2003) 'Empirical research in law' in P Cane and M Tushnet (eds) *The Oxford Handbook of Legal Studies* (Oxford: Oxford University Press)

Ball, R and C Dadomo (2010) 'UKCLE law subject survey: European Union law', http://eprints.uwe.ac.uk/14747/ (last accessed 30 August 2011)

Biggs, J (1996) 'Enhancing teaching through constructive alignment' 32 *Higher Education* 347

Bradney, A (2010) 'The place of empirical legal research in the law school curriculum' in P Cane and H M Kritzer (eds) *The Oxford Handbook of Empirical Legal Research* (Oxford: Oxford University Press)

Boud, D (1995) 'Assessment and learning: contradictory or complementary?' in P Knight (ed.) *Assessment for learning in Higher Education* (London: Kogan Page)

Cane, P and H M Kritzer (2010) 'Introduction' in P Cane and H M Kritzer (eds) *The Oxford Handbook of Empirical Legal Research* (Oxford: Oxford University Press)

Cownie, F (2004) *Legal Academics: Culture and Identities* (Oxford: Hart Publishing)

Dyer, C, S McCrum, R Thomas, R Ward and S Wookey (2008) 'Making contact work: is the Children and Adoption Act 2006 enough for resident parents and children?' *Family Law* 1237

ESRC (1994) *Review of Socio-Legal Studies: Final Report* (Swindon: ESRC)

Healey, M (2005) 'Linking research and teaching to benefit student learning' 29(2) *Journal of Geography in Higher Education* 183–201

Law Society and General Council of the Bar (1999) *A Joint Statement Issued by the Law Society and the General Council of the Bar on the Completion of the Initial or Academic Stage of Training by Obtaining an Undergraduate Degree* (London: Law Society)

Nuffield Inquiry on Empirical Legal Research (2006) *Law in the Real World: Improving our Understanding of How Law Works*, www.ucl.ac.uk/laws/socio-legal/empirical/index.shtml (last accessed 14 September 2011)

Rowntree, D (1987) *Assessing Students: How Shall We Know Them?* (London: Kogan Page)

Trevor-Roper, H R (1969) 'The past and the present: history and sociology' 42(1) *Past and Present* 3–17

Zamorski, B (2002) 'Research-led teaching and learning in higher education: a case' 7(4) *Teaching in Higher Education* 411–27

Part I
Developing Modules and Assessment

2

Socio-Legal Studies Module: The Bristol Experience

Morag McDermont, Bronwen Morgan and David Cowan

Introduction

In this chapter we discuss the standalone Socio-Legal Studies module that has been offered to undergraduate students at Bristol University since 2006. The module was offered initially to second and third-year law students; it is now limited to third-year law students, but is open to students from other departments and schools in the Faculty of Social Sciences and Law. The module is optional but has drawn a healthy number of students in the six years that it has run. The module is not intended to provide the detailed training which we offer at postgraduate level, but seeks to provide students with an encounter with law 'from the outside' through a social science lens. This has required a compromise between an approach based entirely on theory and one on empirical methods and research.

In this chapter we discuss, first, the intellectual rationale behind the module, then we move on to the structure and content of the course. We then discuss the forms of assessment, providing some examples and discussing the students' response to it. Finally, we look at the sort of students that have been attracted to the module and discuss their feedback to the course content.

Intellectual rationale

Deploying theory to seek to understand the 'social' is an integral element of the research interests of many of the socio-legal academics in the Law School at Bristol. We have sought to reflect this intermingling of the theoretical and the empirical in our socio-legal teaching at both undergraduate and postgraduate level. The aims of our undergraduate module reflect this approach and include:

- broadening the methods and approaches to which students are exposed in their first degree by looking at law 'from the outside' through a social science lens;

- fostering the sense that law can be a site for scholarly enquiry (and academic careers);
- fostering enthusiasm for law-related work outside the profession, especially in the policy world.

We have always hoped that the undergraduate module would provide some of our law students with an enthusiasm for taking a more empirical and social scientific approach, and so act as a feeder for our MSc in Socio-Legal Studies. In fact, in the six years of running the undergraduate module, we have only had one student progress from this module to the MSc; this was a student who was awarded one of our 1+3 Economic and Social Research Council studentships.

One of the strengths of this module is that the Law School has a significant number of academic staff actively engaged in socio-legal research who deploy a range of different theoretical and methodological perspectives to enquire into a wide variety of research areas. This unit enables academics to use their own research in the design and delivery of seminars, bringing the topics of study to life and enabling students to see at first hand how academics go about conducting social research in law and integrating social theory into their work (e.g. Cowan, 2004; McDermont et al., 2009). Over the life of the module, around ten academic staff have been involved in delivering elements of the teaching. As we shall see in the next section, it is the research interests and focus of staff that have shaped, and re-shaped, the programme year on year.

Structure and content: a threefold logic

The module has a credit of 20 points (that is, one-sixth of a year's credit). In the University of Bristol model this translates to 20 hours of teaching, delivered in two-hour seminars once a fortnight. Working within this constraint, and that of the combined knowledge and expertise of the socio-legal teaching staff available in any one year, we have deployed a threefold logic to establish the structure of the module and the content of seminars.

Strand 1: thematic organization

The module is organized around topic areas with two or three seminars based around the same theme. In the initial structure, the themes were: Individuals in Dispute; Regulatory Agencies; Corporations; Police; Experts and Expertise. However, this has subsequently been modified to accommodate different staff interests, feedback from students and, most critically, a desire to discuss research ethics more explicitly within the context of a study of scholarly research literature and research design. There are now four themes: Discretion in the Legalised Arenas; Corporations and Corporate Social Responsibility (CSR); Foucault, Expertise and Law; and Ethics and Research Practice. This model is discussed in more detail below.

Strand 2: theoretical perspectives

Over the past few years, we have covered a range of theorists and perspectives – positivism, feminism, legal consciousness,[1] street-level bureaucracy, Weber, Foucault, Marx. The last was specifically introduced following student feedback.

Strand 3: empirical methodologies

We have introduced students to a variety of experimental methods including: use of court records, interviews, postal questionnaires; case studies; genealogies; action research; film analysis; and print media analysis.

Within each broad theme we introduce students to a theoretical perspective, one or more methodological approaches, as well as some of the scholarly work in the theme.

We know that, for the vast majority of law students, socio-legal studies is very different from most of the modules that they have previously studied in the Law School; and, equally, that the assessments will require that they think differently. Therefore, before embarking on the thematic areas, we begin with an introductory seminar which aims to

- introduce the idea of 'socio legal studies';
- introduce the unit, discuss the format of seminars and the modes of teaching to be used;
- provide an overview of the assessments; and
- through the format of a group exercise, stimulate students' thinking about what law is and the myriad of places and spaces where law might be found.

Finding appropriate reading for this lecture has always been, and remains, a difficulty. There is no core text for socio-legal studies (a market gap that maybe someone could fill?). The 'broad church' nature of socio-legal studies means that it has proved impossible to find the ideal material that can introduce the range of perspectives. The difficulties are compounded by the different genealogies of the North American 'law and society' movement and the UK socio-legal approach, the latter starting out as highly empirical and developing into a more theoretically grounded movement (converging with

---

1   Although we accept that it is a moot point as to whether this is a theoretical or methodological perspective.

the law and society approach: see further Cotterrell, 1995; Hutter and Lloyd-Bostock, 1997; and Friedman, 2005).

The approach we have taken has been to introduce some of the debates between lawyers and sociologists, and in socio-legal studies/law and society studies through the first chapter in Steven Vago's, *Law and Society* (2009), and an article that appeared in the first ever number of the *British Journal of Law and Society* (now *Journal of Law and Society*), I D Willock's 'Getting on with sociologists' (1974). This is not a wholly satisfactory solution as the Vago chapter is too focused on US approaches, and the Willock article is somewhat dated and so unable to take account of more recent UK developments. We keep on searching. In addition to these two pieces, we have found it necessary to introduce law students to the political background to much of the UK-based empirical research; for this, Harlow and Rawlings' seminal book *Law and Administration* (2009) is ideal – chapter 2 covers a lot of the ground in language that is fairly familiar to law students.

Using themes to explore different perspectives

As we said in our introduction, after the first year of running the Socio-Legal Studies module we decided to restrict entry for law students to third-years only. This was considered necessary because we felt that, without having studied Jurisprudence (compulsory in the second year), the theoretical perspectives of socio-legal studies would be too advanced for some students (and, in any case, having studied jurisprudence, students would be in a better position to make a judgment as to whether they enjoyed the more theoretical approach). It also had the advantage that students would have studied the (compulsory second-year) Crime, Justice and Society unit, which exposed them to an approach similar to that of socio-legal studies. That unit requires students to embrace empirical research in the field and think critically about the role and value of law. The unit emphasizes the notion of criminalization, both through looking critically at the process by which certain types of behaviour become defined as criminal, and through looking at the discretionary processes through which the law so-defined is (or is not) enforced in practice. Key concerns throughout are the extent to which such criminalization can be considered just, and the way in which societal attitudes and social divisions affect, and are affected by, criminalization.

So, whilst the themes we have chosen to cover in the Socio-Legal Studies module are to a certain extent determined by the research interests of those available for teaching in any one year, we have also tried to cover issues that may have some connection with areas that law students will already have encountered in their studies. For example, Marxist and feminist perspectives are familiar from Jurisprudence; regulatory agencies have been discussed a little in Public Law; and police in Crime, Justice and Society.

Next we discuss the themes as they appeared in our 2010–2011 delivery of this module.

Theme 1: discretion in the delivery of public services

We have attempted to begin the module by looking at perspectives that are utilized across a range of areas of empirical enquiry. Initially, we looked at research connected with individuals' interaction with law through disputes, pairing this with a practical seminar on qualitative research methods; more recently we have begun with a look at the area of discretionary decision-making, using material from administrative law. Our approach has changed over time, in part as a response to feedback from students which indicated that launching into practical research methods at the beginning was too challenging, as well as the changing availability of expertise (bearing in mind the school's research leave policy).

The first seminar pair concerned the ways in which discretion is exercised. We approached the theme in this way in order to provide a link – a bridge – between our students' knowledge and understandings of public law and socio-legal studies. Our purpose has been to demonstrate to our students that, although discretion may be broad, there are always factors which narrow down the exercise of discretion. Internal policies may do so; as may the institutional effects of bureaucracies, both of which – to put it broadly – narrow down the range of possible decisions and reasons. External factors, such as audit and accountability, also have an impact. On the other hand, clear, fixed rules, which appear to have no element of discretion to them, perhaps counter-intuitively may well allow for discretion at the margins. The binary divide between rules and discretion may, in fact, be illusory. In this pair of seminars, then, the very concept of discretion is interrogated along with its exercise.

The first seminar concerned bureaucratic discretion and issues of control; the second required students to think about the developing literature on legal consciousness as a research methodology. The first seminar contained the usual material that one might expect on discretion, as well as a particular focus on street-level bureaucracy. Students were challenged to think critically about the relationship between law, rules and discretion. One key issue for discussion in this seminar was whether 'managerialism' means the death of discretion.

In the second seminar, students were, as already indicated, introduced to part of the legal consciousness literature. They were informed in the reading materials how this literature differs from other aspects of socio-legal studies. Box 1 shows the characterization that was used.

Box 1: legal consciousness as a research method

The socio-legal 'legal consciousness' literature seeks to move away from a 'law-first' paradigm which places law and lawyers in the forefront, turning instead to ordinary life and everyday encounters with law. Researchers are as much interested in what people do not think about law as what they do think, examining how taken-for-granted understandings of law shape possible interactions with (and resistances to) legalized mechanisms and institutions. For Patricia Ewick and Susan Silbey, two of the key proponents of this approach, legal consciousness work means exploring

> commonplace events and transactions to seek the web of legality, conceiving of law not so much operating to shape social action but as social action...to understand how law emerges from these local settings and interactions with the ontological integrity it claims for itself and that socio-legal scholars have for so long attributed to it. (1998, pp. 34–5)

David Cowan's study of homeless persons units suggested that a focus on the institutional encounter and the nature of the communications between welfare applicant (in this case, a person applying for social housing because of homelessness) and welfare bureaucrat (the housing officer) can illuminate how the applicant forms ideas about the nature of the administrative processes, and the possibility or value of challenging the decision (Cowan, 2004). Davina Cooper (1995) moves away from the study of 'ordinary people' to look at how the cultural conditions in local government develop understandings of legality in professionals. In Silbey's most recent work, she suggests that researchers should move to investigating 'the ground of institutional practices'. In institutions, she suggests 'cultural meaning, social inequality, and legal consciousness are forged' (2005, p. 360).

All our seminar materials incorporate questions for discussion. In this seminar, students were particularly engaged by the questions: 'Where is the "law" in legal consciousness studies?' and 'Does legal consciousness scholarship help us understand better the exercise of discretion in institutional settings?'

Theme 2: corporations and corporate social responsibility

We introduced a pair of seminars on companies and CSR as a way of demonstrating how Marxist perspectives can be deployed in socio-legal research. This theme also enabled us to look at comparing different research methodologies in action. The first seminar was entitled 'Law, Organisations and the CSR

Debate'; the second 'From Rules on the Book to Rules in Action – litigation vs regulatory standards'. This seminar pair explored the issues around corporate accountability, departing, however, in two ways from the usual focus taken in company law on the legal duties shaping internal corporate governance: first, by exploring a wider view of the role of corporations in society, one often expressed nowadays as CSR; second, by focusing on *non-legal ways* in which corporations *as organizations* respond to legal pressures in the direction of broader social responsibility. Thus, we have been able to develop the focus in the first seminars by exploring further the ways in which legal issues are often worked out in daily life as non-legal issues or, even when legal, in locations far from courts and lawyers. But this time, rather than applying these ideas to individuals, we applied the ideas to organizations. Students particularly focus on the *McLibel*[2] trial in these two seminars; case readings are mixed with a documentary film[3] and media reports, as well as academic work, such as Vick and Campbell's important paper in the *Journal of Law and Society* (2001).

Questions for discussion included:

- What is the 'event study' method used by Vick and Campbell? What are the pros and cons of its use in evaluating the economic impact of the *McLibel* case? And in evaluating the wider social impact of the case?
- What other kinds of information did Vick and Campbell gather to evaluate the impact of the case? What other kinds of 'legal events' might be investigated by the event study method?
- Compare O'Rourke's (2003) academic article with his policy story in a non-academic magazine (O'Rourke, 2001): what are the pros and cons of turning academic research into 'action recommendations' of the kind in this article? What other kinds of legal issues could be investigated through 'action research'?

Theme 3: experts and expertise: introducing a practical exercise in print media analysis

One of the aims in devising this pair of seminars was to involve students in carrying out research of their own as an element of the module. We did not believe that it would be possible, within the confines of the module and our threefold aims, to provide students with the necessary skills to understand how to conduct either quantitative or qualitative research using human research participants (each of these would have been a module in its own right). Such research would also have required ethical approval, for which

---

2 See *McDonald's Corporation v Steel & Morris* [1997] EWHC QB 366; *Steel and Mossir v UK* [2005] ECHR 103.
3 *McLibel* (1997) directed by Franny Armstrong and Ken Loach.

there was not sufficient time or resources.[4] We therefore devised a practical exercise which required students to investigate a particular area by examining media sources – the internet, newspapers, professional journals and academic specialist journals.

The pair of seminars examined the role that experts and expertise play in legal arenas, particularly within the court setting. Alongside this, the aim was also to introduce students to the work of Michel Foucault and to those who have been influenced by his work. We chose to examine expertise within the legal arena of the court, a subject with which students would have some familiarity, in order to introduce this fairly difficult theoretical perspective. The seminar used Foucault's (1983) essay, 'The subject and power' as a means to examine the ways in which subjectification/objectification operates in the exercise of power. Through Foucault's understanding of 'dividing practices', we could begin to examine how people are 'made up' as experts, by themselves and by others. This allowed students to look at the way experts are used in the court setting as a 'dividing practice', where one set of experts can become divided from another, and experts from lay persons as *in*experts. In the second seminar we hoped that students would be able to deploy Foucault's perspective as a lens to examine a particular case where expertise was called into question – the role of Roy Meadows as an expert (medical) witness in numerous cases involving the cot deaths of babies (see Box 2).

Theme 4: research ethics and research practice

The current focus in social science research on ethical research practices and ethical compliance has meant that research ethics was a central element of our module from early on. In particular, an internal debate within the Law School as to whether third-year students should be allowed to conduct empirical research for their research project, in the absence of training on research methods for law students, propelled research ethics up the agenda.

We have experimented with a number of different formulations for the delivery of teaching on research ethics and research practice. We believe that the current formulation, which treats this as a thematic area taught at the end of the module through three linked seminars, works particularly well as it enables us to cover both substantive areas of research (policing one year, judging another) and theoretical perspectives (feminist research methodologies) alongside ethics.

The first of three seminars in this theme considered research ethics within the context of a specific research area. As far as resources go, here we are in a position of plenty. There are a considerable number of books on research

---

4 Note how this issue was overcome in the family law module discussed in Chapter 3 by setting a single exercise for which the lecturer obtained ethical approval.

Box 2: practical exercise

The aim of this seminar is for you to research the ways in which different groups of professionals and non-professionals reacted to an instance in which expert knowledge has been critical in legal decision-making. You may remember the headlines when Professor Roy Meadows was struck off the medical register by the General Medical Council (GMC) after being found guilty of serious professional misconduct. The GMC decided he gave 'erroneous' and 'misleading' evidence at the trial of solicitor Sally Clark, who was wrongly jailed for the murder of her two sons who died in 'cot deaths'.

Working in groups **before attending the seminar**, using library and internet resources, examine the different reactions to what some might see as a 'crisis' in expertise and answer the following questions:

1   Discuss the reaction of the medical profession.
2   What about the reaction within legal forums? What do judges have to say about the role of medical experts? Was the reaction to Meadows being struck off different in the legal journals from the medical journals? If so, why? Do you think these differences are explained by the differing interests of the professions?
3   Wynne (1989) argues (at p. 27) that 'the particularities of each institutional setting are a key part of the constitution of authoritative knowledge in that setting'. Discuss this in relation to the case of Roy Meadows.
4   What about the parents – how are they portrayed in this drama? Is there a recognition that they too might be 'experts', or have 'expertise'? Did Sally Clark's position as a solicitor make her a different sort of subject?
5   Under the Woolf reforms, opposing parties were encouraged to appoint a single expert witness. Do you think this is a good idea? What might be some of the problems?
6   Does Foucault's essay help in thinking about the role expertise plays in legal settings?

And in conclusion, think about the role of the socio-legal researcher. How do these readings on experts and expertise make you think about the role of the researcher? How do they affect your sense of whether you yourself would wish to develop further the research skills you are learning in this course?

ethics aimed at students. For our purpose, Israel and Hay (2006) *Research Ethics for Social Scientists* strikes a good balance between ethical discussion and practical examples that can engage the students. We also require students to read the Socio-Legal Studies Association, 'Statement of Principles of Ethical Research Practice' (January 2009).

By the end of the seminar we wanted students to understand ethical compliance as something much broader and more important than researchers merely protecting themselves against either claims of unethical behaviour or the risk of withdrawal of funding from institutions that do not have ethical review procedures in place. In the seminar, students explored positive reasons for social scientists to be concerned that research is ethical. By this point in the module most students have come to see the potential for empirical research to produce some longer-term good, and so are happy to subscribe to the view that researchers have an obligation to ensure that the research process should not *harm* those who are being 'researched'. However, the intention has been to take students further than this, setting out arguments against an inalienable right to carry out research; that the best research requires that we gain the *trust* of people or communities we are researching, and that research is designed ethically in order to gain this trust. Finally, we should be concerned about ethical practice because we want others to trust our results – unethical practices could put research findings in doubt.

The seminar then explored the difficult ethical issues that arise when applying ethical principles to research participants in positions of power, particularly when research may cast a critical light upon their activities. Through examining research into policing or judging, the students discuss how far considerations of trust and informed consent outweigh the public interest in the conduct and publication of critical research into the powerful. Through readings that focus on two issues commonly faced by socio-legal researchers – ensuring that research participants are knowing and willing participants, and ensuring the confidentiality of participants – the seminar intended to develop critical thinking about the role research ethics can, should and does play in shaping research into the law and powerful legal actors.

The second seminar in this trio explored research methods through the lens of feminist research methodologies. The feminist perspective follows on from research ethics particularly well because feminist research frequently throws up particularly difficult ethical dilemmas, and because many feminist researchers see ethics as a central element of their work.

This seminar asked what makes a piece of research 'feminist', and what it means to attach this label to a piece of research. Seminar readings and discussion focused on the choice of research methods for feminist research, and some notable ethical dilemmas raised in the context of feminist research. These issues were explored in relation to socio-legal research being carried out by a socio-legal research student in the Law School (see Box 3). This has had the added advantage of enabling students to see how a socio-legal approach is translated into the research arena at PhD level.

Box 3: Seminar 9: researching from/in a feminist perspective

Tanya Palmer's research explores the distinction(s) between sex and sexual violation in order to suggest legal models that may better represent this distinction, particularly where sexual violation occurs within the context of abusive relationships. It does so through analysis of criminal laws on sexual offending, theoretical literature on the issue and empirical research, including interviews and focus groups with police officers, survivors, support workers and lay persons.

The format of the final seminar, which considered issues that arise in formulating a research proposal, was developed in response to students articulating fears about the second piece of coursework in which they are asked to write a research proposal (see below). Developing themes, perspectives and methods from throughout the module, the seminar was intended to help students in considering the components of constructing a research proposal. As preparation for the seminar, students are set some reading (borrowed from our colleagues in sociology) on doing qualitative research, devising a research question, and an article by a law and society scholar which explains clearly the empirical issues in conducting an administrative justice research project. Alongside this reading, they are asked to consider an outline of a research problem (taken from a research bid submitted by one of the academic team). They are told that they will be asked to work in groups in the seminar to design a research proposal to address this research problem and given a set of questions which they should consider – these are the same as those set out in the second coursework question (see Box 5 below). In this way, students begin the process of thinking about how they might design their own research proposal.

We have also followed this with a presentation by a socio-legal academic on a successful research bid, a copy of which has been made available to students in advance. This again allows students to begin exploring the problems and issues that arise in putting together a 'real life' research proposal.

Assessment

From the outset we decided that the module would be assessed by coursework only; we believed that an exam would not allow students to engage in a meaningful way with the range of aims of the module. Students do two pieces of coursework, one half-way through the course (submitted after the Christmas vacation) and the other at the end of the module. It was intended that each piece of summative assessment would be aimed at testing students' ability to engage with different aspects of the module.

The first piece of summative assessment tests the student's capacity to bring theory to bear on secondary empirical literature. For example:

- How does the way in which police/experts/regulatory agencies exercise power shape how law is enforced?
- How can either Weber or Foucault's perspectives on governing assist in understanding the role and functioning of regulatory agencies?

Those students who had enjoyed jurisprudence did well in this type of question, but others struggled. A variation of this was tried recently which really seemed to engage the students. Here the question asked students to use the material from preceding seminars to analyse a film (see Box 4).

Box 4: first coursework question

Imagine that you have been asked to write a film review of EITHER *Erin Brockovich* OR *The Corporation* for a popular current affairs journal that regularly carries articles on law-related issues. Using the socio-legal material from any, or all, of the seminars in this term, write a **2000-word** review discussing and analysing what the film tells us about the operation of law within the context of the subject of the film.

The essay must be **fully referenced** using an accepted referencing system (e.g. Harvard).

This coursework followed on from seminars about the use of discretion and legal-consciousness approaches, as well as topics on CSR and Marxist approaches to analysis. Most of the seminar group appeared to engage with the approach of this question, producing some excellent essays using legal consciousness perspectives and/or the material on CSR.

The second piece of summative assessment is intended to test students' capacity to conceptualize the process and structure of primary empirical research. We have experimented with various methods of assessment including:

- asking students to develop a survey and an interview schedule linked to a piece of research literature;
- writing a research proposal that built upon a practical exercise in an earlier seminar.

Currently, the coursework is set out as a detailed set of instructions on issues to be covered in preparing a research proposal, as shown in Box 5.

Box 5: second coursework question

Identify an issue that you consider needs further research. Your essay should set out the background to such a research proposal, explore why this research needs to be done (where you could utilize some of the research from seminar 7 as justification), how you would carry it out, and what possible problems might be encountered. You do not need to be concerned by resource constraints (however, you might decide that some discussion of resource requirements might be appropriate) – this could, for example, be research that requires a number of researchers, or should be carried out over a number of years.

It is not intended that this essay should be a formal research proposal, but it should address the following questions:

1 What are the aims and objectives of the research?
2 What are your research question(s)?
3 What theoretical perspective would you consider would be most appropriate, and why?
4 What contribution to policy-making would you hope that your research would make?
5 What methods would you use (identify the benefits and limitations of your proposed methods)?
6 What ethical issues do your methods give rise to?

There is no specific weighting attached to each of the above questions – how you approach this essay will depend on your own interests and strengths. However, you are encouraged to draw upon material discussed in the **whole** of the unit.

The word limit for this essay is **3000 words**.

This was the piece of coursework that caused students most anxiety. In feedback, several said it was unlike anything else they had been asked to do as a law student. It gave students much more scope for personal choice than in other modules, and asked for *practical* as well as *theoretical* thought.

In order to overcome students' fears, changes have been made from year to year. In the first years, the research proposal question had been the first piece of coursework students were asked to do. Once we realized the anxiety it caused, we reversed the order to enable students to become more attuned to the requirements of thinking empirically as well as theoretically. We also changed the balance of marks, so that the second piece of coursework accounted for 60 per cent of marks, the first for 40 per cent. (The only way we could achieve this within the confines of University of Bristol regulations was to reduce the word limit for the first coursework essay to 2000 words and increase the second to 3000. This had the benefit of allowing us to expect students to cover more ground in setting out their research proposal.) We began to inform the students in the first introductory seminar what they would be expected to do at the culmination of the module; and this second and final coursework question was made available from the beginning of the seminar series in order that students could begin to consider how seminar material could be incorporated into a research proposal. We also made some first-class essays from earlier years available to students on 'Blackboard' (with the consent of the authors).

A significant outcome of the assessment process in each year was the large disparity in marks between the first and second coursework for some students. Often students who had found the application of social theory somewhat challenging in the first coursework came into their element when designing a research project.

Students: who are they and what do they think?

In this final section, we provide some analysis of the types of student who have chosen to take this module, their grade outcomes, and we consider some of the anonymous feedback which was received from them after the module had been completed.

Type of students

The numbers of students taking this module have ranged from 12 to 30, with an average of 15. The gender balance of students taking this unit generally corresponds with the gender balance of those taking the LLB programme. The module tends to be less favoured by international students, perhaps because of the requirements of their jurisdictions and the apparent preponderance of commercial law interests among that sizeable group.

Students who took our module usually had public law and jurisprudence interests, as well as having their enthusiasm generated by the Crime, Justice and Society unit taken by all students in year two (outlined above). The common parallel modules taken by the students included Medical Law and Law and Gender, although a wide variety of other modules were also apparent. In particular, some students have taken this module as well as commercial/ company law modules to balance out their curriculum. In the main, feedback from the students suggested that they chose the module because of an interest in social theory as well as the contexts of law (and for some, because it was coursework not exam-based).

Even before we restricted the module to third-year students, it was mostly taken by third-years. The module is open to non-law students as well and, in most years, a small number of students from across the Faculty of Social Sciences and Law take the module (usually just one or two per annum). This may seem a disappointing uptake from students outside the Law School, but is explicable by reference to the structure of degree programmes in other schools within the faculty: in those schools, open units are generally restricted to students' first year when this module might be stretching them too far. It appears from our feedback that one or two students from those other schools chose this unit, perhaps mistakenly, on the basis that it would give them an understanding of 'law'. Those students usually left the module after the first seminar.

In each year to date, three or four students have demonstrated sufficient appreciation of the subject to have obtained first-class marks on the module; marks generally follow the expected bell curve for all units. Our impression has been that the weaker students in our module are similarly weak in the rest of their degree programme; equally, students who engage with our module are able to develop their interests and produce outstanding work.

Student responses

Feedback is sought from all students at the end of the seminar series on the standard Law School feedback form. Students are asked to rate the module out of five; practically all seem to rate it at four or five. Particular comments note that tutors are passionate about the sessions they teach, which is particularly gratifying as the module reflects the research interests of such a significant proportion of staff within the school. Students are also positive about academics bringing their own research into the seminar room.

Questionnaire returns also reflect the fact that seminars are lively, with interesting, often wide-ranging debate. However, it is also the case that our questionnaire returns suggested that some students find certain topics more challenging than others, and, consequently, do not feel sufficiently able to engage with the discussion so that the seminars can appear one-sided. Some tutors have sought to get around that problem by providing a short introductory lecture (of about 20 minutes) to introduce the subject and provide a base for more complex analysis; that approach was well-received by the students. The inclusion of some theorists has proved more difficult than others when structuring seminars – in particular, our students have found Weber especially challenging – and, although we teach systems theory on our MSc in Socio-Legal Studies, we have not introduced it at undergraduate level because we regard it as too challenging. Students have nevertheless particularly engaged with the 'street-level bureaucracy' literature, perhaps because of the more grounded approach.

Finally, our students regularly describe the module as exciting and refreshing, putting their other courses in 'context'; but they have also expressed anxiety because, in the main, the module is rather different from the other subjects studied within the LLB curriculum. Particular anxiety has been expressed over the assessments which, again, are different from those faced by the students within the rest of the LLB curriculum. As noted above, they are more open-textured and require the students to identify the object of study, rather than address a pre-defined object. Over the years, we have sought to ameliorate that anxiety through the use of formative assessments and by changing the course structure and seminar content.

Conclusion

It will be remembered that one of our original motivations for developing this undergraduate module was to provide a feeder through to our newly developed MSc in Socio-Legal Studies. As a motivation, it is fair to say that this has not been fulfilled. That having been said, though, we remain totally committed to our undergraduate module for two particular reasons.

First, the student experience appears to have been enriched by studying this module. The foundational subjects studied as part of the LLB at Bristol are a mixture of doctrinal law and contextual analysis (although the degree of 'context' depends on how that word is operationalized by our colleagues). The socio-legal module enables students to reflect on the role and power of law across the curriculum, something which they can take with them into future careers or further study. The quality of work produced by our students also demonstrates their willingness and ability to develop their skills into new arenas.

Secondly, our sense is that our colleagues who teach on the module, and (most certainly) ourselves, are able to use it as a way of positively engaging our research with our teaching commitments. Our sense is that, often, lip service is paid to the link between teaching and research – particularly when research drills ever deeper into a field of study and moves ever further away from the seminar room in the foundational subjects. This module has enabled all of us to indulge ourselves by bringing the passion which we share for our research work to bear in the classroom.

Thirdly, we recognize that socio-legal studies has not been particularly well served by the standard undergraduate law curriculum (or at least not in some universities). This was the point made by the authors of the Nuffield Inquiry on Empirical Legal Research (2006), where they discuss 'the problem of self-replication', 'academic careers in law schools', and the 'culture of legal scholarship' (paras 85–103). It has been our aim to meet those particular challenges head on. It would be wonderful to think that, in future, there would be no need for a standalone socio-legal module because the foundational subjects would incorporate the full range of socio-legal work within their delivery.

References

Cooper, D (1995) 'Local government legal consciousness in the shadow of juridification' 22 *Journal of Law and Society* 506

Cotterrell, R (1995) 'Sociology of law in Britain: a case study' in *Law's Community: Legal Theory in Sociological Perspective* (Oxford: Oxford University Press), pp. 73–90

Cowan, D (2004) 'Legal consciousness: some observations' 67(6) *Modern Law Review* 932

Ewick, P A and S Silbey (1998) *The Common Place of Law: Stories from Everyday Life* (Chicago: University of Chicago Press)

Foucault, M (1983) 'The subject and power' in H L Dreyfus and P Rabinow, *Michel Foucault: Beyond Structuralism and Hermeneutics* (Chicago: University of Chicago Press)

Friedman, L M (2005) 'Coming of age: law and society enters an exclusive club' *Annual Review of Law and Social Sciences* 1:1–16

Harlow, C and R Rawlings (2009) *Law and Administration* 3rd edn (London: Butterworths)

Hutter, B and S Lloyd-Bostock (1997) 'Law's relationship with social science: the interdependence of theory, empirical work and social relevance in sociolegal studies' in K Hawkins (ed.) *The Human Face of Law: Essays in Honour of Donald Harris* (Oxford: Clarendon Press), pp. 20–43

Israel, M and I Hay (2006) *Research Ethics for Social Scientists* (London: Sage)

M McDermont, D Cowan and J Prendergast (2009) 'Structuring governance: a case study of the new organisational provision of public service delivery' *Critical Social Policy* 29(4): 677–702

Nuffield Inquiry on Legal Empirical Research (2006) *Law in the Real World: Improving Our Understanding of How Law Works*, www.ucl.ac.uk/laws/socio-legal/empirical/index.shtml (last accessed 14 September 2011)

O'Rourke, D (2001) 'Sweatshops 101: lessons in monitoring apparel production around the world' *Dollars and Sense*, cover story, September/October, www.dollarsandsense.org/archives/2001/0901orourke.html (last accessed 23 November 2011)

O'Rourke, D (2003) 'Outsourcing regulation: analysing non-governmental systems of labour standards monitoring' 31 *Policy Studies Journal* 1–29

Silbey, S (2005) 'After legal consciousness' *Annual Review of Law and Social Science*, 1:323–68

Socio-Legal Studies Association (January 2009) 'Statement of Principles of Ethical Research Practice', www.slsa.ac.uk/research-area (last accessed 23 November 2011)

Vago, S (2009) *Law and Society* 9th edn (Upper Saddle River NJ: Pearson Prentice Hall)

Vick, D and K Campbell (2001) 'Public protests, private lawsuits, and the market: the investor response to the *McLibel* case' (2001) 28 *Journal of Law and Society* 204–41

Willock, I D (1974) 'Getting on with sociologists' 1(1) *British Journal of Law and Society* 3–12

Wynne, B (1989) 'Establishing the rules of laws' in R Smith and B Wynne (eds) *Expert Evidence: Interpreting Science in the Law* (London: Routledge), pp. 23–46

3
Applied Research Methods and Law Reform: The Leeds Experience

Peter Vincent-Jones and Sarah Blandy

Introduction

This chapter reflects on the experience over the past decade of developing and teaching a compulsory module on research methods in the second year of the LLB at Leeds.[1] While the degree programme is essentially doctrinal in nature, at least one module each year takes a broader approach: Legal Skills in Year 1, this module in Year 2, and Jurisprudence in Year 3. Students may also select from a wide range of options in the second and third years, some of which are socio-legal and/or theoretical (such as Family Law). In addition they may choose elective modules in subjects offered by other schools in the university. However, the compulsory first year diet of Torts, Contract, English Legal System and Constitutional Law does not encourage exploration of 'law in action' as distinct from 'law in books' (Pound, 1910). There is therefore little prior context for the introduction of a socio-legal approach to the study of law in Year 2, or preparation for the idea that legal research might include empirical investigation of the law/society relationship.

Background: from 'research methods' to 'advanced legal research and law reform'

Following a review of the LLB programme in the mid-1990s, students at Leeds were required to take a 10-credit module in Research Methods (RM) in the second year of the degree. A core aim of the module was to help prepare students for the compulsory final-year dissertation. To this end students were asked to devise a proposal for a 'research project' consisting of a title, key research questions, an outline of the research approach and methods necessary to answer them, and an indicative bibliography. However,

---

1 Staff currently teaching on the course are Sarah Blandy, Peter Vincent-Jones (module co-ordinator since 2004) and Julie Wallbank. Other colleagues who have taught on previous versions of the module include Phil Hadfield, Chloe Wallace and Emma Wincup.

the link between RM and the dissertation proved problematic for a number of reasons. RM had to be independently assessed in order to contribute 10 credits to Year 2 of the programme. While the proposal could form the basis of the dissertation, an empirical project would be unlikely to be feasible within the time and resource constraints of an undergraduate dissertation, and the school could not guarantee supervisory capacity for the topic. There were other problems with this early version of RM. For example, students tended to choose the same popular topics, within years and between years, leading to cases of suspected copying and plagiarism. The module was criticized by external examiners who were sceptical that a proposal for a research project could really be assessed independently of its implementation. Finally, the module title was arguably inaccurate and misleading. The focus on developing a research proposal in the assessment did not allow sufficient opportunity for students to acquire in-depth understanding of research methods in the accepted social science sense.

Acknowledging these difficulties, the module was redesigned for the 2005–2006 session with a more explicit focus on empirical research methods and a greater emphasis on specifically socio-legal research. The direct link with the final-year dissertation was broken (though the development of research skills relevant to the dissertation remained a key aim) and the form of assessment changed. Students could choose one among seven topic fields (the law relating to gypsies and travelling people; the effects of employment law and regulations on small businesses; the law relating to co-habitation; the awareness on the part of legal professionals of the Human Rights Act 1998; the law relating to prostitution; the impact of judicial review on administrative decision-making; and the law relating to religious discrimination). In their chosen field, students were asked: (a) to provide a brief overview of the range and type of existing legal and socio-legal research, including a select bibliography of not more than ten key references, explaining how the search for relevant sources was carried out; and (b) to design *either* a quantitative *or* a qualitative research study related to the topic. As part of the latter, students were required to explain key research questions and the research methods intended to be used in addressing them, and to consider any political and ethical aspects that might arise in the conduct of the research.

This version of RM was clearly an improvement in more effectively introducing students to social research methods, and also addressed some of the problems of repetition and suspected collusion associated with its predecessor. However, the module was unpopular due to the low perceived relevance of social research to the 'real' subject matter of a law degree. The element of artificiality continued in the requirement that students design an empirical research project which they knew they would never have to carry out, and using skills they thought they would never have to use in their further academic study or in their careers as lawyers.

For the academic year 2006–2007 the module was revised again with a different philosophy. The emphasis shifted to equipping students with the critical skills necessary to evaluate the arguments of academic writers, drawing on qualitative/quantitative research in specific journal articles selected as 'case studies' in the use of socio-legal research methods. For the assessment, students were required to read Quick (2006). Students were asked, with reference to materials studied in the module: (a) to explain the approach adopted by the author to the subject, and evaluate the research methods employed in the empirical study described in the article; and (b) to evaluate the author's use of empirical data and argument in relation to those data.

This move to a 'critical consumer' model, away from the more traditional social science approach involving research project design, was regarded by the teaching team as a significant step forward. The problem of the artificiality of the earlier assessment exercise was avoided and a better justification of the relevance of the module established. The aim was now to promote a critical understanding of how socio-legal researchers use empirical research methods to investigate the operation of law and legal institutions 'in society'. The module would (it was hoped) increase awareness of the study of law beyond legal rules and doctrine, help develop critical skills, and broaden the range of sources students might use in conducting independent research in preparation for writing extended essays and their dissertation in the final year.

Further experimentation followed in academic year 2007–2008. The adequacy of existing law was subjected to scrutiny, and the emphasis placed on the range of legal/socio-legal methodologies and approaches adopted by legal academics in contributing to law reform debates in fields such as family law, employment law and consumer law. Seminars drew on a range of materials distinguishing: (a) black-letter analysis and arguments for law reform directed at increasing doctrinal coherence, whether through the common law or legislation; (b) the use of empirical data (qualitative and/or quantitative) in support of arguments for policy or legal reform; and (c) comparative legal research suggesting solutions to similar problems drawing on the experience of other jurisdictions. Given the practice of skills associated with the doctrinal approach in substantive law modules throughout the degree, the main focus was on empirical and comparative legal research. For the assessment, students were required to write an essay, critically evaluating the use made in published research of *either* empirical methods *or* comparative legal methods in contemporary debates on law reform in one of a limited number of fields: child trafficking in connection with prostitution; legal aid; contact between children and non-resident parents; and religious discrimination.

This iteration of RM represented an advance over earlier versions in linking different critical approaches to the study of law with arguments for legal reform. However, it was also considered a step backwards in the dilution of the focus on empirical research methods. In retrospect, the attempt to introduce students to comparative methodology at this stage in their academic careers was premature. It was also felt that, while there were benefits in increasing the scope for students to demonstrate independent research in their chosen field, something had been lost in the move away from the requirement critically to evaluate one or two carefully selected case-study articles.

Building on this experience, a new module was approved for academic year 2008–2009. The transition from the earlier focus on social research methods to the present emphasis on socio-legal research and law reform was reflected in the new module title Advanced Legal Research and Law Reform (ALRLR).

The current module: ALRLR

The current module provides 10 credits of a total 120 for the year. It is delivered through four one-hour lectures, one library workshop, and four seminars of one-and-a-half hours' duration. The number of lectures has been reduced from five to four, and the self-learn/virtual learning environment (VLE) component increased, in response to focus group and other student feedback. The first lecture introduces students to 'non-doctrinal' approaches to the study of law and to the difference between empirical legal research and doctrinal analysis. It also introduces students to the quantitative/qualitative distinction, and outlines the range of empirical research methods used in socio-legal studies. The second lecture explains key concepts in quantitative empirical research, drawing on examples in the field of negligence focusing on personal injury claims and the compensation culture. The third lecture adopts a similar structure, introducing students to qualitative empirical research, in this instance illustrated with reference to literature on the impact of judicial review on administrative decision-making. The fourth lecture (by Sarah Blandy) takes the students through the design of an actual study undertaken for the Department for Constitutional Affairs, based on the methodology described in the article by Hunter et al. (2008), pointing out why particular methods were chosen, their advantages and drawbacks.

A detailed handout is provided at the beginning of the course, incorporating a 'workbook' designed to enable students to work independently through set questions and recommended reading. There is no standard textbook, so a range of core materials on doctrinal/empirical legal research and social research methods is made available on the VLE. In addition to such reading, for each of Seminars 2–4 students are asked to evaluate case-study journal articles drawing on empirical research. The case-study articles (one in each of Seminars 2 and 3, and two in Seminar 4) are carefully selected to illustrate the use of a range of empirical research methods by socio-legal academics in the subject areas which should be familiar from Year 1: Tort (negligence), Administrative Law (judicial review) and Contract.

Aims, learning outcomes, transferable skills and rationale

The course aims, learning objectives and rationale set out in Box 1 are reproduced directly from the module handbook.

Box 1: aims, learning objectives and rationale

Module aims

- To develop students' understanding of doctrinal and empirical approaches to the study of law and legal phenomena;
- To equip students with a basic understanding of empirical research methods;
- To enable students critically to evaluate the use made by academic writers of such methods and data;
- To encourage understanding of the importance of empirical research in debates concerning law reform;
- To equip students with advanced research skills in using legal databases and the internet;
- To help prepare students for their final-year dissertation.

Learning outcomes

- An appreciation of the range of approaches to the study of law and legal phenomena;
- A basic understanding of empirical research methods;
- An understanding of the role played by empirical data in debates on law reform;
- The ability to carry out scholarly research using legal databases and the internet; and
- The ability to identify research areas, questions and methods appropriate to the final-year dissertation.

Transferable skills

- Increased self-confidence in oral expression, and ability to 'think on your feet';
- Advanced skills in searching for and accessing relevant literature using databases and the internet;
- Skills in critically analysing and evaluating scholarly publications against specified criteria; and
- Writing skills through preparation of assessed coursework.

Module rationale

In completing your first year of legal studies at Leeds you have acquired a range of discipline-specific skills in learning how to 'think' like a lawyer, including finding, understanding, and applying rules and principles in resolving legal problems. Year 1 was concerned mainly with the 'black letter' or doctrinal tradition of legal scholarship, whose purpose is to analyse and expound the law on any particular subject with reference to primary and secondary sources.

The aim of this Year 2 module is to develop further intellectual skills and expertise in research and critical evaluation appropriate to the second year, and to help prepare for the final year Dissertation. To this end we broaden the scope of legal study to include empirical legal research which focuses on how the law and legal institutions operate in their wider social, economic and political context.

Unlike doctrinal research which involves the study of law 'in the books', empirical legal research is based on the observation of law 'in society'. Empirical legal research is increasingly regarded as vital to improving our understanding of how the law works 'in the real world' (see Nuffield Inquiry on Empirical Legal Research, 2006). We explore how empirical methods are used to generate new knowledge and understanding of law in society in the subject areas with which you are already familiar: Tort, Contract, and Administrative Law.

Two types of empirical research in these fields may be distinguished. On the one hand, quantitative research (literally relating to 'quantity') generates 'hard' and 'objective' data expressed in the form of numbers, percentages, or numerical values, which may be manipulated in various ways through statistical analysis. On the other hand, qualitative research (literally relating to 'quality') produces 'soft' data in the form of words or pictures, whose meaning is more 'subjective' and dependent on interpretation.

While quantitative research typically involves the use of methods such as surveys and questionnaires, qualitative research is associated with methods such as interviews and participant observation. However, the quantitative/qualitative dichotomy should not be exaggerated. Much socio-legal research is likely to involve a combination of types of empirical research. And the same empirical method (for example the postal questionnaire) may be used to generate both quantitative and qualitative data.

Doctrinal research and empirical legal research should be regarded as complementary rather than mutually exclusive. Many of the journal articles to which you will be referred in this module combine doctrinal and empirical socio-legal analysis. Both approaches may be critical of existing law and be accompanied by arguments for legal reform/revision – whether by means of legislation or judicial development through the appellate courts.

A further common feature of legal and socio-legal research, whether doctrinal or empirical, is that its conduct is increasingly governed by codes of ethics designed to protect a range of individual and societal interests in the research process.

Doctrinal research, empirical legal research and research ethics

Following a library workshop in which students practise advanced research skills in accessing databases and literature searching, the first seminar is intended to set the scene for subsequent investigation of the use by academics of social research methods in the substantive areas of negligence, judicial review, and contract. The assumption is that students will be familiar with the legal content of these topics from their first-year studies, enabling them to concentrate on methodological issues. A key learning objective at this stage is for students to develop an understanding of essential distinctions – between doctrinal and empirical legal research, and between quantitative and qualitative research.

While the quantitative/qualitative distinction has proved generally unproblematic, many students have considerable difficulty in grasping the peculiar character of the black-letter study of law as a system of legislative rules and judicial doctrines, as taught in the core curriculum in Year 1, and the difference between this dominant tradition and the study of law in society. In preparation for the seminar, students are referred to extracts from McConville and Hong Chui (2007) and asked: 'What is doctrinal legal research? Who does this type of research, for what purposes? What steps are involved in carrying out this type of research? What is empirical legal research? What is the difference between empirical legal research and other "non-doctrinal" approaches to the study of law?'

Having established the relatively narrow scope of the doctrinal approach, the foundations are laid for exploring the complementary nature of empirical legal research, illustrated in arguments for the reform of legal rules based on evidence of their operation and effects 'in the real world'. The idea that the socio-legal study of law might involve a *combination* of doctrinal *and* social research, rather than a focus on social research to the exclusion of legal doctrine, has helped establish the relevance of the module within the

LLB programme.[2] The increasing involvement of staff in teaching ALRLR who have both experience in empirical socio-legal research and academic and/or professional backgrounds in the discipline of law has been a major step forward in this regard. Earlier versions of the RM module were taught by experts in social research methods who (through no fault of their own) lacked legal training and were unfamiliar with the empirical literature in law, and so unsurprisingly were not best placed to explore the links between these aspects of socio-legal research.

The first seminar also encourages students to reflect on why, and for whom, empirical legal research is important. In this connection, students are referred to the Nuffield Inquiry report (2006) and to the Law Commission's website.[3] They are asked what types of research the Law Commission undertakes in discharging its responsibility of ensuring that the law is as 'fair, modern, simple, and as cost-effective as possible'. The remainder of the seminar explores the nature of research ethics in legal research. Students are asked to apply the Socio-Legal Studies Association (SLSA) 'Statement of Principles of Ethical Research Practice' (2009) in considering whether the research described by Carolyn Hoyle in her piece on 'Ethical and Methodological Issues in Researching Domestic Violence' (Hoyle, 2000) was ethically conducted.

Empirical legal research in negligence, judicial review/administrative discretion and contract

For the second seminar (Understanding Quantitative Empirical Legal Research) students are invited to explain what they understand by key concepts in quantitative research such as reliability, replicability, validity (distinguishing internal validity and external validity), generalizability and causality. They are also introduced to the concept of triangulation. This is followed by consideration of the advantages and limitations of secondary analysis of quantitative data, with specific reference to official statistics in the legal and criminal justice fields. Students are asked: 'Why are official statistics on crime likely to be unreliable, and how does the British Crime Survey attempt to avoid this problem?' Students are invited to compare this example with other contexts (such as probation, prison, judicial statistics) which illustrate other problems in the secondary use of quantitative data gathered by government agencies. The rest of the seminar focuses on critical evaluation of a socio-legal article using secondary quantitative analysis, contributing to the

---

2 Of course, we recognise that much empirical socio-legal research has nothing to do with legal doctrine in the sense here defined. Similarly, only a certain type of socio-legal research has direct implications for the reform of law or legal institutions. However, all the case-study articles used in the ALRLR module have such characteristics, at least to some degree.

3 www.justice.gov.uk/lawcommission/index.htm

compensation culture debate (Lewis et al., 2006).[4] A checklist is provided to encourage students to work through the article systematically and to identify key issues, as follows:

1 Is the approach doctrinal, empirical, or a combination?
2 What aspect of law, or what 'problem', does the research address? What are the main research questions? What are the researchers trying to find out? What 'gap' in our knowledge does the research seek to fill?
3 Is the research qualitative, quantitative, or a combination of these types (n.b. triangulation)? Is the research 'primary' or 'secondary'? If quantitative secondary research, is there any use of official statistics?
4 What empirical methods, or techniques, are the researchers using to address their research questions (n.b. triangulation)?
5 What empirical data are produced by the methods used?
6 Are the data produced by the research methods reliable? Is the research replicable? Have the researchers spelt out their procedures so that the results are capable of replication?
7 How do the researchers analyse the data? What analytical methods do they employ? How are the raw data presented or manipulated, and in what form?
8 Assuming the data to be reliable, are the results of the research 'externally valid'? How representative is the *sample* (that segment or part of the phenomenon that the researchers are trying to study)?
9 Where research data are claimed to show a causal relationship between 'x' and 'y', does the claim hold water; does 'x' really explain or cause 'y'? Are inferences 'internally valid'?
10 What ethical issues were at stake in this research? Did the researchers conform to any ethical code, e.g. SLSA 'Statement of Principles of Ethical Research Practice' (2009)? What ethical principles *should* they have observed?
11 How convinced are you by the authors' overall argument and conclusions based on the empirical research? What are the implications of the research for legal reform, either explicitly addressed by the authors, or implicit? What does the research contribute to our understanding of law in this field? How successful is it in filling 'gaps' in knowledge?

The third seminar (Understanding Qualitative Empirical Legal Research) follows a similar pattern. Students are invited to explain key qualitative research concepts, and to consider why (according to social research

---

4 Other journal articles in the field of tort/negligence drawing on empirical research methods that have been found suitable include Gray and Sharpe (1973), Dingwall et al. (2000), Lewis et al. (2002), Williams (2003; 2005), Morris (2007) and Hand (2010).

methods experts referred to in the core reading) criteria such as reliability and validity have to be adapted or differently applied in this context. The reasons concern the very different aims of qualitative researchers, who as a rule are not claiming to produce findings that are generalizable to other social settings, or to 'measure' social reality with the same degree of accuracy as their quantitative counterparts. Accordingly, while all other points on the checklist for evaluation of the qualitative case study article (Halliday, 2000a)[5] are the same, prompts 6, 8 and 9 differ from those in the previous exercise. So rather than ask whether the data produced by the research are 'reliable' and 'capable of replication', the question is whether they are 'dependable' or 'auditable' (whether the research has been carried out in a manner likely to convince an independent auditor or peer reviewer of their trustworthiness: Lincoln and Guba, 1985). Again, instead of asking whether the results of the research are 'externally valid' and whether the sample is 'representative', the focus here is on the extent of 'thick description' and 'transferability' to other contexts. And, finally, in place of the concern with 'internal validity' and 'causality', the parallel question for qualitative research is whether the results are 'credible' in the sense of being feasible, or likely to be believed by others. Here the empirical focus is on the impact of administrative law, in particular judicial review, on the exercise of discretion in decision-making by local authorities implementing homelessness legislation.

For the final seminar (Understanding Empirical Research on Contract), students are asked to evaluate two articles, one quantitative (Vincent-Jones, 1993) and the other qualitative (Beale and Dugdale, 1975).[6] Whereas in the previous two seminars some of the answers to checklist questions are obvious from the seminar's focus on either quantitative or qualitative research, here no clues are provided as to the nature of the empirical research, so students are required independently to demonstrate understanding of key distinctions and to determine and apply the appropriate criteria for evaluation.

By the end of the module, therefore, the same evaluation technique will have been practised on four occasions across the three different subject fields of Tort, Contract, and Administrative Law. The intention is that students will thereby have acquired a range of critical consumer skills necessary to understand how socio-legal arguments about law and law reform are made on the basis of empirical research, and that these skills should be transferable and of practical use in their independent research for assessed essays and their final-year dissertation. The critical skills element is reinforced by the assessment,

---

5 Empirical studies of judicial review/administrative discretion include Halliday (2000b), Machin and Richardson (2000) and Sunkin et al. (2007).
6 On the empirical socio-legal study of contract, see also Macaulay (1963) and Lewis (1982).

which adopts a similar format to the seminar exercises. Students are required to write a 2500-word essay:

> With reference to research methods concepts studied in this module, evaluate the argument of the author(s) in one of the following articles, paying particular attention to (i) the methods employed and the use made of empirical data, and (ii) the contribution of the research to the understanding of law in the given field.

For 2010–2011 the articles were: Pick and Sunkin (2001) and Williams (2007).[7]

In addition to the written assignment, for the 2011–2012 session an element of oral assessment has been introduced, weighted 15 per cent of the total mark. Students are informed in the module handbook:

> We aim to encourage an open and relaxed atmosphere in which everyone has the opportunity to learn by participating in discussion. For each of seminars 2–4 you will be assessed according to the following criteria:

> - Preparation: We expect you to bring notes to the seminar so that we can see how you have prepared answers to the set questions. Space has been provided in the Workbook for you to make notes for seminar preparation (if you do this electronically, you are expected to bring a printed copy to the seminar).
> - Contribution to discussion: We expect you to make relevant points in participating in and contributing to discussion, but also to show sensitivity to others in the class by responding to them in a respectful and constructive fashion. Listening carefully is just as important as speaking clearly. A good seminar participant will not dominate discussion.
> - Quality of content: We expect you to demonstrate orally your familiarity with the module materials, and your knowledge and understanding of key methodological issues and concepts. You will not be penalised for making mistakes or for being wrong, indeed learning from mistakes is one of the benefits of open discussion.
> - Quality of expression: We are looking for clarity, fluency and conciseness in your oral expression. The ability to 'think on your feet' and respond appropriately to unanticipated situations, comments or questions is a core transferable skill.

---

7 The assessment articles for 2011–2012 were Halliday (2000b) and Hand (2010).

Discussion and conclusion

Following a lengthy period of experimentation, the ALRLR module in its present form is more or less established as part of the LLB at Leeds. In summary, the module has evolved through four phases with different aims:

- As originally envisaged, RM sought to equip students with skills necessary for devising a research proposal in preparation for their final-year dissertation.
- In the second phase students were encouraged to carry out independent research in one of a number of fields of socio-legal studies, and to devise a research proposal using empirical methods in their chosen field.
- Phase 3 saw the introduction of the critical consumer model, in which the aim shifted to equipping students with critical skills necessary to evaluate the arguments of academic writers, drawing on qualitative/quantitative research, in specific journal articles selected as case studies in the use of socio-legal research methods.
- The final step in the development of ALRLR builds on this core requirement of critical evaluation, but with specific reference to the use made by the authors of empirical research in arguments contributing to contemporary socio-legal debates including those on law reform.

The evolution has been far from unproblematic, and the module might have been abandoned at various times over the past ten years due to a range of factors including student dissatisfaction, lack of staff engagement and concerns about the negative impact on National Student Survey. There is no doubt that the publication of the Nuffield Report in 2006 and the increasing interest in broadening the scope of the law curriculum have reinforced the school's commitment to retaining an element of social research methods training in the degree programme. While ALRLR is undergoing further development and there is work still to do in convincing some students of its value and relevance, there are encouraging signs that the investment in time and resources is being rewarded: recent feedback from students has been more positive; external examiners have been enthusiastic; there has been a consistently high proportion of first-class marks in the last three years; and most recently, assessment of seminars has transformed the experience of teaching the module and resulted in an apparently improved experience for students.

The absence of examples of established practice either within the UK or internationally on which to draw continues to be a major problem. At the time of writing, Leeds is unusual if not unique in requiring LLB students to take a compulsory course incorporating socio-legal methods in their second year. The development of the module has been a matter of trial and error, with a number of (what have turned out to be) wrong turnings. A related difficulty has been the lack of suitable teaching materials. While there are excellent introductory books exploring the nature of socio-legal studies (Travers, 2010), and some books dealing specifically with aspects of research methods for law (McConville and Hong Chui, 2007), there appears to be nothing suited to the particular requirements of ALRLR. For our purposes, the problem with established texts on social research methods (e.g. Punch, 1999; Burns, 2000; May, 2001; Bryman, 2008; Kalof et al. 2008) is that they are written for a social science audience, and do not include socio-legal examples or address the crucial nature of the relationship between empirical and doctrinal research.[8]

There is also the continuing difficulty of striking a balance between the emphasis on social research methods and the substance of socio-legal analysis in the areas studied. As has been seen, the main purpose of the module is to equip students with transferable skills which are repeatedly practised in relation to selected case-study fields both in seminars and in the assessment. The rationale for the focus on negligence, contract and administrative law is that students should be familiar with the doctrinal aspects of these core areas from the first year, and should be receptive to a socio-legal approach which complements their black-letter knowledge of law. The assumption is that students will naturally be interested in questions such as whether and how business people use contract law in practice; whether there exists in Britain a damaging compensation culture with too many negligence claims; and whether bureaucratic decision-making conforms to the lawyer's ideal of administrative justice. However, the idea that students acquire a basic understanding in Year 1 which they carry into Year 2 has in many cases proved over-optimistic. More fundamentally, the separation of doctrinal and socio-legal knowledge implicit in this model of undergraduate legal education is debatable, raising the question of whether it might be better to incorporate a socio-legal element into substantive subjects from the outset. While socio-legal methodology might be regarded ideally as forming just one part of a more general socio-legal approach to the study of law, the opportunities for such study are limited by the constraints of the undergraduate curriculum, which remains overwhelmingly doctrinal. Against this background, a module which necessarily concentrates on methodological issues cannot expect to generate much interest in a broader socio-legal approach, although each year it seems to have this beneficial effect on some students.

Various challenges will need to be met in consolidating the achievements of ALRLR to date. An important factor in the school's re-commitment to the module in 2007–2008 was the willingness of established staff with appropriate socio-legal experience to teach it. As has been seen, we consider it

---

8 On the relationship between legal and socio-legal method more generally, see, however, Dobinson and Johns (2007); Salter and Mason (2007).

essential that teaching is undertaken by staff with legal backgrounds who have conducted empirical research in their own fields. However, course delivery remains heavily dependent on the input of two or three senior academics with such experience. There is a general reluctance of staff to become involved in teaching on the module, despite its acknowledged importance as a compulsory element in Year 2 of the LLB programme. It is vital that lessons learned from the development of ALRLR from its origins in RM are not lost, and that a critical mass of appropriately qualified and motivated staff is developed and maintained.

There is also a need for further fine-tuning and experimentation. The module's present structure and content have been the result of a number of compromises. For example, one drawback with the critical consumer model and associated assessment is that students are confined to critiquing a limited range of articles, and do not have the opportunity to undertake research in a topic area of their own choosing. This limitation is avoided only to some extent through incorporation of an element in the assessment addressing the 'contribution of the research (described in the article) to the understanding of law in the given field'. Many students find this aspect of the assessment difficult, probably because of fundamental problems in seeing the relevance of socio-legal research. Nor can it be claimed that ALRLR leads on to the dissertation in the same way as would a module requiring students to undertake independent research in preparing a dissertation proposal. Another problem with the current model is that that an author's presentation of empirical research in a journal article tends to provide only limited information on the research methods employed in a prior empirical study. The consequence is that much of the evaluation can only be speculative and must take the form of identifying conditions that would need to have been satisfied in order (for example) for the research to be considered ethical, or for the data to be regarded as reliable or dependable. We might get round this problem by using research reports, which include greater detail on research methods, in place of journal articles as the subject matter for evaluation. But this would undercut the objective of developing skills in evaluating socio-legal arguments that draw on empirical research, which are transferable and enhance the capacity for 'critical reading' in the remainder of the degree programme.

A final limitation of the critical consumer approach to empirical socio-legal skills training is that any article published in a peer-reviewed academic journal is unlikely to be methodologically incompetent. Given the absence of obvious 'mistakes', there is a limit in the extent to which an evaluation can be expected to be critical. On the other hand, there is no research design that could not be improved by more time and resources, and the evaluation exercise in its present form has succeeded in developing students' understanding of how the range and quality of empirical socio-legal research is inevitably hampered to some degree by such practical constraints.

Although the majority of law students at Leeds continue to base their final-year dissertations on what might be described as 'doctrinal' subject matter, a significant minority choose topics which require at least some discussion of 'law in society', and a number of dissertations are genuinely socio-legal. The generally high standard of dissertations suggests that even the more resistant students develop through ALRLR useful transferable skills, for example in searching databases and reviewing scholarly literature, and in engaging with a wide range of source material. The module also provides students with the opportunity to practise critical skills, both in oral contributions to seminars and in writing for the assignment, in a form that does not exist elsewhere in the curriculum. Beyond this, we hope that Leeds students will complete the module with a greater appreciation that the study of law can embrace both doctrinal and non-doctrinal approaches, and that socio-legal research has a distinctive contribution to make to the better understanding of law and its further development and reform.

References

Beale, H and T Dugdale (1975) 'Contracts between businessmen: planning and the use of contractual remedies' 2 *British Journal of Law and Society* 45–60

Bryman, A (2008) *Social Research Methods* 3rd edn (Oxford: Oxford University Press)

Burns, R B (2000) *Introduction to Research Methods* (London: Sage)

Dingwall, R, T Durkin, P Pleasance, W Felstiner and R Bowles (2000) 'Firm handling: the litigation strategies of defence lawyers in personal injury cases' 20 *Legal Studies* 1–18

Dobinson, I and F Johns (2007) 'Qualitative legal research' in M McConville and W Hong Chui (eds) *Research Methods for Law* (Edinburgh: Edinburgh University Press)

Gray, R J and G S Sharpe (1973) 'Doctors, Samaritans and the accident victim' 11 *Osgoode Hall Law Journal* 1–29.

Halliday, S (2000a) 'The influence of judicial review on bureaucratic decision making' (Spring) *Public Law* 110

Halliday, S (2000b) 'Institutional racism in bureaucratic decision-making: a case study in the administration of homelessness law' 27 *Journal of Law and Society* 449–71

Hand, J (2010) 'The compensation culture; cliché or cause for concern?' 37 *Journal of Law and Society* 569–91

Hoyle, C (2000) 'Ethical and methodological issues in researching domestic violence' in R King and E Wincup (eds) *Doing Research on Crime and Justice* (Oxford: Oxford University Press)

Hunter, C, J Nixon and S Blandy (2008) 'Researching the judiciary: exploring the invisible in judicial decision making' 35 *Journal of Law and Society*, Special Research Issue, 76–90

Kalof, L, A Dan and T Dietz (2008) *Essentials of Social Research* (Maidenhead: Open University Press)

Lewis, R (1982) 'Contracts between businessmen: reform of the law of firm offers and an empirical study of tendering practices in the building industry' 9 *Journal of Law and Society* 153–69

Lewis, R, R McNabb, H Robinson and V Wass (2002) 'Court awards for loss of future earnings: an empirical study and an alternative method of calculation' 29 *Journal of Law and Society* 406–35

Lewis, R, A Morris and K Oliphant (2006) 'Tort personal injury claims statistics: is there a compensation culture in the United Kingdom?' *Journal of Personal Injury Law* 87.

Lincoln, Y S and E G Guba (1985) *Naturalistic Inquiry* (Beverly Hills CA: Sage)

Macaulay, S (1963) 'Non-contractual relations in business: a preliminary study' 28 *American Sociological Review* 55–67

Machin, D and G Richardson (2000) 'Judicial review and tribunal decision making: a study of the Mental Health Review Tribunal' *Public Law* 494–514

May, T (2001) *Social Research: Issues, Methods and Process* 3rd edn (Buckingham: Open University Press)

McConville, M and W Hong Chui (eds) (2007) *Research Methods for Law* (Edinburgh: Edinburgh University Press)

Morris, A (2007) 'Spiralling or stabilising? The compensation culture and our propensity to claim damages for personal injury' 70 *Modern Law Review* 349–78

Nuffield Inquiry on Empirical Legal Research (2006) *Law in the Real World: Improving Our Understanding of How Law Works* (London: Nuffield Foundation)

Pick, K and M Sunkin (2001) 'The changing impact of judicial review: the independent review service of the Social Fund' (Winter) *Public Law* 736–62

Pound, R (1910) 'Law in books and law in action' 44 *American Law Review* 12–36

Punch, K F (1999) *Introduction to Social Research: Quantitative and Qualitative Approaches* (London: Sage)

Quick, O (2006) 'Prosecuting "gross" medical negligence: manslaughter, discretion, and the Crown Prosecution Service' 33 *Journal of Law and Society* 421

Salter, M and J Mason (2007) *Writing Law Dissertations* (Harlow: Pearson Education)

Socio-Legal Studies Association (January 2009) 'Statement of Principles of Ethical Research Practice', available at www.slsa.ac.uk/research-area

Sunkin, M, K Calvo, L Platt and T Landman (2007) 'Mapping the use of judicial review to challenge local authorities in England and Wales' *Public Law* 545–67

Travers, M (2010) *Understanding Law and Society* (Abingdon: Routledge)

Vincent-Jones, P (1993) 'Contract litigation in England and Wales 1975–1992: a transformation in business disputing?' 12 *Civil Justice Quarterly* 337

Williams, K (2003) 'Doctors as good Samaritans: some empirical evidence concerning emergency medical treatment in Britain' 30 *Journal of Law and Society* 258–82

Williams, K (2005) 'State of fear: Britain's "compensation culture" reviewed' 25 *Legal Studies* 499–514

Williams, K (2007) 'Litigation against English NHS ambulance services and the rule in *Kent v Griffiths*' *Medical Law Review* 153–75.

4

Innovations in Assessment: Family Law at Sheffield

Penelope Russell

Introduction

In this chapter I will describe the way in which one institution, namely the University of Sheffield, has managed to combine socio-legal research with assessment within the undergraduate curriculum. It was devised over a decade ago by my predecessor, Catherine Williams, with two aims: to enhance student learning; and to provide large data sets for further research. In this chapter I will focus solely on the former.[1]

I have only been coordinator of the module for the last year and I have grappled with some issues relating to the socio-legal assessment, not all of which have been resolved. The combination of assessment and socio-legal research provides a number of benefits but these are inevitably limited by the resources of an undergraduate programme. These benefits, limitations and issues will be explored later in the chapter.

The assessment is within the Family Law module of the LLB programme. It comprises an essay question to be answered over a six-week period on an unsupervised basis, what we call a 'coursework project'.

The Family Law module carries 20 credits; the University of Sheffield LLB programme requires that 120 credits must be accumulated in each academic year, divided between two semesters.

The inclusion of a coursework project within the assessment regime of the module means that there are a range of assessments: the coursework project carrying 40 per cent of the overall marks and examination and seminar performance carrying the balance of marks. Having a range of assessments benefits both student and tutor. For the student, it has the benefit that a broader range of skills and knowledge is tested and there is greater opportunity to do well. For the tutor, there are a number of different assessments

---

1 For a very helpful explanation of the research aspect, see Potter and Williams (2007).

staggered over time so the marking is varied and spread over a period, which aids tutor concentration.

The coursework project has an additional requirement that each student must carry out empirical research in order to answer the essay question. The research is of the most basic variety, namely each student is provided with a pre-prepared questionnaire to which they find ten respondents. A survey method was chosen because it is simple to administer and provides standardized responses, which aids the marking process. It is also less invasive than other forms of empirical research, with fewer ethical concerns.

The questionnaire sets out a number of scenarios that are fictional but realistic. Each scenario is usually a variation on a theme. By way of illustration, examples can be given from previous years, all in the context of family law. The most recent was a consideration of the division of property on divorce. The question paper asked students to examine critically, using subsequent case law and survey results, a statement made by Lord Nicholls in *White v White* [2000] 2 FLR 981 that fairness prohibits discrimination between the roles of husband and wife. The survey requested respondents' view of a fair division of the capital and income of the marriage in scenarios of varying lengths of marriage and nature of contribution. Students were asked to use the survey data to consider whether Lord Nicholls' approach accords with the views of their respondents. Earlier questionnaires have set out scenarios seeking respondents' opinions on whether unmarried fathers should have parental responsibility for their children and whether cohabitants should have the right to inherit their deceased partner's property, as well as respondents' views on transcultural adoption.

Including empirical research within the coursework assessment sends a clear message to students about the value and importance of socio-legal research. Knight (1998) states: 'Assessment is a moral activity. What we choose to assess and how shows quite starkly what we value.' (p. 13) It places socio-legal research at the heart of the undergraduate experience and ensures that it has the full attention of students. This and other benefits will be explored later in the chapter, but firstly I will set out the mechanics of organizing the coursework project.

Method

The first step is to select the topic: something interesting, perhaps controversial, that students and their respondents can relate to. The questionnaire is essentially a public opinion survey, as all that can be sought in the circumstances is respondents' views of the law, not their experiences of the effects of the law. This is because students would find it difficult to locate respondents with the necessary experience and there would also be difficult ethical issues to overcome. The questionnaire topic must be one that a member of the public can understand and express an opinion about. Ideally it would be something currently in the news but it must be borne in mind that there is an inevitable delay (perhaps up to a year) between the writing of the materials and their release to students. This delay is caused by piloting and then by internal ethics and scrutiny approvals.

The next step is to write the questionnaire. This throws up interesting design questions. Usually it comprises a number of factual scenarios upon which respondents are asked for their opinion. Should the questions be open or closed, seeking qualitative data or quantitative data? Obviously open-ended questions seeking qualitative data can yield more interesting results and greater insights, but restricting the questions to tick box answers means that the process is simpler and there is less risk of contamination of the results by the student interviewer. The latter is of particular concern as the students tend to interview family and friends and therefore the relationship may inhibit an honest verbal response. I would suggest that the best design is the inclusion of tick-box options in order to provide an essential structure, with the addition of a few open-ended questions to give respondents some opportunity to explain their choice of option in their own words if they wish.

As well as the scenario questions, the questionnaire includes a data request for personal information about the respondents including their marital status, gender, age and occupation, but excluding their name or any other identifying characteristics. Additional questions can be included, such as parental status or property ownership, depending on the nature of the research topic. Thought can also be given to seeking information about social class which could be addressed by asking about employment, housing type and/or household income. This provides the students with helpful information when interpreting the survey results and allows a more detailed and complex analysis.

Obviously, care must be taken when drafting the questionnaire to ensure that the meaning of the scenario questions is clear to both the student researchers and potential respondents. In particular, the terminology should be comprehensible to a layperson and technical language should be avoided. Piloting should reveal any lack of clarity or potential misunderstanding which could affect the validity of the survey results. Amendment can be made to the questionnaire at that point.

Once the questionnaire has been finalized, the next step is to seek generic ethics approval. On the prescribed application form it is explained that the nature of the research project is educational, the empirical research is being carried out by students in order to answer an essay question and the objectives of the research project include giving students experience in collecting and analysing survey data.

The submission of the ethics application includes the provision of an information sheet and consent form. This not only forms an important part of the students' introduction to the practice of empirical research and ensures that full consent is freely given but also minimizes the risk of fabrication of responses, as the consent form requires a signature and it is anticipated that it would be more difficult to fabricate ten different signatures than to obtain responses to the questionnaire. The consent form should also be signed by the student researcher but, in order to maintain anonymity for the purposes of the assessment, students are asked to write their registration number instead of their name on the forms.

The question paper for the coursework project must also be drafted. This sets out the essay question and the learning outcomes for the assessment, stating for example that candidates are required to conduct a survey using a pre-prepared questionnaire and to incorporate the findings into the essay, to include an explanation and evaluation of the survey method as well as interpretation of the survey results. The importance of explicit learning outcomes cannot be overemphasized as they aid transparency of academic expectations for the benefit of the students and promote equality of opportunity. They ensure that the assessment goals are clear and should therefore reduce any student uncertainty and worries about what is expected of them. Also, drafting the learning outcomes is a valuable process for the tutor as they impose a requirement to articulate exactly what it is that the students should be learning, a more difficult issue than would initially appear.

At around the time of release of the materials to students, a lecture is given solely about the coursework project. This is good practice as the novel nature of the coursework project can cause anxiety and it is hoped that a clear explanation about the assessment will lessen this. Students can be wary of innovative forms of assessment, so it is important that the coursework project is introduced to them in a confident and accurate manner. The lecture also gives very basic research training and guidance about the conduct of socio-legal research including steps to minimize interviewer bias. It provides an introduction to concepts such as validity and reliability, suggesting that the students should take into account the implications of the size and characteristics of their sample. At the end of the lecture, preliminary reading about socio-legal research is recommended, including parts of Colin Robson's 'real world research' (Robson, 2011). In particular, students are told that they must not interview anyone under the age of 18 or share respondents, to avoid burdening anyone unduly. In the lecture, the students are shown one of the questionnaire scenarios on a Powerpoint slide and asked to vote on the outcome by a show of hands, thereby provoking an emotional engagement with the issues raised in the scenario.

The students are told that they must find ten respondents to answer the survey. Regarding the selection of respondents, there are inevitable ethical issues. The expectation is that they will approach family and friends, yet this can cause concerns that consent is not being freely given. On the other hand, there are safety issues if strangers are being approached, even in public places. The students are also asked to read out the questions to each respondent rather than allowing them to complete the questionnaire on their own. This is so that they can obtain some meaningful qualitative data, as well as deal with any queries about any of the questions.

The students then have six weeks in which to obtain respondents to the questionnaire, analyse the survey results and write up their coursework project essay. The essay is submitted, along with the completed questionnaires and signed consent forms.

Marking is by way of the usual School of Law assessment criteria for marking an essay, with a mark being given out of 100. These are the criteria applicable to all assessments within the law school. One advantage of this is that the students are familiar with it so they have some awareness of the standards required in their written work. The standard law school criteria are designed to cover the assessment of an essay but some modification of the materials is needed to ensure and show that the marking does reflect the additional requirements of the empirical research. This is done by the drafting of a feedback sheet, which is made available to students prior to starting the coursework and is explained during the coursework project lecture. The feedback sheet makes specific reference to the socio-legal elements of the coursework project – the analysis of the survey results – which the standard law school marking criteria do not. Thus, good essays will include: 'Systematic analysis of the survey results incorporating the results into the essay'.

Once the marking is complete, generic feedback is made available and specific written feedback is given to each student. One-to-one feedback is also available if requested.

Benefits

In order to introduce students to socio-legal research in a meaningful way, it is highly desirable that it is in the form of assessment. Assessment by its very nature is highly motivating; assessment's central role in the experience of learning is well-documented: 'Assessment is at the heart of the undergraduate experience. Assessment defines what students regard as important, how they spend their time, and how they come to see themselves as students and then as graduates.' (Brown and Knight, 1994, p. 12) It is integral to learning and its importance to learning cannot be overestimated.

Assessment has a huge impact on the learning process. Rather than being an end in itself, it is an impetus for learning. Boud (1998) states: 'Assessment is the most significant prompt for learning.' (p. 37) It always leads to learning and we need to ensure that the learning is what we are seeking. It has long been recognized that assessment can be used strategically as it determines how students focus their learning (Rowntree, 1987). By requiring empirical research as part of the assessment of the module, it ensures that students do spend at least some of their time on such research.

After this year's coursework project, I carried out a written survey of the family law students to find out their views of it. The vast majority thoroughly enjoyed doing the research, saying that the human aspect had stimulated their interest. Empirical research can bring the subject alive and enable students to think about the law from a different perspective. This was reflected in the survey responses, one student commenting: 'It enabled me to think about whether the law is satisfactory rather than writing an essay solely on the position of the law.' The students were easily able to engage with the assessment task as it is meaningful research in a realistic context, enabling them to see the implications of the law in practice. Further comments included: 'It's clearly relevant to society so the questionnaire was a good idea.' and 'It was good to get public opinion on the law.'

From the survey results and the finished projects, it appears that the coursework provides an authentic and productive vehicle for the students' efforts. It captures their time and attention, introducing them to a new method and new concepts. The project provides them with a valuable learning experience, introducing them to socio-legal research and requiring them to show awareness of methodological issues. One student commented: 'I thought the idea of incorporating a questionnaire was a good idea and a nice break from the norm.' Also, due to the novel nature of the empirical research and a different question being set each year, the risks of plagiarism are greatly reduced.

There is recognition within pedagogical literature that the method of assessment can encourage a deep approach to learning (as opposed to a surface approach to learning), which then produces better outcomes and maximizes student achievement. It can give students 'a sense of involvement, challenge and achievement together with feelings of personal fulfilment and pleasure' (Ramsden, 2003, p. 57). I would argue that the coursework project has elements that would support a deep approach to learning. For example, the topic is of personal interest to students and so it encourages them to extract personal meaning from the exercise. Also, the form of the essay question supports a search for connection between the black-letter law and the results of the survey.

It can be argued that it is impossible to appreciate an area such as family law without carrying out socio-legal research. Family law is by its very nature empirical: it has an essential human aspect which cannot be ignored. By doing the coursework project, students are able to apply the abstract principles to practical situations and appreciate the effectiveness of the law in context. Arguably, it would be inappropriate to assess understanding of such a social subject in isolation from its practical context as it is generally recognized that there should be alignment of learning, teaching and assessment (Biggs, 2003): we cannot teach family law as a practical subject without assessing the same.

The final benefit of the inclusion of socio-legal research in assessment relates to the acquisition of skills. The coursework project poses a challenge for students as it requires them to try something new, such as interviewing family and friends. The assessment is not simply evaluating the skill of memorization but also higher cognitive functions such as analysis and evaluation (Bloom, 1965). It enables the display of skills required by the Quality Assurance Agency (QAA) for Higher Education.[2] These include, amongst others, the ability to use and evaluate numerical information and to engage in research which involves non-legal sources and materials. These skills are of long-lasting benefit to the students as they can be of use to them in different contexts after graduation. The nature of the coursework project also supports learning as a lifelong process: the students are expected to work autonomously, being given responsibility and expected to exercise choice over certain aspects of the research project. One student commented: 'As the coursework was different to that of other modules, my research skills developed and ability to apply results to facts increased.'

Limitations

It is highly desirable that opportunities for student autonomy and innovation are maximized, as this is linked with greater student engagement and achievement and thereby deeper approaches to learning (Prosser and Trigwell, 2001, p. 68). However, the coursework project can only be an introduction to carrying out socio-legal research, as it omits the initial step of survey design. The project is only concerned with the end result, as the students are given a pre-prepared questionnaire and research question. Ideally, the students would select their own research topic and design their own research instrument but this is impossible on any undergraduate module, given the time available and number of students involved. One insurmountable hurdle would be ethics approval: it would not be possible for ethics approval to be given to each individual student project.

---

2 'Subject benchmark statement for law' set out the minimum standard for a graduate with an honours bachelor's degree in law. See www.qaa.ac.uk.

The main characteristic of autonomy is that students take responsibility for their own learning and there are many theoretical opportunities for this to be supported. Boud (1988) suggests a number of such opportunities (p. 23), but some are not feasible on an undergraduate programme. These include identifying learning needs, setting goals, selecting the learning project and determining the assessment criteria. On the other hand, there are some autonomous actions available to students, namely they are able to plan their learning and learn outside the institution (when conducting the survey). They do not have the opportunity to design the research instrument, but they are expected to evaluate the one used. A further option is to suggest that they reflect on the learning process but, given that they are conducting empirical research and submitting an essay, it may be unduly onerous to also require the completion of a reflective diary about the process.

Given that the students have no input into the selection topic or research method, I have tried to find other ways to increase their engagement with the questionnaire provided to them and to support innovation.

Firstly, they are encouraged to collaborate with others. This is desirable for a number of reasons. The QAA lists the ability to work in a team as one of the skills expected of a law graduate. Also, collaboration is another way in which innovation can be encouraged and can provide moral support and maintain motivation amongst the group. In the lecture, the students are told that they can compare results with fellow student researchers and include this within their essay. This is not obligatory as it is dependent on the cooperation of others and is not entirely within their control.

Secondly, they are given freedom as to sample selection. They are required to find ten respondents but can select the characteristics of the sample. This enables students to pick a particular type of respondent, if they wish. The students who chose to do this seemed to particularly relish the experience, as it enabled them to test a hypothesis – for example, that older women would have a certain opinion about the law, in comparison with others with different characteristics.

Thirdly, I try to support innovation by designing the essay question so that it is as wide as possible, with the intention that the students can simply choose to deal with one aspect of it, supported by part of the data. I do this by the inclusion of a quotation with an instruction to carry out critical analysis. However, this then conflicts with another limitation, namely that of the word limit, which is set centrally by the university based on the credit rating of the module. Some students in my survey did not appreciate that they could simply answer one aspect of the question and complained that the question was too wide for the word limit. What poses an opportunity for one student can be cause for anxiety in another. Next year, I will try to reduce such anxiety by making the element of choice clear to the entire cohort, not only those who attend the coursework project lecture, by the provision of written materials.

Resource issues mean that the coursework project is inevitably an artificial process. For example, the students are only expected to obtain ten respondents, but such a small sample size impairs the significance of the results and has the consequence that meaningful quantitative analysis is not possible. Ten seems to be the optimum number in terms of practicality, yet it could be said to be undermining the authenticity of the research. In my survey, a couple of students raised concerns about this, querying the value of the research, one writing: 'I did not really see the value of the research (it was so unrepresentative).' If it appears that the small number of respondents is impairing the students' emotional engagement with the project, it could be suggested that they pool results so that a larger data set is produced, although this would have to be on condition that analysis of the results remains an individual exercise so that collusion is avoided.

The resource issues and inevitable limitations have implications for the marking of the coursework project. In empirical research, the sample size should be as large as possible, but the marks allocated within the assessment cannot reflect this: students are not awarded marks to reflect their sample size. Almost all students interviewed the required number of ten respondents, but a couple of students located significantly larger numbers. No additional marks were awarded to them. This is because, if marks were awarded for obtaining a larger sample size, it puts pressure on the entire cohort to find a larger number, which is unrealistic and undesirable. In other words, the marking of the assessment cannot accurately reflect good socio-legal practice.

This approach can be contrasted with the selection of the characteristics of the sample. Extra marks were awarded to students who selected a sample with particular characteristics in order to test a hypothesis, although it may be difficult for international students to carry out a similar exercise. The extra marks were awarded on the basis that students are showing awareness of methodological issues, which is one of the learning outcomes for the assessment.

Issues

By including empirical research within the assessment of the module it sends a clear message to students about the value and importance of socio-legal research, yet care has to be taken to ensure that the socio-legal aspects of the assessment are not overlooked. If explicit mention is not made of the socio-legal aspect within the assessment materials, this can give students the impression that it can be and possibly should be given a lower priority.

Making explicit the importance of the socio-legal elements of the assessment is achieved by the design of the assessment materials, supported by the message given to students in the coursework project lecture. To try to promote the socio-legal aspect, I have included specific reference to it at a number of points. The learning outcomes in the project instructions specifically require the students to incorporate the data results into the essay, and to include an explanation and evaluation of the survey method as well as interpretation of the survey results. Also, a pre-prepared written feedback sheet makes specific reference to the use of the survey results. This feedback sheet is made available to the students prior to starting the coursework and is shown on a Powerpoint slide in the project lecture.

Nevertheless, one issue with which I have grappled is the extent to which the coursework project assessment should reward the socio-legal aspect of the assessment. This is because the project has two separate aspects: an analysis of the black-letter law plus the results of the survey. What proportion of the marks should be allocated for consideration of the survey results? How much of a penalty should be suffered if the survey results are not fully considered?

The assessment criteria and feedback sheet both allow holistic marking, so there is no breakdown of the marks for each aspect; each essay is rated as a whole of its components. The difficulty is that marks can be seen to reflect importance: a failure to specify marks for the socio-legal aspect of the essay would not challenge any misconception that the socio-legal aspect may be less important than the black-letter element. The risk is that, if it is not clear that marks are specifically allocated for the socio-legal aspect, then the students can feel able to sideline this approach and all the submissions end up being traditional legal essays illustrated with a smattering of empirical data. This is a particular risk given the predominance of the doctrinal approach on the undergraduate programme; for most students, all they have experienced is the black-letter law of their textbooks and journal articles. The temptation for them is to write what they are familiar with, thereby marginalizing the socio-legal aspect of the assessment.

Personally, I do not wish the empirical element to be a supplemental bolt-on to a basic black-letter essay; instead, it should be a fundamental part of it. There is an unofficial approach within the marking team, whereby a script will certainly be awarded a lower classification if it does not deal adequately with the survey data. This is justifiable, given the terms of the essay question and learning outcomes, explicitly requiring a consideration of the survey results. However, the nub of the issue is the meaning of 'adequate': how much of an inclusion satisfies this requirement?

This links with the structure of the essay. I am not prepared to prescribe a structure for the essay, for a number of reasons. One reason is that I wish to encourage a range of responses that would make the assessment more of a valid exercise. The structure of the essay is central to the strength of the argument within the essay. It is essential that students choose their own structure so that its coherence and appropriateness can be judged. In addition, I try to maximize student engagement with the project by giving the students as much freedom as possible to approach the essay in whatever way best suits them. A final reason is that I wish to avoid the tedium of marking 180 identical essays!

On the other hand, some of the students struggle with how and how much to incorporate their survey results. One student commented in my survey: 'I didn't feel confident that I was using it as expected.'; another wrote 'I lacked confidence and was not sure what the examiner wanted me to talk about.' I therefore propose next year to make a number of past essays available so that the students can see the variety of possible approaches to the structure of the essay. This will be accompanied by a clear message that, provided the survey results are fully incorporated into the essay and the structure supports the argument being made, every approach is right.

Another aspect is the treatment of ethical issues. I explain in the lecture that the students should cover ethical issues within the essay, as part of evaluating the survey method. Despite this, consideration of ethical issues is not specified in the learning outcomes or on the feedback sheet. This is because the coursework project is primarily an assessment of family law and ethical issues are not central to the evaluation of the survey results, unless they affect the outcome. The consequence of this is that, by and large, ethical issues tend to be overlooked in the student essays. This is an illustration of the extent to which the design of the assessment materials determines the student learning. The difficulty is that I do not feel entirely comfortable with ethical issues being ignored and this appearing to be condoned.

My desire to maximize student freedom conflicts with the understandable need of some of the students for the tutor to be in control of the task. Students can tend to feel anxious when they have too much independence and responsibility, as it can cause uncertainty about whether or not their approach is correct. This is an unavoidable conflict but it can be reduced by giving clear guidelines to the students of what can be prescribed, together with a consistent message (Brown and Glasner, 1999). In addition, the willingness of each student to engage with the freedom depends to some extent on their past experiences and maturity (Higgs, 1988). It is therefore worthwhile considering the amount of student freedom that is desirable in line with the level of the student intake. The family law module is only available to second and third-year undergraduates, so the maximum amount of freedom is realistic and desirable in terms of the students' abilities and confidence.

On the whole, the students appeared invigorated by the new challenge, yet such freedom also creates an increased demand for support, reassurance and approval. Over the six-week period, the process was undeniably labour-intensive because I gave emotional and practical support to students pursuing their own individual approach to the essay question. The support involves a lecture, scheduled group drop-in sessions, email, electronic discussion board queries and one-to-one meetings with certain students who need additional back-up. Overall, the students seemed to benefit from the experience but admittedly some also felt stressed by it. The exercise is motivating for all but perhaps too motivating for some.

Conclusion

The coursework project is an attempt to incorporate socio-legal research into the undergraduate curriculum, by placing it at the very centre, namely within the assessment of the module. The positive student response alone means that it is valuable and worthwhile but there are other important benefits such as the prioritization of learning about socio-legal research and the acquisition of skills. Nevertheless, it is also important to recognize the limitations of the project: given the resource issues on an undergraduate programme, it can only be an introduction to socio-legal research. The students are only able to select a sample, implement the project and analyse the data; they cannot be involved in the selection of the research topic or design of the research instrument. The coursework project also highlights some of the tensions between the competing ideologies within law-school teaching, namely the priority that should be accorded to socio-legal analysis or black-letter evaluation. It also reveals the tension for the tutor between the ideal of giving students complete freedom to approach their essay in whatever way they choose and the reality of the work required to support anxious students in a novel endeavour.

References

Biggs, J (2003) *Teaching for Quality Learning at University* (Maidenhead: Open University Press)

Bloom, B (1965) *A Taxonomy of Educational Objectives* (New York: McKay)

Boud, D (ed.) (1988) *Developing Student Autonomy in Learning* (London: Kogan Page)

Boud, D (1998) 'Assessment and learning: contradictory or complementary?' in P Knight (ed.) *Assessment for Learning in Higher Education* (London: Kogan Page)

Brown, S and A Glasner (eds) (1999) *Assessment Matters in Higher Education* (Buckingham: SRHE and Open University Press)

Brown, S and P Knight (1994) *Assessing Learners: Higher Education* (London: Kogan Page)

Higgs, J (1988) 'Planning learning experiences to promote autonomous learning' in D Boud (ed.) *Developing Student Autonomy in Learning* (London, Kogan Page)

Knight, P (ed.) (1998) *Assessment for Learning in Higher Education* (London: Kogan Page)

Potter, G and C Williams (2007) 'Two birds, one stone: combining student assessment and socio-legal research' 40 *Law Teacher* 1–18

Prosser, M and K Trigwell (2001) *Understanding Learning and Teaching* (Buckingham: SRHE and Open University Press)

Ramsden, P (2003) *Learning to Teach in Higher Education* (London: Routledge Falmer)

Robson, C (2011) *Real World Research* (Oxford: Blackwell)

Rowntree, D (1987) *Assessing Students: How Shall We Know Them?* (London: Kogan Page)

Part II
Socio-Legal Studies in the Foundation Subjects

5
Land Law and Equity and Trusts

Rosemary Auchmuty

It is a curious paradox that, while both equity and land law[1] would seem at first glance to be natural objects of socio-legal study, concerned as both are with values and power relations, the black-letter approach tends to dominate our syllabuses and textbooks, with only the barest nod in the direction of historical context and a smattering of policy. The focus of these courses is the *legal rules*, and most of us are content if, by the end of the module, our students can apply the correct law to the facts of a problem question and give competent advice. This is hardly surprising. Both equity and land law are regarded as 'difficult', technical subjects which students find alien and inaccessible. In the face of rising failure rates, teachers face the challenge of making them as straightforward as possible, while yet covering sufficient content to satisfy the professional requirements laid down by the Joint Academic Standards Board. If there is one skill above all that the law degree offers students, it is the skill of 'thinking like a lawyer' – of being able to identify the relevant legal issues in a given problem and apply the correct law to solve it. Many of us conclude that if we send our students out into the world with this skill in the area of property law, where it is so often lacking, this is a significant achievement. And so it is. But it is not enough.

Our aim should be to turn out graduates who know the law but who also take a view on its appropriateness and effectiveness – on its very justice. That view should be based not on the mechanical application of rules, nor on gut feeling and 'opinion', but on rational and informed arguments supported by evidence. This is the rationale for socio-legal perspectives on property law, without which any useful evaluation of the law is impossible.

---

1 This chapter covers both land law and equity and trusts because, first, the subjects overlap, and, second, some teachers cover certain topics in property law (such as trusts of the family home) in equity while some include them in land law. Even those programmes in which land law precedes the study of equity and trusts must introduce students to the history of equity and the trusts at the start of land law, so the subjects are complementary and often indivisible.

First principles

Although socio-legal perspectives might appear to be an 'add-on' to a standard rule-based syllabus, they are better conceptualized as a *different approach altogether*. A comparison of two books on the same area of law will demonstrate the differences between the doctrinal and the socio-legal approach. Mark Pawlowski and James Brown's *Undue Influence and the Family Home* carefully analyses the large body of case law, whose lack of consistency is deplored by the authors; they conclude by calling for a 'coherent statutory code' (Pawlowski and Brown, 2002, p. x). Belinda Fehlberg's *Sexually Transmitted Debt: Surety Experience and English Law* focuses rather on the parties involved in the cases – the banks, lawyers and the sureties themselves – to expose law's failure to take account of the complexities of intimate relations and the difference between commercial and conjugal motivations (Fehlberg, 1997, p. 71). For Fehlberg, the problem is not the incoherence of the law but *the unjust effect of its operation on women*. She challenges the judges' universal assumption that the family home should always be available as security for business loans, and suggests that the way forward is a programme of education to empower women to resist their husbands' demands (pp. 281–2).

Fehlberg's work shows that a socio-legal perspective is about seeing law in its social setting. For socio-legal scholars, laws do not exist in their current form because those are correct or the only possible ones but because they are artefacts constructed out of a dozen or more factors rooted in the politics, economy, demography and social mores of the place and time as well as the personalities concerned. Knowing this means that we cannot accept legal rules at face value; we think about what social forces produced them, how they impact on different groups, what alternatives are possible and desirable. We accept law's authority, of course, but not necessarily its truth or its justice. We identify injustices in the law and the legal process, and we argue for reform – in the pursuit not of the abstract consistency often favoured by the doctrinal lawyers, but of justice for all. Sometimes we throw up our hands and argue that the best prospects for justice lie outside the law altogether.

Methodologies

Once we view law as a product of a particular social context, we are free to analyse it according to a range of disciplinary methodologies. No longer restricted to legal method, we can turn our interpretive gaze outwards to disciplines with the potential to illuminate our study of law in different ways. Socio-legal study in the UK looks to the arts and humanities as well as the social sciences. Historical method is an obvious starting-point, partly because so much of property law derives from the past – most equitable remedies, for example, can be traced to particular social problems the law needed to solve – but also because law as a discipline derives much of its authority from past precedent. Legislation and cases can be interrogated through the various lenses of literary criticism; there is a flourishing 'law and literature' scholarship in which property law has proved a fruitful object of study (for example, Watt, 2009). Biographies of judges cast light on the role played by personality and background in judicial decision-making (Heward, 1990); geographical research and photographic analysis contribute that sense of place so central to land law (Massey, 1994; Layard, 2010); architectural and art historians have provided hitherto unconsidered insights into the legal process (Moran, 2009; Mulcahy, 2010).

From the social sciences, contemporary issues such as the rise of unmarried cohabitation (relevant to the study of trusts of the family home) will draw on, but also invite, sociological and demographic research (Firth, 2009). An important methodology is the fact- and opinion-finding survey which, carefully analysed and interpreted, can yield useful data for policy-makers and critics of the law (Lewis, 1999). Granted that there is limited space within our core Land Law or Equity modules to permit extensive engagement with empirical research of this kind (and if we do introduce it we need to guard against misuse of data or unethical attempts by students to conduct their own research), nevertheless empirical work is basic to an understanding of society and law, and to dispelling the myths, misconceptions and uninformed opinions that too often pass for authority in legal work.

I am conscious that drawing on disciplines from the arts, humanities and social sciences to inform our teaching and research in law may make us guilty of dabbling, and encouraging students to dabble, in scholarship we do not properly understand. Given that historians, literary critics and art historians study for years to become experts in their fields, one may wonder what gives lawyers – notoriously narrowly educated in a discipline indifferent to any authority but its own – the authority to poach untrained into the territory of others. To this I would say that, although there is indeed a risk that we will get it wrong, just as non-lawyers may get legal method wrong, many of us are in fact educated in other disciplines, our students may have more extra-legal knowledge than we give them credit for (since we rarely have occasion to draw on it in the law degree), and we are all capable of learning new skills. And surely any exposure to alternatives to black-letter law is better than none.

The ongoing benefit for students of learning about socio-legal approaches and techniques in the first or second year of their LLB, where much property law teaching is located, is that they may feel inspired by their experience to choose to write a dissertation in the area in their final year, and will have the skills to do this competently. I have often come across students keen to research a socio-legal aspect of property law but with no idea of how to go about it or what has already been written on the subject. At least, if they meet socio-legal scholarship in a core module, they will have a better sense of the huge range of scholarship out there and the possibilities for original engagement. And this may lead to postgraduate work in the field, and the broadening out of the socio-legal research community about which disquiet was voiced by the Nuffield Inquiry on Empirical Legal Research in 2006 (Genn et al., 2006).

Empirical research

How do we use these perspectives? Let us take empirical socio-legal research as an example (though the techniques can be adapted to any methodology). A good starting-point is to introduce students to model examples – for example, Belinda Fehlberg's (1997) work on undue influence mentioned above or that of Anne Barlow and her colleagues (2005) on cohabitants' understandings of their property rights. Students can use the findings simply for what they reveal about the statistics, attitudes and experiences of the respondents, but a tutorial or coursework exercise could develop their skills by, for example, asking them to consider how much the data and analysis in the chosen body of research have influenced judgments or policy documents such as Law Commission reports (e.g. Law Commission, 2007). Not only does this help students see the impact (or otherwise) of socio-legal work, it may also expose judicial propensities for deciding cases on the basis of unevidenced assertions about social attitudes or realities (for example, Potter P's remarks on marriage in *Wilkinson v Kitzinger (No 2)* [2006]),[2] a revelation that should impel students to question the objectivity of law-making. Since students may often 'feel' that judges are out of touch with reality, this kind of comparison will give them the evidence we are always asking them to provide for their beliefs and feelings.

A second way that model articles can be used is to draw attention to the methodological issues in undertaking this kind of research. Such a consideration will be imperative if you or your students entertain any idea that they themselves might do some empirical work, but it is also a useful exercise in its own right. Of course in a substantive law subject this can only be done in the most basic fashion, but it will hone their analytical skills and introduce them to a methodology they may wish to develop further in a dissertation or postgraduate work. For example, students could consider how representative

---

2 'It is apparent that the majority of people, or at least of governments, not only in England but Europe-wide, regard marriage as an age-old institution, valued and valuable, respectable and respected, as a means not only of encouraging monogamy but also the procreation of children and their development and nurture in a family unit (or "nuclear family") in which both maternal and paternal influences are available in respect of their upbringing.' (para. 118)

any given sample of interviewees might be and how questions are devised to answer the particular research questions of the project. They must be made aware of ethical issues such as the impact on interviewees of asking questions of a personal nature and the need for confidentiality and anonymity. An apparently neutral question about property distribution on the breakdown of a relationship, for instance, might cause distress to an interviewee who has suffered such a breakdown; something on mortgages might upset a person whose home has been repossessed. Students will take note of the technique used by Barlow and many others of asking their target sample to comment on hypothetical fact situations which effectively distance the question from personal experience.

From analysing the methodological considerations it is but a short step to actually *doing* a small piece of survey research. The pioneering work of our colleagues at Sheffield[3] and Greenwich – where students' findings from a coursework task on property allocation on relationship breakdown were actually used by the Law Commission in its study – demonstrate that survey research undertaken by students may produce genuinely useful results. There are several property law issues your students could investigate (and you would doubtless choose whatever is current) but much depends on your cohort: a question on home ownership might be inappropriate in an area where people mostly rent, and if most of your students live in halls there will be a limited sample of relevant people they can interview. The task of drawing up hypothetical fact situations could be a class exercise, which incidentally has the merit of letting students see what it is like for lecturers to write problem questions for tutorials or exams (the next step, of course, is for them to *mark* them) and may well have the effect of sharpening up their own problem-solving skills.

Making it relevant

We can (and most of us do) contextualize our discussion of cases in lectures and tutorials with a bit of history, some statistics, a picture or some biographical information about the judge concerned but, although these may help students to grasp the issues and perhaps fix the cases more clearly in their minds, they may subsequently discard this additional information as irrelevant detail of no *legal* significance. We need to embed the socio-legal perspective in the module structure itself. This means, of course, requiring students to demonstrate an understanding of the socio-legal context and approach to property law as a *learning outcome* for the module and *assessing* it appropriately. Students are very focused and will readily identify *what really matters* (that is, what is to be assessed); indeed, one of the skills we teach them is how

---

3 See Potter and Williams (2007) and the discussion in Chapter 4, above.

to separate out the relevant from the irrelevant when it comes to legal issues. Socio-legal analysis must therefore be relocated in the relevant.

One way to do this is to focus on the *current* and the *local*. Many of us use newspaper articles, photographs or documentary footage to draw students' attention to the law in practice. There is always coverage of some celebrity who has left an enormous bequest to her pet dog or cat which you can use to illustrate anomalous purpose trusts in your Equity module. When we introduce this kind of real-life example we remind students that law is about real people (and real places when it comes to land law), and thus alert them not only to the expected recognition of the problems they create for law but also to what they suggest about national character, class, gender assumptions and so on. It is always worth looking out for newsworthy items to enliven a class and get them to think about how and why the law develops in the ways it does, especially if you can catch it at the precise moment that it is developing.

Fixing on the *local* also brings the law home in a memorable way. The early pages of Clarke and Greer's admirable textbook, *Land Law Directions* (2010), include photographs (many taken by Clarke herself) of landmarks in the Greenwich area where they teach. I particularly like the juxtaposition of the *Cutty Sark* and *Gypsy Moth IV* which invites students to apply the 'degree of annexation' test to determine whether each monument is a chattel or part and parcel of the land (pp. 14–15). For my own students, the fact that the Pye of *J A Pye (Oxford) Ltd v Graham* [2002] was (and still is) a major property developer around Reading gives the case particular resonance: they can imagine the large tracts of Berkshire farming land soon to be turned into housing estates; they can see what the estates look like. These prompts are valuable aids to understanding and memory but they also encourage students to reflect on the social consequences of legal decisions and priorities for their own local community.

The central importance of history

Most property law textbooks start out with a brief history of key concepts – equity and the trust, tenure and estates – intended to explain the reasons for the peculiar forms that survive today. This desire not simply to explain but to *justify* present law in past developments derives from old methods of teaching the subject, when a chronological format of the law's development was used rather than today's exposition of current principles and authorities. Early property law textbooks compromised by introducing each topic with a concise history, 'for the purpose of explaining some of the more intricate of the modern rules', as the author of *Topham's Real Property* explained (Topham, 1911, p. v). This systematic treatment is less often seen today, where history is confined to an early chapter and largely ignored thereafter.

Of course we need the historical context; without it, English property law would make even less sense than it already does to many students. Indeed, I would argue for the inclusion of much more history, especially recent history. But the version we have in most textbooks – the history of ruling-class men, without controversy, nuance, or anything after the late nineteenth century – hardly fits the bill. The 1925 legislation is covered, of course, but we learn little about its context and rationale. If a socio-legal enquiry is to be followed, it must start here.

The textbook accounts we are generally offered are, for the most part, antiquated, self-justifying, uncritical and partial. They are antiquated because they are based on the often discredited works of eighteenth- and nineteenth-century legal writers and judges, not on the researches of more recent scholars using modern historical methods. They are self-justifying because the authorities they rely on have selected and manipulated the sources to produce the desired story of progress to the present. They are uncritical because they make no effort to apply modern scholarly techniques to this received version of history. By justifying the present by reference to the past, they produce an unabashed 'Whig' version of history – that ideology beloved of the Victorians but long abandoned by serious historians – that sees the present state of things as culmination of a more or less linear process of improvement. They have little conception of 'the past' as something that can change as fresh light is cast upon it by new research; textbook writers may conscientiously update each new edition of their text, yet we rarely see any alterations to the historical sections. These accounts are, finally, partial, in both senses of the word: they are incomplete, and they favour certain actors in history. When law students were all destined to become ruling-class men, such histories told a reassuring tale well-adapted to their world-view. They are totally unsuitable for the law student of today.

The problem is that law, as a discipline, has traditionally recognized no sources but its own. Thus, for the legal scholar, the writings of Coke and Blackstone must necessarily be more authoritative than those of a contemporary, non-legally trained historian – especially when she happens to be American, as many scholars working in this field are. This is in spite of decades-old critiques of the great men's methodologies and misogynistic bias by, for example, Stopes on Coke (1894, pp. 99–107) and Beard on Blackstone (1946, pp. 77–95). While most of today's legal scholars – and indeed judges – are not quite so dismissive of extra-legal resources as they used to be, they still tend to be unaware of developments in history-writing and the huge body of relevant scholarship out there that would temper – or even contradict – the received accounts.

This ground needs to be cleared *before* students embark on further socio-legal explorations because, without it, they will have a very imperfect understanding of the society that produced our laws, they will continue to dismiss or undervalue non-legal sources, and they may fall into the same uncritical, descriptive, self-serving trap that so many textbook accounts do. The way that textbooks present history may lead students to assume, as many people do, that history is no more than a collection of facts that speak for themselves. The reality is that history is *an interpretation* of *particular* facts – just like legal judgments, in fact! Once students grasp this truth about both disciplines, they will be well on the way to understanding the socio-legal approach.

Two shifts are therefore needed. First, legal sources should be seen for what they are – historical documents, products of a particular social context and an individual author or group of authors with an intended goal and audience. Students need to recognize that, because of the circumstances of its creation, an English law rarely takes the form its authors would ideally have chosen, let alone the form preferred by other stakeholders and campaigners on the issue. Judge-made law is shaped by precedent, legislation by politics, and both, usually, by compromise.

Second, the traditional exposition of the development of English property law must be critiqued and rethought. The problem with Whig history is that it represents legal developments as a tale of progress from complexity and injustice to greater simplicity and justice, with the terms often elided – that is, simplicity is seen as conferring justice. (This is particularly true of accounts of registered land.) While it is acknowledged that we are far from reaching this goal – apart from anything else, society keeps throwing up new challenges to keep the courts and Parliament on their toes – there is always a sense that law is essentially benevolent and *will get there in the end*. It is easy to see why this form of history appeals to lawyers; as historian Susan Staves explains:

> Because legal history has usually been done by judges and law professors involved in a system which society requires to produce articulate defenses of the justice and rightness of current legal institutions, legal history has most often been celebratory, explaining how the law was more and more beautifully adapted to the needs of society, more and more reflective of absolute justice. (Staves, 1990, p. 9)

The effect is to stifle criticism of both present and past, since both are seen as natural developments or, where there has been a substantial break with the past (as with registered land, for example), as reforms which are *inevitably* positive. It is almost impossible now to mount a critique of registered land (O'Donnell and Johnstone, 1997, pp. 85ff.).

This representation of legal history has two important consequences. First, it erases the power struggles, the opposition to reform and the agency of the campaigners who ultimately succeeded, or not. Students are led to believe that the law has evolved through internal reform rather than as the result of radical movements – feminism is an obvious example – or external pressures. Second, it presents an image of contemporary law as essentially just, or at least moving towards justice, and conversely of past law as less just, simply because it was based in a less just society. This excuses, as well as misrepresents, the past – but also the present. Some reforms have *not* made for greater justice, and some past injustices need further explanation.

How are we to persuade students that the textbook account is inadequate? The textbook is *the* Authority in many of our classrooms; for most students, what appears in a book published by Oxford University Press *must* be more reliable than something said by their obviously biased lecturer in class. My response would be, first, to produce your revised version of history in your lecture handouts, together with an extended reading list to act as evidence and scholarly support for your assertions. Second, I would devote a lecture or seminar to explaining the historiography of property law (that is, the ways different historians have approached writing its history) and techniques of historical method, and demonstrating how historical method can usefully be used to interpret legal sources. Extracts from received accounts, more critical approaches and relevant cases could be reproduced, with appropriate questions, for class discussion. In my experience, students love this kind of work; it really engages them. They have an opportunity to think rather than simply absorb and to make suggestions without worrying about whether they have the 'right' answer.

Third, build history into all your teaching. Take the topic of charities, for example. After the complexities of constructive trusts and the perhaps tedious detail of administration of trusts, the law of charities, which most of us teach towards the end of the course, comes as something of a light relief, with its clear and intelligible principles, accessible subject matter, interesting case law and relevant policy considerations. Even so, there is a sense in many textbooks of the inevitability of its development from the Statute of Elizabeth to the Charities Act 2006 that invites critical interrogation. The books tell us that the familiar classification derives from an era in which charities provided most of the social services now largely delivered by the state; yet how often do we seize this opportunity to explain to our students – or ask them to find out for themselves – how the welfare state evolved, how fiercely reforms were fought for and how strongly they were resisted by vested interests, and how great a difference state control made to people's lives (Wilson, 1977). It goes without saying that such knowledge is particularly useful at a time when the process looks likely to be reversed.

Following through the development of particular charitable categories will help make students aware of the political content in legal policy. Take education, for example. Students may not be aware that free secondary education only became available after the Second World War, transforming the lives of large numbers of boys and, especially, girls, who were more likely to have to forgo schooling in families with limited funds. For the first time in history, these working-class young people were able to transcend the barriers that had previously doomed them to a lifetime of poorly paid, menial work and go on to further training, higher education, careers and the comforts of middle-class existence – including the chance to own their own home. Free, state-provided education did this – yet the well-to-do at private schools and Oxbridge have continued to cling to their privileges as charities. Finally, and critically, I would set a piece of assessed coursework about one aspect of property law history you have mentioned in your lecture, again with a list of references to assist research (for students will not be familiar with this kind of resource). Alternatively, your coursework could be a repetition of the class-room exercise, with a different set of extracts and questions.

An example

I will illustrate the shortcomings of textbook accounts of property law history and how they might be addressed by focusing on their treatment of gender – a topic which, as I will later explain, could be picked up as one of several themes to be followed through in the syllabuses of both Land Law and Equity and Trusts. I have chosen gender partly because this is my personal research interest, but also because it is such an egregious instance of the partiality of most property law histories. It is no exaggeration to say that it is only by recognizing the significance of gender that one can properly understand the history of equity and the rationale for many of the devices still in use today.

Women are rarely mentioned in the historical accounts of the development of equity, but one place where they do generally make a brief appearance is in discussions of the usefulness of the trust in *ameliorating the economic position of married women*, as A W Scott put it (Scott, 1922, p. 457), and countless text-book authors have echoed. Such explicit reference to gender difference in the substantive law, unusual today since substantive legal differences no longer exist, used to be an automatic feature of textbook accounts of property law. Today this history will be reduced to an explanation that, before the Married Women's Property Acts, the common law vested a married woman's property in her husband, leaving her not simply in a vulnerable economic position, but practically without legal personality at all. Blackstone's famous dictum may be quoted:

> By marriage, the husband and wife are one person in law; that
> is, the very being or legal existence of the woman is suspended

during the marriage, or at least is incorporated and consolidated into that of her husband; under whose wing, protection, and *cover*, she performs every thing. (Blackstone, 1765, p. 441)[4]

Equity, however, enabled a man to settle a sum on his wife or daughter for her personal use after her marriage, free from interference from her husband. Marriage settlements became almost a prerequisite for marriage in the propertied classes and were accordingly protected for policy reasons. Equity's intervention is thus represented as *a good thing,* because it protected powerless wives from greedy husbands and gave them a measure of financial independence.[5]

The protection of wives from greedy husbands or (these days) partners is a theme our students will see returning again and again throughout the history of the equitable jurisdiction right up to *Stack v Dowden* [2007] and beyond. Yet here it appears out of nowhere, and is immediately dropped without further discussion. There is never any space to ponder the extraordinary common law principle that gave all a woman's property to her husband, or to consider why she needed to be protected from him. What did this say about English marriage? What did it say about English *men?* What did it say about the justice of the law, or whose interests it served?

Then take the strict settlement, which may rate a mention in these textbook accounts not just as an important application of the trust principle in the seventeenth and eighteenth centuries but explicitly as a means of benefiting women by enabling men to dispose of their land on death otherwise than by strict primogeniture. Once again, this is portrayed as *a good thing;* primogeniture (in England meaning leaving property to the eldest son) is obviously unfair to younger sons and daughters, and the trust enabled provision to be made for them too.

The historical reality was somewhat different. Twenty years ago, Eileen Spring queried the received version of legal history that held that the strict settlement both improved the financial position of daughters and showed that the eighteenth-century family had become more egalitarian and caring (as argued by, for instance, Stone, 1990). By focusing on the heiress-at-law, a person most of us never knew existed, she demonstrated that the significance of the strict settlement was that the law developed not to protect women, but

---

4   Blackstone disliked the equitable jurisdiction and so overstated married women's powerlessness. The huge authority of his *Commentaries* as a source of law provided the basis for what Mary Beard describes as the great 'fiction that women were, historically, members of a subject sex – "civilly dead," their very being suspended during marriage and their property, along with their bodies, placed under the dominion of their respective "lords" or "barons"' (Beard, 1946, pp. 84–5).
5   But only a measure, since a 'restraint on anticipation' was almost always imposed on the trust property, making it impossible for a woman to draw on the capital; she could only use the income.

for precisely the opposite reason – to do them out of their common-law entitlement (Spring, 1993, p. 9).[6]

It is well-known that land descended to the eldest son in common law,
but it is less well-known that, in the absence of a son, land descended to
the daughters – not just the eldest, but all of them in equal shares. Drawing
on demographic evidence, Spring calculated that about one-third of landed
estates should have gone to women in common law under this rule. In fact,
less than ten per cent did – because the strict settlement enabled fathers to
divert the property *away from* their daughters in favour of collateral males.
So the strict settlement, far from providing a generous portion for daughters, 'aimed first and foremost at limiting the interest of the heiress-at-law'.
Spring's conclusion is stark:

> Clearly the history of the heiress in gentry and aristocratic fami-
> lies is of a great downward slide. From once succeeding according
> to common law rules, she came to succeed about as seldom as
> possible. With the strict settlement of the eighteenth century she
> reached her nadir... In short, English landowners had moved from
> lineal to patrilineal lines. (Spring, 1993, pp. 18–19)

What this demonstrates is that the notion that the common law was
always stacked against women, and that equity's interventions always served
to improve their position, is wrong on both counts. In fact the process was
one of common-law rights for women being undermined by masculine
exploitation, in turn leading to equitable protection followed by backlash, as
those who controlled law-making manipulated both law and equity to serve
reforming and reactionary ends. This is a process not unfamiliar to those who
have studied the ebbs and tides of equitable protection for women in later
generations, including our own.

Students get the impression that those women of yesteryear were relatively powerless or passive in their dealings with property, yet Tim Stretton's
study of an Elizabethan court of equity reveals the extent to which they were
prepared to go to court to try to protect their property rights – which, in
truth, they needed to (Stretton, 1998). Maria Cioni (1985) traces the ways
that women helped to develop particular forms of relief through their use
of the Court of Chancery in the same period. But then Susan Staves shows
how the courts misused the law to curtail and even deprive women of their
entitlement to a whole range of property rights including dower, jointure,
pin money and maintenance allowances (Staves, 1990). It is clear, then, that
there is a lot of research out there which, while it certainly complicates the
easy textbook tale, yet casts useful light on the development of the law. By

---

6 I am grateful to O'Donnell and Johnstone (1997) for alerting me to this example.

including this detail at the start, we would not only make history more inter-esting and relevant to our students, we would better prepare them for the complexities and contradictions of equity's relationship with law in their property law studies.

An opportunity to introduce the nineteenth-century women's movement, which most students have scarcely heard of, is provided by the Married Women's Property Acts. Why do our textbooks skim over this momentous development in English legal history, which one historian has suggested 'carried through one of the greatest expropriations and reallocations of prop-erty in English history' (Holcombe, 1980, p. 27; see also Holcombe, 1983)? If mentioned at all, it will be as a reassurance to students that the gender discrimination of the common law had been done away with – the usual tale of progress – and that nothing more need be said on the subject. (And nothing will be.) In fact, as any text of the actual period would tell you (in a section entitled 'Persons under disabilities as to property' – see, for example, Strahan, 1908, p. 377), the Acts did not give married women the same rights to their property as those enjoyed by men or single women. Instead, their property was treated as if it were held under a trust; hence, married women could not bind themselves personally for their debts, which made other parties reluc-tant to deal with them. It goes without saying that textbooks never mention the 30 years of campaigning by Victorian feminists for a Married Women's Property Act that would actually give married women the same rights as men and single women (Auchmuty, 2008); the Acts are presented (as always) as an instance of the law reforming itself.

In my last institution we used to set a class exercise in which tutorial groups were divided into government and opposition and asked to debate, as if in an 1870s Parliament, the merits of giving married women control over their own property. Those who opposed the measure had to rehearse all the justifications for the status quo while those in favour could either promote the Bill eventually enacted (essentially a showpiece for the integration of equity into the English courts through the Judicature Acts) or argue for the feminist equal-rights position. Students prepared by reading both secondary sources and extracts from the debates in Hansard and feminist literature of the time reproduced for them in a study pack. It was good fun and unthreat-ening because it all happened in the past, but it gave the students an idea of how those with privileges use law to defend their position, while yet demon-strating the potential of law to respond (albeit in a half-hearted and piece-meal way) to social change and radical demands.

Of course, the Married Women's Property Acts did little to facilitate women's *access to* property, so that for the vast majority of women, who had no property, their effect was more symbolic than material. It was not until 1949 that the last vestiges of coverture were swept away in the Restraint on

Anticipation Act, and arguably not until *Williams & Glyn's Bank v Boland* [1981] – that is, more than a century after the first Married Women's Property Act – that the courts finally recognized that married women might have separate rights from their husbands in the home. If this revelation is less shocking to our students than to those of us who have lived through the changes, it should perhaps alert them to the slow acceptance of equality principles in law and the tenacity with which those with power cling to their legal privileges.

Clearly, a history of equity and land law that includes these issues is not just a history with women added but a completely different story. It is a story which should interest our students – consider the popularity of costume dramas with property law plots like *Downton Abbey* – and will get them started on drawing out the recurrent themes of the law's development. Most importantly, it will alert students from the outset to the pitfalls of unthinking reliance on equity's protective jurisdiction and of faith in law's evolutionary progress towards justice and equality.

Themes and topics

It is obvious that certain topics in property law lend themselves better to socio-legal perspectives than others. In equity and trusts, charities are an obvious candidate; in land law, mortgages; straddling the boundaries of the two, we have trusts of the family home. The drawback of the topical approach is, however, its patchiness: *now* you see a socio-legal perspective; *now* you don't. My preference would be for a *thematic* approach. Here you can structure your modules in your usual way but you will establish, at the outset, a set of themes you want your students to pick up and develop as you progress through the topics. Your assessment will be devised around one or more of these themes. In this way, socio-legal concerns are seen to be pervasive, and property law assumes a coherence that binds together what might otherwise appear to be a collection of disparate subjects.

An example

'The law of land comprises a crystallised expression of values... cast in sharp relief against the landscape of the law.' (Gray and Gray, *Elements of Land Law*, p. 4). With reference to one or more areas of land law, and referring to cases and statutes where appropriate, identify the key values or aims promoted by English land law and evaluate the balance struck between them.

We have tried this in a small way at my own institution. We were keen for students to acquire, as well as an in-depth knowledge of selected topics, a sense of land law *as a whole*, its history, structure, common themes and the policy concerns driving its development. So we introduce these themes and policy concerns at the start of the module, to be returned to, where relevant, as we proceed through each individual topic; and they are drawn together in the final class. Students' understandings are assessed in a compulsory essay question in the final exam, the title of which they have been given early in the module, and material for which they have (we hope) amassed throughout the year. The first time we tried this, we were delighted with the results; almost all the student cohort really did seem to have a notion of land law as a body of law that did, in fact, proceed according to some loose but identifiable principles and policies.

The pre-seen question we ask is inevitably couched in very broad and general terms because it is intended to encompass the whole of what we teach. But it would also be possible to go into more depth on *one* particular theme in a piece of coursework or essay question in the exam, and here some socio-legal investigation that might be too detailed for the general syllabus will be appropriate. It is not unusual, for instance, for teachers of Land Law or Equity and Trusts to set an essay question or coursework in the area of implied trusts of the family home, focusing perhaps on whether unmarried cohabitants would be better served by a statutory regime of the family-law type (such as that recommended by the Law Commission in 2007), or simply whether the implied trust rules are satisfactory. These questions stray into socio-legal territory but are often answered by students on the basis of minimal socio-legal knowledge, which is hardly surprising when you consider how little attention is given in property law textbooks to empirical research. Many students end up making their critical judgment on the basis of personal opinion rather than any evidenced arguments. Those who read the Law Commission Report and the case law before *Stack v Dowden* will recognize that the proposed statutory regime is intended to protect vulnerable women. But the claimant in *Stack v Dowden* was a man: did this make a difference? Immediately the way that law deals with *gender* reveals itself as a significant theme that could be placed under the microscope in this context. So too could the theme of the way the law negotiates *conflicts between commercial bodies and private individuals or groups* – including how property law purports to strike a balance between the protection of land as investment and land as home, the extent to which it is prepared to recognize property-based human rights, or equity's role in the regulation of commerce (dealt with more fully when you cover the commercial uses of constructive trusts). A slightly different pervasive theme is that of *culture*, which runs through the case law in a way that is largely invisible because it involves asking questions rarely asked by doctrinal lawyers. Who are these litigants? What are their understandings of their property rights? How do these affect their experience of the law? These themes will be further discussed below, but I make no claim for their being the only or the best themes to pursue; they are simply the ones that seem most obvious and accessible to me.

Culture

Let us start with culture, because culture goes to the heart of conceptions of property. Just as different national jurisdictions view 'property' and 'property law' very differently (reading the multiple judgments of the European Court of Human Rights gives immediate insight into this – see e.g. Auchmuty, 2009), so too do different cultural and ethnic groups and, within these, people of different genders or classes. The challenge for any jurisdiction which encompasses such diverse elements is to decide how far that difference should be respected and accommodated. In the past there was no problem: English law was sovereign both at home and throughout the British empire. But with the more recent recognition of the rights of dispossessed indigenous people, and the growth of multi-culturalism and respect for minority ethnic groups, efforts have been made to recognize or integrate alternative legal systems or even to accord jurisdictional power in certain areas of law.

Ideas about property are particularly culturally specific, so the intersection of two very different conceptual frameworks may lead to conflicts of law and policy. Catharine MacKinnon drew attention to the problems associated with this kind of cultural relativism in an essay about a Native American woman's attempt to have her children counted as members of her own pueblo for the purpose of inheriting tribal communal land. The relevant tribal law stipulated that the right extended to the children of a Santa Clara man who married a woman from outside the pueblo but not to the children of a Santa Clara woman who married a man from outside – a classic example of patrilineal descent. By ruling that this was a question of tribal sovereignty, the United States Supreme Court found itself permitting violations of its own gender equality principles. Yet the very fact that the Native law favoured men's property entitlements over women's, as MacKinnon observed, was due to colonial influence; it was not an original tribal principle. She wrote:

> I raise this case because it poses tensions, even conflicts, between equality of the sexes, on the one hand, and the need to approach those questions within their particular cultural meanings, in an awareness of history and out of respect for cultural diversity and the need for cultural survival, on the other. (MacKinnon, 1987, p. 65)

Similar arguments are sometimes heard in the United Kingdom about the role of Sharia courts in resolving family disputes among British Muslims. Bringing these issues to students' attention disturbs any complacency about 'rights' as an unqualified good. It alerts them to issues of competition and hierarchy in rights and encourages them to reflect on their own values and politics around ethnicity and gender.

Culture can be introduced to Land Law students at the very start of the module. Though most courses and textbooks plunge straight into a description of the way English law defines land and property rights, some seek to locate this viewpoint in a comparative context. Pointing up the arcane peculiarities of the English system when set against other legal regimes is a useful way to fix them in students' minds, but it also establishes a critical, questioning tone. 'Each society develops its own cultural attitudes to its land,' wrote Kate Green in her pioneering short text (Green and Cursley, 2001, p. 6). That the English way of doing things is not the only one, nor necessarily the best, is not a bad message to give students at the outset.

If you or your colleagues have the expertise, comparisons can be made with a civil law jurisdiction such as Scotland or, if you have an Erasmus exchange arrangement, one of those countries; or a case study can be selected from the well-documented Native Title disputes of North America. Many western US states retain significant elements of Spanish and Mexican land law as well as Native-American practice. In New Mexico, for example, successive ruling groups

> saw the land, and its applicable laws, in different ways... Native-American Pueblos relentlessly organized the natural world round them to reflect fundamentally religious values. Hispanos placed their conception of land on the hard rock of human use and, as a result, tied property directly to life-giving rivers, largely disregarding the rest. (Hall, n.d., p. 48)

The Hispanic land-owning system was communal, an arrangement that sat uncomfortably with 'the peculiar American view of property as a marketable commodity' imposed when the 'Anglos' took power: 'This fundamental disagreement meant that the legal systems of all New Mexican sovereignties had great difficulty resolving land disputes.' (ibid.)

The case study most familiar to English land lawyers is that of the Australian Aborigines, whose claims to their native land came into conflict with those of the white colonizers deriving their authority from English law. Reading the case law, students can see for themselves just how different are the conceptions of the native Australians and the common law – incompatible in almost every respect. *Milirrpum v Nabalco Ptd Ltd and the Commonwealth of Australia* (1971) demonstrates the incomprehensibility of the indigenous view to the common lawyer, until a shift in cultural awareness produced recognition in *Mabo v Queensland (No 2)* (1992). But this was the beginning, not the end, of land law's problems in this area. Much of the disputed land had been 'owned' by white Australians for generations; they would not give it back to the Aborigines without a struggle, or at least substantial compensation. What if it was valuable mining land, as the Nabalco property was? Compensation would not be adequate. And what if the land was now populated by hundreds of separately owned homes in the middle of a city? A consideration of such conflicting rights will alert students to the significance of land's economic value in law. It will introduce them to another recurrent theme in property law, discussed later in this chapter: how law reconciles competing commercial and private interests.

In this case, what was a landmark decision in recognizing both the fact of colonial expropriation and the validity of a very different system of land rights ended in a compromise that demonstrates very clearly the role of property rights in perpetuating an existing power structure. Where the tribal lands claimed were not considered useful for any other purpose, the Australian government was happy to return them to the descendants of the relevant tribes. Where this was not the case, the Aborigines were compensated with other land. Since this land had little economic value, the government lost little in the gesture – and the Aborigines gained little, too. The decision not to compensate them with money rather than land was justified on the grounds that the Aboriginal relationship to land was not an *economic* but a *spiritual* one; indeed, this was identified as the key difference between their view and that of the common law. O'Donnell and Johnstone note:

> Giving land to 'traditional' Aborigines so that they may preserve their spiritual links with it in no way unfairly advantages them economically because there is little or no economic or material advantage in it. To the extent that Aborigines step outside of the 'traditional' [i.e. by claiming economic compensation such as a white Australian would expect] they cease to be authentic and hence become less deserving of land rights...Seen in this light, *Mabo* holds little promise: it is primarily about the legitimation of the existing system of landholding and title, and at the same time as it recognises Native Title it explicitly provides a formula for its extinguishment. (O'Donnell and Johnstone, 1997, p. 81)

The 'Native Title' cases, fascinating for their content alone, also provide students with valuable insights into the *fact-finding process* in legal disputes, something which, we hope they will come to appreciate, often determines the legal principles that are laid down and applied. In *Milirrpum*, the court purported to identify the salient features of the Aboriginal conception of property ownership; having set them against those of Australian law, the court drew the inevitable conclusion that the latter could not include the former. But how did it find out what the Aboriginal conception was? The case report reveals that claimants from the Aboriginal communities who did not speak English were cross-examined through an interpreter who did not speak all of their languages. Moreover, the questions asked, proceeding from the common law point of view, were often meaningless to the witness, while the questions that might have elicited a more accurate picture were not asked, because these dealt with legally irrelevant matters. Finally, by disqualifying hearsay evidence, the court ruled out much Aboriginal testimony about tribal beliefs and practices, for the Aboriginal culture is an oral one and knowledge is passed down from generation to generation not in writing but by word of mouth. How fair, then, was this trial?

Culture tends to disappear from our property law curricula after this cameo appearance at the start; even those of us who want students to be aware of alternative conceptions of property find it hard to sustain a comparative approach across an entire module. But there is no reason why you should not revisit the theme when you consider the selection of 'relevant' facts and the testimony of witnesses in the case law of subsequent topics such as undue influence or the family home (Auchmuty, 2001; 2002). Which facts are deemed relevant, and why? What is understood, and not understood, and why? Whose story is being told? *What is missing?* Although cultural details may be suppressed as irrelevant, thus removing them from the public record, and although judges are less inclined to comment on culture than on other factors such as gender or class, an important technique of the socio-legal approach is keeping your antennae tuned to spot references to, or assumptions about, cultural difference. Our students, when requested to do the same, may turn out to be even more culturally sensitive than we are because of their personal circumstances, and we can learn from them.

Culture can be the factor that determines the outcome of the case. In one of the eight appeals in *Royal Bank of Scotland v Etridge (No 2)* [2001], the claimant was a Hasidic Jew whose husband had persuaded her to agree to mortgage the family home as security not simply for certain property speculations, as she thought, but for all future borrowings. She claimed that she would never have agreed to an 'all-moneys' clause, but the House of Lords decided that a woman from her cultural background could not oppose her husband and would leave all financial decisions to him. This finding – which could have been taken to fulfil the twin tests of manifest disadvantage and reposing trust and confidence in her husband – was used by the court to *deny* her a remedy: such a woman, they held, would always have done what her husband wanted, so there could be no undue influence forcing her to act against her will. Thus are MacKinnon's warnings about cultural relativism borne out – and incidentally the intersection between the two themes of culture and gender brought home to students – and students given an opportunity to consider whether they would have decided this case differently (see my alternative judgment in Hunter et al., 2010).

Culture also underlies much of charity law. Through a study of its cases, students gain an insight into what society has deemed worthy of financial and legal privilege across the 400 years from the Statute of Elizabeth to the present. In the beginning, for instance, charities for the advancement of religion meant repairs to Anglican churches and little else (Mitchell, 2010, p. 262). Little by little our worldview changed: charitable status was accorded to other Christian faiths, to other monotheistic religions, to faiths with many gods and eventually to faiths with none (*Sacred Hands Spiritual Centre's Application for Registration as a Charity* [2006]). While religious organizations, like all applicants for charitable status, must prove public benefit, the law privileges religion on the ground that 'it is better for man to have a religion – a set of beliefs that takes him outside his own petty cares and leads him to think of others – rather than no religion at all' (*Holmes v A-G* 1981). But even that principle has been weakened by the provision in the Charities Act 2006 s. 2(2)(l) for recognition of charities for the advancement of moral or ethical belief systems.

This area of law is full of contradictions which are fun for students to unpick. Why, for example, was charitable status not accorded to the Carmelite nuns in *Gilmour v Coats* [1949]? As His Eminence Cardinal Griffin explained, 'the daily prayers and mortifications which the Carmelite Nuns...offer for their neighbour...advance religion and are of inestimable benefit to their neighbour in bringing to those who are ignorant of them or have rejected them the gifts of God and the graces to obtain them' (at p. 431). That may be so, responded Lord Simonds: 'But it does not follow from this that the court must accept as proved whatever a church believes. The faithful must embrace the faith believing what they cannot prove: the court can only act on proof.' (at p. 446)

The principle is clear enough: religious bodies must demonstrate their benefit by, at the very least, conducting some of their activities in public. But this requirement itself, as O'Donnell and Johnston point out, imposes a 'Protestant ethic' of doing good in the community (O'Donnell and Johnstone, 1997, p. 28). Immediately, then, contemplative orders are barred. The rule is rooted in the history of charity law but sits awkwardly with a professed acceptance of all beliefs. Behind *Gilmour v Coats* lies a long saga of British suspicion of Roman Catholicism with its foreign rites and leadership, its celibate priests and sisterhoods that lured women away from their rightful destiny as wives and took their money (see, for instance, the famous undue influence case of *Allcard v Skinner* [1887]). That public policy retains its force in this area of law is apparent from the lengthy rejection by the Charity Commissioners of charitable status for the Church of Scientology in 1999.

The Charity Commission's policy statements are available online and provide a fruitful source of material for coursework tasks since they set out the basis and development of each area of law. Almost any area of charity law will serve – for example, the evolution of ideas about charities for animal welfare from the horses-and-hounds era to the 'higher feelings' justification for pet charities (but will 'public benefit' ever encompass benefit to the animals themselves?) or the evolving conception of 'political purposes'. Students can be asked to analyse the glib generalisations that besprinkle these documents – for example, this statement from the *Analysis of the Law Underpinning the Advancement of Religion* (2008, para. 2.11):

> The law needs to be interpreted in the light of...the changed religious, social and cultural landscape of England and Wales...particularly the habits of society, contemporary ideas and conditions and current ideas of social service.

This very general and uncontroversial assertion, of a type commonly seen in legal essays, calls for a careful unpicking of just what changes have occurred in the religious, social and cultural landscape and what contemporary habits, conditions and ideas of social service – especially in the current political climate – might be. And *this* lends itself to empirical research, delving into social history and trawling through newspaper libraries.

Gender

Although property law is all but gender-neutral in its substantive rules today, gender remains an important and pervasive consideration in both the development of its principles and their application. Women as a group are absent from large swathes of the syllabus but, when they do appear, it is always as the 'other', and usually as the victim. What we rarely get is a sense of a *gender dynamic*, the relationship between men and women – a relationship so frequently of frank exploitation that one suspects that, since it reflects so badly on men, this might even be a deliberate omission. Reading cases on undue influence or family home disputes, students will readily identify that the law has a problem with women who allow themselves to be pressured or drift into unwise situations. By focusing on *gender* as a theme, however, rather than *women*, they will see that the problem is not the women *per se* but their assumed and actual gender roles and the contrasting material situations of men and women. That these ideas, behaviours and material situations are in process of change even as we speak is, of course, one of the fascinating aspects of this topic, but it does prompt recognition that today's students may not fully understand the gender dynamics of previous generations – a topic rarely explored in our textbooks, which tend to skate over contemporary history and assume that the identification of men with paid work and women with housework and childcare is universal rather than a blip in our particular history.

Discussions of gender often arouse hostility among students. There are always those for whom a reference to women in two successive lectures offers evidence of the lecturer's bias against men. But I have found that if you make gender just one of several pervasive themes in the course, there will be less resistance, partly because the recurrence gives it greater credibility (not helped, however, by its absence from the textbooks), but partly, too, because engagement with the themes is a learning outcome of the course and will be assessed. And of course the theme will be picked up with enthusiasm by other students, to whom the idea of looking into the sexes' different experiences of property law holds much appeal. A useful teaching device is to ask students to focus not on the unfortunate women in these cases but on the *men*. This helps to deflect any criticism that you give too much attention to women in law. If you ask questions such as *Why has the man in this case behaved in this way? What is the law's response to his actions?* Even *Do you think it is appropriate? What do you think the law's response should be?*, you change the focus from protecting the 'victim' to naming the cause of her problems and revealing how power relations become embedded and perpetuated in society.

The abolition of the presumption of advancement in s. 199 of the Equality Act 2010 (not yet in force at the time of writing) offers a topical opportunity for socio-legal investigation, if only to force students to look beyond the obvious rightness of formal equality to the reason for the presumption's existence and the purpose it originally served (Auchmuty, 2007). A coursework title we set on this topic this year elicited unevidenced (and sometimes incorrect) generalizations about women's economic position in both the 'ancient' (*sic*) past and the present, combined with ignorance of the social changes that led to the weakening and eventual abolition of the presumption, and even a complete misunderstanding of *Tinsley v Milligan* [1993], where one student advocated the *extension* of the presumption of advancement to same-sex couples on equality grounds. This kind of kneejerk reaction to the availability of rights as an automatic remedy is a consequence of the rise of the rights culture following the coming into force of the Human Rights Act 1998, discussed below.

Where the theme of gender has most obvious application is in the topic of trusts of the family home. Here we quickly realize the difficulties caused by the textbook silence on recent history (that is, the history of the past 50 years or so), alluded to earlier in this chapter. The classic cases of *Gissing v Gissing* [1971], *Pettitt v Pettitt* [1970] and *Burns v Burns* [1984] may as well have taken place in the Victorian era as far as most of our students are concerned; they all happened in the past, and either things are different now (the old tale of progress) or nothing has changed, an impression reinforced by the frequent references to these decisions as authorities for later case law. On the one hand, it is undoubtedly true that our understandings of home ownership and of men's and women's relationship to the home, the workplace and each other have been transformed in the last half-century, yet, as Baroness Hale's judgment in *Stack v Dowden* and subsequent litigation would seem to suggest, it would be wrong to see women's difficulties as quite resolved. We have moved on, but we are not there yet; things are different, but somehow the problem remains. I have noticed that some textbook writers have given up mentioning cases from the 1970s and 1980s in the realization, perhaps, that their facts are no longer relevant to today's conditions and may be misinterpreted by students who lack a grasp of gender relations and housing policy in the relevant period.

I would take the opposite approach: I think these cases are worth discussing as part of the hidden heritage of gender expectations underpinning the law in this area. Such an exercise will immediately expose the importance of context in legal decision-making. Specifically, it will raise the issue of *agency* in any given place and time, encouraging students to consider whether the women in those cases 'chose' to contribute less in purely financial terms to the home, whether they 'chose' to stay home and look after the children, or whether they did these things because of a lack of affordable childcare, unequal pay or bars in employment or, above all, social expectations. Moreover, in 'choosing' the homemaker role, did they anticipate forgoing an interest in the family home? Can we blame them for getting this wrong? *Are we wrong to trust those we love?* Understanding the past will enable students to consider how far things have changed. Here they can draw on their own experience alongside the facts of contemporary case law and other sources, and perhaps even undertake some empirical research. As I have said before, if we want them to engage with potential reform in this area, we want them to produce assessments based on considered evidence, not impressionistic opinions.

Research into the social context of *Gissing* and *Burns* will make clear to students that the twentieth-century equitable rules confining shares in the family home to those who made *financial* contributions to the property were potentially unfair to women who, because of the social factors mentioned above, were less able to make such contributions. This will in turn reveal how such rules have tended to perpetuate existing structures and keep property in the hands of men. Students will see how each judicial attempt to make the law 'fairer' to women provoked hostile reactions from those who contended that equity was being employed in too free or unprincipled a manner, leading to a narrowing or even blocking of the reform. In light of this knowledge, students might be cynical about Lord Neuberger's preference in *Stack v Dowden* for those clear and predictable resulting trust rules that just happen to have worked so well for men in the past. Yet it might also lead them to side with him; with women's changing economic position today, maybe the certainty of strict rules equally applied is just what is needed.

It follows that it is only with this background knowledge that we can make proper sense of a case like *Stack v Dowden*, a judgment that has divided critics in much the same way as those earlier cases. Students, like judges, seem to find *Stack v Dowden* a difficult case to apply. They often revert to common-sense ideas about deservingness and financial contributions, bypassing all the social factors that Baroness Hale endeavoured to bring into the equation. But those social factors are the key to her very different approach; Hale wanted the court to confront the reality of people's lives and the way they arrange their affairs within a committed relationship. Only by asking these questions can they (and our students) get to the heart of the parties' intentions.

What makes the case so interesting as a paradigm is that, both in its facts and in its law, *Stack v Dowden* is the product of 40 years of social change, much of it (let us not forget) fuelled by feminism. Prior to the 1970s, Ms Dowden simply could not have been in the position she was; a woman like her could not have existed as litigant. She could hardly have been an electrical engineer (that was a man's profession), and she could hardly have earned more than her partner: women did not have equal pay and were informally barred from senior positions, especially those which involved overseeing men. Once the children came along, she would have married their father, or at least pretended (as Mrs Burns did) that she was married to him; her home would not have been in joint names, but solely in his; and she would have been coming to court just to get a share, not a larger one. Students need to know this, for most of them will have grown up in an era of formal gender equality and have not yet, perhaps, come up against the informal barriers that still remain in many areas of life.

One way to help them to understand this is to ask them to research and compare the social setting of *Burns* and *Stack v Dowden*. To do this, they must be made as aware as Baroness Hale is (since she has lived through the period in question) of the long history of privileging of men in property claims, the profound social and economic changes in women's position over the period from *Gissing* and *Burns* to the present, the parallel changes in patterns of property ownership and mortgage practice – homes acquired since *Boland* have tended to be in joint names – and the steep decline in marriage and rise in cohabitation, themselves a consequence of divorce reform and women's increased access to paid employment as an alternative form of support – all of which Ms Dowden's case exemplifies. Such an investigation lends itself to a group exercise, ultimately leading to a presentation, perhaps with each member of the group taking a different topic to research and present. Students could also consider the significance of the background and personality of Baroness Hale herself, and her position as the only woman ever to sit in our highest court. Apart from the standard biographical references, you could refer your class to her pioneering co-authored study *Women and the Law* (Hoggett and Atkins, 1984) and note her contribution to the *Feminist Judgments* book (Hunter et al., 2010); what does this say about her? An interesting exercise would be to compare and contrast Hale's approach to women's property claims with that of another very different champion of their rights, Lord Denning.

Ms Dowden's situation looks in so many respects like that of Mrs Burns: long-term cohabitation, several children, relationship breaks up and she wants her share. But how different the gender dynamics are – and thus the outcome. Notwithstanding Baroness Hale's attempts to make the law fairer for women, Ms Dowden won for precisely the same reasons that Mr Burns did – because she held the financial power in the relationship. *So what is the way forward for women? And where does this leave men?* These are the final questions for students to consider, questions that have more than academic interest for them because they concern their own futures, as well as the future of the law. After such a study, no student should be able to complain that property law is dull and irrelevant.

Balancing commercial and private interests

One of the challenges of incorporating socio-legal perspectives into our teaching is that sociological data so quickly become out of date. In teaching the topic of mortgages over the past 25 years, for example, I have repeatedly had to amend my notes to deal with repeated booms and busts, periods of easy cash and property sales followed by recessions and repossessions. It seems that there is always a mortgage scandal of some kind in the news. But this can be a boon, too: because there is always something novel and topical to focus on, mortgages are a splendid topic for socio-legal investigation. Moreover, they provide the clearest example of the way English land law tries to deal with the conflicting rights of commercial bodies (mortgagees) and private individuals (home owners).

First we had the crisis over overriding interests and whether they could *really* bind mortgagees. The House of Lords' decision in *Boland* obliged conveyancers to change their practice. Their exaggerated concerns were only partially assuaged by the House of Lords' ruling in *City of London Building Society v Flegg* [1988] that overriding interests could be overreached. The combined effect of *Boland* and *Flegg* was to make purchasers and mortgagees very keen for the family home to be put in joint names, with both co-owners signing the mortgage agreement, to avoid any possibility of being caught out by any unsuspected overriding interest. This in turn led to a new problem with undue influence as husbands found themselves having to exert pressure on their wives to get them to agree to re-mortgaging the home where, in the past, they would simply have gone ahead without consulting them (as Mr Boland did). Undue influence consumed the courts for a good decade from the lead-up to *Barclay's Bank v O'Brien* [1994] to *Royal Bank of Scotland v Etridge (No 2)* [2001] and beyond.

What this recital of legal highlights reveals is that, whatever the issue, and however great the public outrage, the lender always calls the tune. Attempts by courts or legislators to provide greater protection to home owners or occupants are either minimal – for example, the two months' grace now afforded to unauthorized tenants of mortgage defaulters under the Mortgage Repossessions (Protection of Tenants) Act 2010 – or ineffective, as with Lord Browne-Wilkinson's guidelines for preventing undue influence in *O'Brien*. Efforts made to invoke the Human Rights Act 1998 in defence of defaulting mortgagors have come to nothing (*Horsham Properties Group Ltd v Clark* [2008]).

Why are lenders so apparently untouchable? There is a great deal of material out there, from newspaper reports to policy statements, demographic and statistical evidence, and all manner of sociological and economic commentary, to assist students in identifying the factors responsible for the current 'balance' of power. Questions they could consider are whether there should be more control and regulation, and whether this would make a difference; whether more could be done to prevent home owners from losing their homes, and from making unwise financial decisions in the first place; if so, how? They could examine the situation in other jurisdictions where, for example, home ownership is neither common nor officially endorsed, the mortgage industry is more highly regulated or loans for business purposes are not permitted to be secured on family homes.

Coursework in this area could take many forms. Students could read and compare the Court of Appeal and House of Lords decisions in *Flegg*, an exercise which directly confronts the problem of conflicting legal and policy principles and how different courts may choose to resolve the conflict in different ways. They could write an alternative judgment to the existing judgments in cases like *Flegg, Etridge* or *Horsham*, developing the law or applying it differently to the facts as the situation demands. This would need some preparatory training, but the *Feminist Judgments* book (Hunter et al., 2010) offers an excellent illustration of how it might be done. They could draft some statutory provisions, modelling their efforts on real legislation or Law Commission proposed Bills.

Undue influence case law offers some of the best examples of the 'balance' in action. When discussing the *Etridge* guidelines, students could be asked to consider whom the rules are intended to protect and whom they *actually* protect. This should lead to discussions about how co-owning wives (it is nearly always wives) might be *better* protected against undue influence, about which there is a large body of literature. They could be given an undue influence problem to analyse, with a supplementary exercise requiring them to write the solicitor's letter to the surety in the problem, following the *Etridge* guidelines. Some preparatory discussion about the appropriate style, tone and form for client letters would be needed here. To vary the exercise, and to confound gender expectations, you might make the client a *man* who leaves all financial decisions to his businesswoman wife. Or you could also make him (or her) an immigrant, alerting students (who may of course know this from personal experience) to the possibility that home ownership may have a particular significance for those already displaced from their homeland. Analysing an Australian case, *Australia v Amadio* (1983), O'Donnell and Johnston (1997, pp. 31–53) make the point that immigrants, facing discrimination in the job market, are more likely to go into business on their own, and thus more likely to need to borrow money against the security of their home; they are also more vulnerable, through lack of familiarity with the language and/or legal culture, to fraud or poor practice, as the English undue influence cases also demonstrate (Auchmuty, 2002).

Bankruptcy provides another example of the law's privileging of commercial rights over private. Students learn that the Insolvency Act 1986 s. 335A takes family circumstances into account but prioritizes the interests of creditors, unless those circumstances are 'exceptional'. *Re Citro* [1991] is authority for what is included in this description:

> As the cases show, it is not uncommon for a wife with young children to be faced with eviction in circumstances where the realization of her beneficial interest will not produce enough to buy a comparable home in the same neighbourhood, or indeed elsewhere. And, if she has to move elsewhere, there may be problems with schooling and so forth. Such circumstances, while engendering a natural sympathy in all who hear of them, cannot be described as exceptional. They are the melancholy consequences of debt and improvidence with which every civilised society is familiar. (at p. 157)

It is worth getting students to consider what Lord Justice Nourse is really saying here. First, that the predicament of the bankrupt's wife and children is not exceptional (in fact, it is quite usual); and second, that it is due to debt and improvidence. But *whose* debt and improvidence? By omitting to specify agency here, the judge subsumes wife and children into a generalized blame, though they might in fact be (and probably are) entirely without responsibility for their situation. In any case, students might note, simply because a situation is familiar does not mean it is right, or even tolerable.

What gives support to a critical reading of *Re Citro* is a dissenting judgment by Sir George Waller, who calls into question the 'balancing' of private and commercial claims and agrees with the trial judge that sale should be postponed because the children 'were very much at the critical stage for their education' (at p. 163). Here is a convincing reason for enjoining students to read cases in full; dissenting judgments show them what might have been, what possibly should have been, and what might yet be. They also offer a model for the alternative judgment exercise mentioned above, demonstrating how the same law can be applied to produce a different (some would say fairer) result following different precedents or emphasizing different facts.

Turning to equity and trusts, O'Donnell and Johnstone note (1997, p. 23) that a surprising amount of the syllabus we teach centres on business. Students learn, for example, about the trust as a means of regulating family wealth (and of avoiding tax) and equity as imposing standards of conduct on professional trustees and company directors. An initial exploration of equity's conscience-based jurisdiction and its role in protecting the vulnerable is quickly left behind as we move on to specific uses of the 'discretion' with their fairly fixed rules and strict liability application in the commercial context.

What we teach, however, seems curiously at odds with what we know (and what the media tells us) about actual behaviour in the business world. Here we see the same resistance as in the mortgage industry to regulation of standards and protection of investors and clients through the availability of property-based remedies. Equity's interventions are portrayed as needlessly restrictive, impeding the free development of commerce, curbing risk-taking and over-protective of investor or client. To such critics Lord Millett famously observed:

> There has never been a greater need to impose on those who engage in commerce the high standards of conduct which equity demands. The common law insists on honesty, diligence, and the due performance of contractual obligations. But equity insists on nobler and subtler qualities: loyalty, fidelity, integrity, respect for confidentiality, and the disinterested discharge of obligations of trust and confidence. It exacts higher standards than the marketplace, where the end justifies the means and the old virtues of loyalty, fidelity and responsibility are admired less than the idols of 'success, self-interest, wealth, winning and not getting caught'.

He went on with astonishing prescience (this was written in 1998): 'It is unrealistic to expect that employees can be given incentives through enormous bonuses without undermining their business ethics.' (Millett, 1998, p. 216).

As the banking crisis unfolded a decade later, my students found that Millett's views on the fiduciary relationship not only illuminated the abstract ideals of equity but *politicized* them. At the time he was writing, undue influence preoccupied the courts. Millett expressed 'serious misgivings' about the way the law was applied in these cases and how it was 'manifestly failing to give adequate protection to the wife or cohabitant who acts as surety' (p. 220). His statement continues to be relevant, and no doubt some other controversy will present itself when you come to teach this area, in the context of which you can ask your students for a critical analysis.

Human rights, once thought to have little application to property law, are now assuming more and more significance in a range of areas we cover. Though human rights disputes essentially pit private rights against public ones, they are often invoked in the commercial context. My experience indicates that human rights are most usefully introduced in the Land Law module in a separate session that not only sets out the relevant substantive rights under the European Convention on Human Rights (ECHR) but also reminds students of what they have doubtless been taught elsewhere but have probably forgotten or discarded at module's end, about the court structure, the ways Convention rules are applied, the state's defences, and the possibility of horizontal as well as vertical effect. Examples of their application can be drawn from areas of property law that will not be dealt with in detail on the course, such as housing law, leaving the case law relevant to your Land Law syllabus – for instance, *Pye v Graham* [2000] and *Horsham* – to be discussed in their specific context. This dual approach will help to reinforce both the principles and recognition of the pervasiveness of this theme.

But human rights also lend themselves to critical discussion per se. No treatment of the subject would be complete without consideration of what a human right *is* and, specific to property law, why there is no guaranteed right to property in the Convention (Harris, 1999). Here students could usefully be introduced to some statistics of property ownership worldwide, by region and by gender. Here, too, a consideration of the different cultural approaches to home *ownership*, again by reference to statistics and policy statements, can give students some idea of our relatively ethnocentric reverence for owning rather than renting. Students could discuss which other property rights, besides ownership, are candidates for protection in law. Indeed, there is something to be said for getting them to think about these matters *before* you outline the actual substantive rights, to bring home more starkly the gap between the ideal and the reality. Human rights have become so institutionalized now that one sometimes feels people have forgotten what purpose they are meant to serve. When half the world does not have enough to live on, is it right that a millionaire's wealth should be protected by *human rights* legislation?

Pye v Graham, to be discussed when you come to adverse possession on your course, provides the perfect opportunity to revisit the meaning as well as the law of human rights. Here the courts had good technical reasons for not finding for the applicant but the case inevitably raised the wider issue of how far human rights law *should* protect large wealthy companies with easy access to legal advice who simply sleep on their rights. In the old days before the coming into force of the Land Registration Act 2002 my classes used to enjoy spirited discussions about the morality of adverse possession (Auchmuty, 2004). Today's students are much less likely to be conscious of the arguments in its favour now that the Register is king. But even those who get exercised by the idea of land theft must have difficulty sympathizing with J A Pye and Company once they read the facts of this case and consider which was the more *deserving* party.

All this will lead students, I hope, to ponder the drawbacks and limitations of a rights culture. Since most of them will have grown up taking human rights for granted, they may find it hard to credit that anyone might seriously argue against them. Yet there was a robust critique at the time of the incorporation of the European Convention into English law which drew attention to the hierarchical and competing nature of rights, their partiality and reifying effect (Kingdom, 1992). Students could be asked to read and discuss the critical literature; alternatively, you could draft a suitable problem and get students to debate or write opposing arguments or role-play the issues.

Many students dislike the overlapping subject-matter of Land Law and Equity and Trusts. They would find it easier if the syllabuses were entirely separate and self-contained for ease of learning and knowing which rules to apply. Of course, as we tell them, life is not like that. Your client is not going to be interested in whether she has a land law or a trusts claim; what she wants from you is the correct legal analysis and the appropriate remedy. And the chances are that her claim involves principles from both areas. By the end of the year, however, students are going to have to face the fact that not only does Equity cross over into Land Law, it penetrates into many other areas. This is demonstrated by the work we do on equitable remedies. I have always found this a difficult topic to teach effectively. It can feel disconnected from the rest of Equity and Trusts, however much one tries to represent it as 'coming full circle' from the discussion in the introductory classes of equity and its 'new rights, new interests, and *new remedies*'. We are obliged to teach it: the professional bodies require it and, if we really want our students to be able to think like lawyers, we need to ensure they can follow through their analysis of legal issues and advice with a consideration of relevant remedies. Unfortunately, even if we focus on remedies in their property law applications, we cannot escape the possibility that a discussion of injunctions, for example, will take us into legal areas such as tort or intellectual property on which our knowledge of the substantive law may be hazy.

'Equitable remedies' has two good points, however: the cases are generally interesting, and it is one of those areas in which the law is actually developing, unlike many other topics in the Equity syllabus. As I write, the press is alive with criticisms of what journalists call 'super-injunctions', granted to protect the privacy of celebrities, with the Prime Minister quoted as saying:

> What's happening here is that the judges are using the European convention on human rights to deliver a sort of privacy law without parliament saying so... [whereas] what ought to happen in a parliamentary democracy is parliament – which you elect and put there – should decide on how much protection do we want for individuals and how much freedom of the press and the rest of it. (Boycott, 2011, p. 6)

Quotes like this provide a useful opportunity to engage students with the theme of commercial versus private rights. I would flash them up on a Powerpoint slide and ask students to analyse the statement. I would not ask for opinions at the outset – this too often invites uninformed 'belief' – instead, focus on the quote. What is the Prime Minister's view of the place of the European Convention on Human Rights in English law? (What *is* its place? – quick revision.) Is he concerned about its role or about the judges' interpretation of the law? Or is he (like many other politicians) simply cross because judges have power to make law at all? Is he right to be concerned?

These questions go to the heart of constitutional law, but they also go to the heart of equity. Injunctions are *equitable* remedies, imposed at the court's discretion, but only according to clear principles laid down in previous case law. (What *are* these principles? – another opportunity for quick revision.) We cannot know what precise facts prompted the Prime Minister's outburst in this case – the whole point of these injunctions is to suppress reporting of the facts – but newspaper accounts hinted that it was the usual claim under Article 8 of the ECHR (respect for home and family life) instigated by a male celebrity to hush up an embarrassing extra-marital affair. So here we note the increased use of this article, one with links to property law, and recall the discussion we have had on the meaning of a 'human right' and how far it should extend to *this*. But we can also reflect on whether the law *should* protect the media's commercial interest in newsmongering or the individual's interest in suppressing details of his private life.

Conclusion

There will always be students who feel more comfortable with clear rules and certain answers than with questioning and critique, and who sympathize with those judges who feel 'compelled' to follow precedent whatever the justice of the outcome or decline to develop the law into hitherto untrodden territory.

These are the students who dislike overriding interests because they spoil the mirror-like perfection of the Land Register and agree that Lord Denning's idea that the constructive trust should be imposed wherever conscience and justice demand is very bad law indeed.

On the other hand, there will be students in your class who are so attracted to the idea of equity as the bearer of justice that they find it hard to let go of their illusions when presented with the reality in specific situations. Socio-legal knowledge can be effective in tempering both extremes. It forces the idealists to confront the subjectivity of 'conscience', very evident in Lord Denning's judgments, while making it impossible for the rule-lovers to ignore the differential impact of those rules on equally deserving claimants. Where once the victims could be ignored as unfortunate casualties of an otherwise worthy system, today our students' attachment to rights principles such as equality and respect for diversity makes it harder for them to dismiss the critique out of hand.

And what if some students resist? Remember that, if you integrate socio-legal perspectives into your learning outcomes, content *and* assessment, they are less likely to dismiss them as an irrelevant distraction to the real business of learning the law. Your aim should be to maintain the momentum across the whole syllabus, to keep asking those socio-legal questions in lectures and tutorials – *Why is the law like this? Whose interests does it serve? Does it work well for everyone? Could it be improved – and, if so, how?* – until the students learn to ask these questions automatically of every legal principle and decision they meet. And follow up with the *How can we find out?* (the methodological question), and *How can we be sure of our analysis?* (the evidential one).

You do not need to know all the answers yourself. The sheer volume of literature available in our teaching areas can be overwhelming. It is hard enough to stay on top of changes in the substantive law before even starting on the socio-legal scholarship. But no one expects you to be an expert in everything. When deciding what to include in your module, just play to your strengths and interests. Start with your areas of expertise and share your insights and enthusiasms with your students – surely, what is meant by 'research-led teaching'. If you have coursework, frame it around one of these topics. I know colleagues in other law schools who are housing or company law specialists whose students, presented with case studies in their areas, feel pleased and confident that they are working with cutting-edge scholarship. *My* students get stuck with the examples in this chapter. You will doubtless work out your own.

Cases cited

Allcard v Skinner [1887] 36 Ch D 145
Australia v Amadio (1983) 151 CLR 447
Barclay's Bank v O'Brien [1994] 4 All ER 417

Burns v Burns [1984] Ch 317

City of London Building Society v Flegg [1988] AC 54

Gilmour v Coats [1949] AC 426

Gissing v Gissing [1971] AC 886

Holmes v A-G *The Times* 12 February 1981

Horsham Properties Group Ltd v Clark [2008] EWHC 2327

J A Pye (Oxford) Ltd v Graham [2002] 3 All ER 865

Mabo v Queensland (No 2) (1992) 175 CLR 1

Milirrpum v Nabalco Ptd Ltd and the Commonwealth of Australia (1971) 17 FLR 141

Pettitt v Pettitt [1970] AC 777

Pye v Graham [2000] 3 WLR 242

Re Citro [1991] Ch 142

Royal Bank of Scotland v Etridge (No 2) [2001] 4 All ER 449

Sacred Hands Spiritual Centre's Application for Registration as a Charity [2006] WTLR

Stack v Dowden [2007] UKHL 17

Tinsley v Milligan [1993] 3 All ER 65

Wilkinson v Kitzinger (No 2) [2006] EWHC 2022 (Fam)

Williams & Glyn's Bank v Boland [1981] AC 487

References

Auchmuty, R (2001) 'The fiction of equity' in S Scott-Hunt and H Lim (eds), *Feminist Perspectives on Equity and Trusts* (London: Cavendish)

Auchmuty, R (2002) 'Men behaving badly: an analysis of undue influence cases' 11 *Social and Legal Studies* 257–82

Auchmuty, R (2004) 'Not just a good children's story: a tribute to adverse possession' 63 *Conveyancer* 293–307

Auchmuty, R (2007) 'Unfair shares for women: the rhetoric of equality and the reality of inequality' in A Bottomley and H Lim (eds), *Feminist Perspectives on Land Law* (London: Glass House Press)

Auchmuty, R (2008) 'The Married Women's Property Acts: equality was not the issue' in R Hunter (ed.) *Rethinking Equality Projects in Law: Feminist Challenges* (Oxford: Hart Publishing)

Auchmuty, R (2009) 'Beyond couples? *Burden v the United Kingdom* (2008)' 17 *Feminist Legal Studies* 205–18

Barlow, A, S Duncan, G James and A Park (2005) *Cohabitation, Marriage and the Law: Social Change and Legal Reform in the 21st Century* (Oxford: Hart Publishing)

Beard, M R (1946) *Woman as Force in History: A Study in Traditions and Realities* (New York: Macmillan)

Blackstone, W (1765) *Commentaries on the Laws of England* vol. 1 facsimile edn, S N Katz (ed.) (Chicago: Chicago University Press)

Boycott, O (2011) 'Cameron reveals unease over judges creating a privacy law', *The Guardian*, 22 April.

Charity Commission (2008) *Analysis of the Law Underpinning the Advancement of Religion*, www.charitycommission.gov.uk/library/

Cioni, M (1985) *Women and Law in Elizabethan England with Particular Reference to the Court of Chancery* (New York: Garland)

Clarke, S and S Greer (2010) *Land Law Directions* 2nd edn (Oxford: Oxford University Press)

Fehlberg, B (1997) *Sexually Transmitted Debt: Surety Experience and English Law* (Oxford: Clarendon Press)

Firth, L (ed.) (2009) *Marriage and Cohabitation: Issues* vol. 166 (Cambridge: Independence)

Genn, H, M Partington and S Wheeler (2006) *Law in the Real World: Improving Our Understanding of How Law Works* (London: Nuffield Inquiry on Empirical Legal Research)

Gray, K and S F Gray (2008) *Elements of Land Law* 5th edn (Oxford: Oxford University Press)

Green, K and J Cursley (2001) *Land Law* 4th edn (Basingstoke: Palgrave)

Hall, G E (n.d.) 'Land litigation and the idea of New Mexico progress' in M Ebright (ed.), *Spanish and Mexican Land Grants and the Law* (Manhattan KS: Sunflower University Press)

Harris, J W (1999) 'Is property a human right?' in J McLean (ed.) *Property and the Constitution* (Oxford: Hart Publishing)

Heward, E (1990) *Lord Denning: A Biography* (London: Weidenfeld & Nicolson)

Hoggett, B and S Atkins (1984) *Women and the Law* (Oxford: Blackwell)

Holcombe, L (1980) 'Victorian wives and property: reform of the married women's property law, 1857–1882' in M Vicinus (ed.) *A Widening Sphere: Changing Roles of Victorian Women* (Bloomington: Indiana University Press)

Holcombe, L (1983) *Wives and Property: Reform of the Married Women's Property Law in Nineteenth-Century England* (Toronto: University of Toronto Press)

Hunter, R, C McGlynn and E Rackley (eds) (2010) *Feminist Judgments: From Theory to Practice* (Oxford: Hart Publishing)

Kingdom, E (1992) *What's Wrong With Rights? Problems for Feminist Politics of Law* (Edinburgh: Edinburgh University Press)

Law Commission (2007) *Cohabitation: The Financial Consequences of Relationship Breakdown* no 308 (London: Law Commission)

Layard, A (2010) 'Shopping in the public realm: the law of place' 37 *Journal of Law and Society* 412–41

Lewis, J (1999) *Cohabitation and the Law: Individualism and Obligations* (London: Lord Chancellor's Department)

MacKinnon, C A (1987) 'Whose culture? A case note on *Martinez v Santa Clara Pueblo* (1983)' in *Feminism Unmodified: Discourses on Life and Law* (Cambridge MA: Harvard University Press)

Massey, D (1994) *Space, Place and Gender* (Cambridge: Polity Press)

Millett, P J (1998) 'Equity's place in the law of commerce' 114 *Law Quarterly Review* 214–27

Mitchell, C (2010) *Hayton and Mitchell: Commentary and Cases on the Law of Trusts and Equitable Remedies* (London: Sweet & Maxwell)

Moran, L J (2009) 'Judging pictures: a case study of portraits of the Chief Justices, Supreme Court of New South Wales' 5 *International Journal of Law in Context* 295–314

Mulcahy, L (2010) *Legal Architecture: Justice, Due Process and the Place of Law* (Abingdon: Routledge)

O'Donnell, A and R Johnstone (1997) *Developing a Cross-Cultural Law Curriculum* (London: Cavendish)

Pawlowski, M and J Brown (2002) *Undue Influence and the Family Home* (London: Cavendish)

Potter, G and C Williams (2007) 'Two birds, one stone: combining student assessment and socio-legal research' 40 *Law Teacher* 1–18

Scott, A W (1922) 'The trust as an instrument of law reform' 31 *Yale Law Journal* 457

Spring, E (1993) *Law, Land and Family: Aristocratic Inheritance in England, 1300 to 1800* (Chapel Hill: University of North Carolina Press)

Staves, S (1990) *Married Women's Separate Property in England, 1660–1833* (Cambridge MA: Harvard University Press)

Stopes, C C (1894) *British Freewomen: Their Historical Privilege* (London: Swan Sonnenschein)

Stone, L (1990) *Road to Divorce: England 1530–1987* (Oxford: Oxford University Press)

Strahan, J A (1908) *A General View of the Law of Property* 5th edn (London: Stevens)

Stretton, T (1998) *Women Waging Law in Elizabethan England* (Cambridge: Cambridge University Press)

Topham, A F (1911) *Topham's Real Property* 2nd edn (London: Butterworth)

Watt, G (2009) *Equity Stirring: The Story of Justice Beyond Law* (Oxford: Hart Publishing)

Wilson, E (1977) *Women and the Welfare State* (London: Tavistock)

6

Contract Law: Socio-Legal Accounts of the Lived World of Contract

Linda Mulcahy[1] and Sally Wheeler[2]

Introduction

The law of contract is ideally suited to teaching from a socio-legal perspective. While doctrinal scholars place primary emphasis on the text, socio-legal researchers prefer to focus on context. They look, in particular, at the extent to which the formal rules of contract are considered legitimate or useful by those for whom they are designed. A wide range of empirical studies of the 'lived world of contract' now exist across time, industries and legal systems which suggest that contract law is not always used in the ways anticipated by doctrinal lawyers. Whilst textual analysis remains important, these findings have challenged the academy to consider the legitimacy of laws of contract which do not always reflect the practices and needs of the commercial sphere. They also encourage us to look beyond what Macaulay (2003) has called the 'paper deal' to the range of extra-legal normative frameworks which bind and govern commercial relationships. Research suggests that phenomena such as trust, co-operation and a good reputation can be as effective in making a commercial deal work as the threat of litigation or liquidated damages clauses. In short, socio-legal accounts of contracts encourage scholars to be more modest in their claims about the centrality of law in successful business deals.

Despite this active interest in the lived world of contract, it could be argued that socio-legal accounts of contract remain under-represented in textbooks written for students. There are a few notable exceptions but most popular textbooks continue to present contract doctrine as a series of rules with their own jurisprudential and internal logic. In other instances, there is a tendency to discuss empirical studies as an 'add-on' to discussions of doctrine by way

---

1 Professor of Law at London School of Economics and Political Science. Please address correspondence to l.mulcahy@lse.ac.uk.
2 Professor of Law at Queen's University Belfast. Please address correspondence to s.wheeler@qub.ac.uk.

of providing some context but little direct challenge to the canon. Used in this way, socio-legal studies is presented as representing a different world of contract which is of some relevance to hard law but should not be allowed to detract too much from the learning of it. In this chapter we argue that a socio-legal approach can, and should, play a much more central role in our analysis of case law. In particular we attempt to demonstrate that socio-legal approaches can be used as a powerful tool to critique the credibility of contract jurisprudence and imagine different ways of conceiving of exchange. Our position is that legal formalism has tended to encourage the spurious idea that law is in some way autonomous, an end in itself, rather than a means to a legitimate social order.

It is undoubtedly the case that legal doctrine can provide insights into the commercial world. It is after all partly produced as a result of observation of social practices and engagements with the very real commercial problems brought before the courts by litigants. But doctrinal analysis can only be enriched when we have something to compare each case with besides another case. Our concern is that formal legal analysis often provides only a selective and partial view of commercial practice which ensures that the problems presented to the courts fit within pre-defined doctrines. These may be valued for the certainty that they appear to bring but they are in danger of attempting to produce an imagined vision of the social world rather than reflecting it. A close reading of doctrine encourages students to critique the internal logic of law and to decide whether its reasoning is compelling and consistent. In this chapter we attempt to demonstrate how socio-legal scholars can use the same law reports but ask different questions of a case. Why did the parties come to law in the first place when other ways of solving their dispute were possible? Do the rulings of the court have legitimacy within the commercial community they were originally designed to serve? Is there evidence that the values reflected in doctrine are shared by contractors? How do judgments represent the commercial sector? What elements of common commercial practice and commercial litigation are rendered invisible by the ways in which cases are presented and reported?

A wide range of literature on the lived world of contracts already exists for those attempting to approach the subject from a socio-legal perspective. Rather than revisit this material we have chosen to consider how this wealth of information might help an undergraduate student to understand how socio-legal analysis can be used in the reading of a case and how it places that case in a broader context. Instead of 'cherry picking' a case that neatly reflects the problems that socio-legal researchers might have with doctrine, the authors have selected the first contract dispute to appear in the Appeal Cases at the time we began this project. We think this demonstrates the breadth of possibilities for the undergraduate curriculum offered by context-based study. Using it as a case study, we consider how this dispute might be analysed through a socio-legal lens. In the first section of this chapter, we explain the factual matrix of the case and set out the approaches that were taken to deciding it as it progressed through the court system. In the second section, we go on to discuss the sort of questions that a socio-legal scholar would pose about this case.

The facts of *RTS v Müller* are complicated and there are four implications of this for teaching purposes. Firstly, this offer and acceptance case is much more complex than the usual diet of cases about flick knives, bullfinches and smoke balls which we offer to undergraduate students. It reveals the rather artificial nature of generations of exam papers in which telex machines break down and messages left on answer machines are not heard. Instead, it immediately introduces students to the much harder reality of incomplete contracts in a commercial setting. Empirical accounts of the lived world of contract suggest that incomplete contracts are quite common and that many commercial deals would not pass the test of contractual formation or variation if challenged in the courts. Despite this, substantive sections on incomplete contracts remain rare in textbooks or lecture programmes. Secondly students might be asked to read and rewrite the convoluted account offered by the Court of Appeal which attempts to explain how the dispute between the parties erupted and got to trial. The importance of how a legal story is told is being given increasing recognition by scholars (Hunter et al., 2010) and this exercise could provide students with the opportunity to reflect on what messages selective and expert legal narratives might convey to the lay reader of cases.

RTS v Müller could also be used to encourage students to research the impact that procedural law has on the presentation of issues. The original hearing in the Technology and Construction Court was called to try preliminary issues only with the expectation that the litigation would be disposed of in a timely and relatively cheap manner. The fact that the case eventually went to the Supreme Court and that there was parallel litigation dealing with issues around costs demonstrates that these goals were not achieved in this instance. Viewed in the round, *RTS v Müller* provides students with a case study in the efficiency and effectiveness of the Woolf reforms and offers opportunities for cross-modular learning. Finally, the case gives students the possibility of looking at the operation of a standard form contract in the business sector. We tend to present standard form contracts to students as falling into two separate categories. In the first classification, we characterize standard forms to students as devices which are commonly an attempt to avoid negotiations and protect business interests when offered to consumers. In the second classification, we present them as exemplars negotiated by trade associations or professional bodies at national level by and for members of the group.

Students are encouraged to be less concerned by these contracts because the parties are of approximately equal bargaining strength. Our presumption is that, as a result, they are usually fair but this does not mean that they are without their problems. Less regularly discussed in undergraduate courses but deserving of attention are the ways in which the latter type of contract may still be the subject of extensive negotiations in order to ensure that it is customized for a particular local deal.

The facts of *RTS v Müller*

Müller is a producer of dairy products for the retail food industry and is famous for the fruit and cereal 'corner' yoghurts which appear on many supermarket shelves and are much loved by one of the authors. RTS was an engineering company which supplied automated packaging equipment to the food industry. Müller wanted to install two automated food packaging lines in its factory and sought out RTS with a view to negotiating a 'design, build and install' contract. In other words, it involved the design of a customized machine which would meet the very specific needs of a particular business. Contrary to the discrete contracts on which we often focus in our teaching, the parties never thought that there would be a single moment of performance evidenced by delivery. Performance was assessed over time and according to whether the equipment built and installed passed a series of factory tests based on speed, reliability and integration with other equipment.

Müller and RTS initially made contact with a view to striking a deal for the supply of customized machines in 2000. Discussions continued in subsequent years, particularly from December 2003 onwards. It was understood that RTS was not to be the sole supplier of equipment but was to be in charge of constructing the packing lines as a complete engineering installation with the equipment from other suppliers integrated into the equipment it was to supply. The parties exchanged frequent 'quotations' which appear to have dealt with the technical engineering specifications required for the project. In August 2004, Müller raised the issue of contract terms and asserted that it wished to contract on its terms but RTS recommended that Müller should use MF/1. This is a standard form contract issued originally by the Institution of Electrical Engineers, now merged with the Institution of Incorporated Engineers to form the Institution of Engineering and Technology (IET). Müller sent a list of amendments to MF/1 to RTS. RTS rejected these amendments.

The parties edged very slowly towards a deal. Müller told RTS in February 2005 that it had been awarded the contract. It then issued a letter of intent to RTS. This set out the contract price of approximately £1.6 million and asked RTS to commence work on the project. The letter asserted that a formal contract would be presented for signature in due course based upon Müller's amendments to MF/1. The letter of intent was to govern dealings between the parties for the four-week period up to the detail of the main contract being agreed. This period was later extended until May and it was not until July that the parties reached an agreement about the amendments to MF/1 ('the MF/1 conditions'). Clause 48 of MF/1 was particularly relevant as it was a 'subject to contract' clause. It asserted that no contract could come into existence until it had been signed and exchanged with the other party. No signed exchange ever took place.

Around August 2005, the parties agreed to change the arrangements for the delivery and installation of the automated food packaging lines in the hope that by doing so Müller would be in a position to fulfil an order it had just received from a national supermarket chain. This appears to have put pressure on the parties and their business relationship. In November 2005, this strained relationship was evident as a dispute arose about the performance testing of the automated lines because the new machinery did not, in Müller's view, meet the quality standards it required. Müller had already paid 70 per cent of the agreed price but at this stage declined to pay anymore. RTS claimed the outstanding 30 per cent of the contract price based either on the agreement made in July or in the alternative on a *quantum meruit* for work done. This claim was countered by one from Müller for £3 million for damages because the equipment RTS had supplied did not, in the company's view, reach the performance standard it thought it was paying for. RTS's counter to this was that MF/1 and the amendments agreed to it limited its liability for delay to pre-agreed 'liquidated' damages of 3.5 per cent of the total price and its liability for the equipment's failure to pass performance tests to 2.5 per cent of the contract price. Müller argued against the incorporation of MF/1 because it wanted to claim damages that were potentially higher than the amounts allowed by the liquidated damages clauses.

The judgments

The issue at trial was the nature of the agreement between the parties. Each of the three courts which determined the issue came to a different conclusion. The trial of the preliminary issues ordered by the High Court required the judge to determine what, if any, was the contract between the parties. Mr Justice Christopher Clarke in the Technology and Construction Court found that the letter of intent formed a contract between the parties for its agreed duration. That contract came to an end on a date agreed between the parties in May. Thereafter the relationship between the parties was again one of contract with the terms of the contract derived from post-May email exchanges between the parties. He determined that certain clauses, most notably the MF/1 conditions, were not incorporated into the contract because there was no exchange of signed contracts.

In the Court of Appeal, the complexity of the fact pattern and the application of law to it is illustrated by the fact that RTS changed its line of argument as to whether a contract existed between the parties. Its new position was that there was no contract. The Court of Appeal accepted this argument and held that no contractual relationship between the parties came into existence after the expiration of the letter of intent agreement. The Court of Appeal found that the parties had 'to all intents and purposes' agreed upon the applicability of the MF/1 conditions to their relationship but that the failure of the parties to comply with clause 48 as regards signature and exchange prevented not only the MF/1 conditions becoming part of the contract but any contract at all coming into existence. For clause 48 not to have this effect there needed to be an express waiver of it by the parties. It followed that if there was no contract in place there was no obligation for RTS to pay damages for breach.

In the Supreme Court, it was decided that a contract *had* come into being after the letter of intent had expired and that the MF/I standard terms were incorporated in it. The Supreme Court supported the position of the Court of Appeal that the parties had agreed the MF/1 conditions. However, a different view was taken of clause 48 since it was felt that waiver of the term was possible to infer from the communications between the parties and their actions. It was argued that the variation in August was recognized by both parties and was not seen as being in any way subject to contract. As a result, the parties were in a contractual relationship with each other. It was found that a contract came into being after the parties realized that the letter of intent had expired and once they had discussed terms prior to the variation in August.

Issues raised by the case

Formation of contract

Students analysing *RTS v Müller* may well be confused by the apparently irrational behaviour of the parties in this case. Standard problems set for undergraduates involving the distinction between offers and invitations to treat, equivocal or ambiguous responses to offers, unopened emails and incomplete voicemails encourage law students to believe that a contract has usually been formed; it is just a case of determining when. Many of the judicial pronouncements about offer and acceptance they will be asked to read will lead them to the conclusion that formation problems arise through lack of planning and formality; one might even suggest stupidity and commercial naivety. In line with this approach it was with something of a sense of frustration that the trial judge, Mr Justice Christopher Clarke commented in the

Technology and Construction Court that this was 'another example of the perils of proceeding with work under a letter of intent', while Lord Clarke of Stone-Cum-Ebony warned in his judgment that 'the moral of the story is to agree work first and to start work later'. Socio-legal accounts of the lived world of contract suggest such comments are misconceived. Empirical studies have revealed that many long-term commercial relationships are often not planned in the ways anticipated by doctrinal analysis. This suggests that it might be more prudent to see such cases as the norm rather than the exception and to reconsider the requirements of the formation doctrines as a result (Lewis, 1982). Lord Denning's attempts to do so (see, for instance, *Butler v Ex-Cell-O* [1979] and *Gibson v Manchester Council* [1979]) did not always meet with judicial approval, though the fact that three courts in this case applied the same doctrines in three different ways suggests that there is considerable scope for a revisiting of current concepts of offer and acceptance.

Socio-legal studies have found that lengthy negotiations resulting in detailed planned contractual documents are much more likely to take place where high-risk, complex, expensive items such as aircraft are involved (Beale and Dugdale, 1975). But even where large-scale commercial transactions are involved *RTS v Müller* suggests that approaches to contract formation may be much more haphazard than the courts or even socio-legal scholars anticipate. Describing the formalities of contract formation in complex construction cases involving a plethora of documents such as collateral warranties, novations, parent company guarantees and licences, Hughes and Bradbury (2009) have suggested that the inevitability of last-minute changes in the market place are such that the parties may even execute signature pages in advance of the final agreed version of the contract or transfer the signature page from a previous draft in order to save time. *RTS v Müller* demonstrates that even when negotiations are detailed, take place over a number of years and involve experienced in-house counsel the exact moment of formation of a contract and the terms on which it is based is extremely difficult to identify.

The Court of Appeal judgment in *RTS v Müller* presents us with an up-to-date example of the clash of norms between formalist doctrine and what empirical evidence suggests is not an unusual situation in commercial practice. It presents us with an uncomfortable scenario involving a complex commercial arrangement involving millions of pounds in which there is a shared understanding on a range of issues where the Court of Appeal was able to determine that there was no enforceable contract once the letter of intent agreement had expired. It soon becomes apparent that what may seem sensible to a lawyer could equally well be seen as an unnecessary transaction cost in the business sector where time is often of the essence. Extensive negotiations resulting in a diet of clear contractual obligations and responsibilities can be expensive to produce, especially where a valued, long-term commercial relationship exists between the parties and a dispute is seen as unlikely by the parties. Significantly, placing stress on formal rights and obligations may even be seen as a sign of distrust or as commercially naive in an ever-changing market.

It is also the case that whilst contract jurisprudence has long placed a high value on certainty, socio-legal scholars have been keen to emphasize the central importance of flexibility in the commercial sector. It is far from unusual for the parties to a contract to begin to perform their obligations as RTS and Müller did before all the terms of the agreement have been reached. This is, for instance, the problem that occurs in 'battle of the forms' cases. Moreover, research suggests that the parties commonly engage in extra-legal adjustments to the original deal which alter performance as the deal progresses. The Supreme Court considered that RTS and Müller had done exactly that in this case when they waived clause 48. Even Lord Clarke of Stone-Cum-Ebony acknowledged in his judgment that the behaviour of RTS and Müller did not represent an unusual way to do business (p. 756).

What research suggests, and *RTS v Müller* provides an example of, is that parties who do not plan are not necessarily naive or acting irrationally when they begin and continue to perform without a formal contract in place to reflect shared understandings or assumptions. Socio-legal accounts of contract suggest that it is good relations and profit margins rather than legal rights and duties that are uppermost in the minds of contracting parties (Macaulay, 1963). Drawing on such accounts, it has been argued by relational contract theorists that co-operating in the course of a long-term commercial relationship is more likely to lead to mutual wealth maximization than not co-operating. This idea of 'solidarity' reflects the importance of seeing commercial agreements as being geared towards mutual futures, interdependence and a plethora of shared goals. It is not contended that in accepting these ideals, the parties abandon their own interests. It is intelligent rather than blind trust which is most effective in such contexts. In the words of classical economics, co-operation and flexibility promote utility maximization rather than undermine it (Macneil, 2001). In this case it is clear that Müller trusted RTS enough to forward the company 70 per cent of the agreed price and to proceed to do business with it without a signed contract in place. Indeed, it seems likely that the reason this case was brought to trial was the problem of too much trust. The critical mistake made appears to be that Müller paid 70 per cent of the price but had got far less than 70 per cent of the work completed. This left the company vulnerable if quality issues arose. A far better approach would have been to link staged payments in percentage terms to the work completed and judged acceptable. Moreover, as the deal progressed, Müller seems to have become distracted from finalizing a formal deal by its desire to fulfil the highly lucrative order with a major supermarket chain.

Significantly, neither RTS nor Müller appears to have been overly concerned about the absence of a contract for most of their relationship. They did not, as is often suggested by doctrinal lawyers, need a fully negotiated contract in order to plan their relationship or enhance their trust in the other party. If the machines produced by RTS had reached Müller's quality standards the potential lack of a contract would, like many of the other business deals discussed by empirical studies, have remained under the legal radar. The parties only turned their attention to the need for a contract which favoured them on breach when the machines designed by RTS did not meet the quality threshold expected by Müller. The parties did not denounce the importance of the contract; they spent a lot of time negotiating contract terms but only started arguing about what had been agreed when both sides needed to minimize their losses: in RTS's case by restricting the amount claimed in damages and ultimately rejecting liability and in Müller's case by seeking to recover damages from RTS. This raises some important issues about the lived world of contract which have been the subject of much debate between socio-legal scholars and 'new formalists' (see, for instance, Bernstein, 1992). The latter have drawn on empirical studies of the commercial world to argue that much socio-legal work has neglected the importance that legal rules can play in planning for, and dealing with, the aftermath of an unsuccessful relationship. It is argued that while techniques such as blacklisting within an industry may be as effective as litigation when bringing a recalcitrant contractor to account, contract law is particularly valuable when it comes to the endgame. Work in this genre encourages us to recognize that disputing contractors may be less worried about their reputations in a buoyant market in which it is easy to find people to contract with or even in a depressed market where there is little likelihood of future contracts but serious problems with cash flow. In these situations, a resort to law allows each party in a dispute to claim contested resources in line with clearly defined and public rules. As the new formalists have suggested, it was mainly during the endgame of the relationship that RTS and Muller made reference to formal contract norms in an attempt by both parties to use the courts to minimize their losses.

These alternative accounts of what binds the parties together in a commercial relationship explain the difficulty that the courts often have in containing commercial behaviour within the doctrinal handcuffs available to judges. More particularly, they explain the convoluted efforts of the judge at first instance to fit the events surrounding the issuing of the letter of intent into the structure of offer, counter offer and acceptance in the Technology and Constriction Court in attempting to explain the behaviour of RTS and Müller by reference to formalist expectations. Viewed from a socio-legal perspective, this case provides an example of the fact that contracts are far from being the static agreements suggested by the formalist approach in which all rights and obligations can be determined at the 'moment of responsibility' when an acceptance exactly matches an offer. Commenting on Anglo-American approaches to contract formation, Macneil has argued that contract formation is much more akin to a dimmer switch, whereby contractual obligations slowly evolve, than to the instant on–off creation of liability envisaged by doctrine (Macneil, 2001). In short, contract formation in the commercial sector is complex and messy; behaviour and express intentions are often indeterminate. Agreements commonly arise from an extensive and tangled trail of correspondence and negotiation involving conduct, written documents and discussions in which mirror image theory or fresh consideration may play little part. As Atiyah (1989) suggested some decades ago, there is a clear danger that doctrine has become too pragmatic and divorced from more abstract concepts of agreement.

Avoiding law?

In addition to revealing the divergence of formation doctrines and practice *RTS v Müller* draws our attention to the way in which commercial parties may actually plan to *avoid* the imputation of a contract. Much was made in the Supreme Court of the fact that intention to create legal relations is often easily inferred in cases where performance has already commenced and the contract price has been agreed. It has long been the case that the law presumes an intention to create legal relations in such commercial agreements. However, in line with the theoretical underpinnings of neoclassical doctrine, with its respect for freedom to contract and freedom from contract, intention can also be negated by an express statement to the contrary. The devices which have been developed to reflect such a repudiation are letters of intent, comfort letters, framework agreements and subject to contract clauses, all of which signal that a final formal agreement has not yet been concluded. Though unpopular in some sectors of the business world, the case of *Baird v Marks & Spencer* (2001) provides the business sector with a salutary reminder of the extent to which an express intention to avoid the imposition of a contract continues to be respected by the senior judiciary. In the current case, two contract avoidance devices, the letter of intent and subject to contract provision, were used to avoid the imputation of an agreement.

Viewed from another perspective, letters of intent are often used as a declaration that the parties are in the process of negotiating and as a symbol of a preliminary commitment to each other. They can come in a number of forms but are in essence a communication expressing a serious intention to enter a contract at a future date. They may take the form of a non-binding statement of the future intentions of both parties; an 'if' contract or good faith proviso which creates binding contractual rights if certain conditions are met. They may also been seen as a complete 'preliminary' contract as was found in *RTS v Müller*. Either way, this device is used where there are good reasons to start work in advance of the finalization of all of the contract documents being agreed, and this technique is commonly employed in cases of commercial urgency. The letter provides an important safeguard of legal rights whilst the contract documents are being completed. In the present case, the parties used the letter of intent to outline Müller's intention to proceed with the project as set out in their offer. The Supreme Court recognized a contract based on the letter of intent and was only able to search for a final contract once it had established that the preliminary letter of intention agreement had expired and the subject to contract clause had been waived.

Letter of intent

1   Whole agreement price £1,682,000
2   Work to commence immediately in order to meet 30 September deadline
3   Full contractual terms to be based on Müller's amended form of MF/I contract
4   Full terms and relevant technical specification to be finalized, agreed and signed within four weeks of the date of the letter
5   Prior to agreement on full terms only Müller will have right to terminate the project and contract
6   If Müller terminates, it will reimburse RTS for reasonable demonstrable out-of-pocket expense up to date of termination.
7   Müller will not be liable for any loss of profits, contracts, anticipated savings, data, goodwill and revenue or other indirect costs arising from termination
8   No further remedies available on termination

Rather than rushing towards the moment of responsibility, these devices demonstrate that it is commercial parties, and not the courts, that have developed ways of suspending or avoiding the importation of a final contract. These mechanisms are commonly used where time is of the essence and work needs to proceed but there is still a requirement to conduct investigations or raise finance, or where legal departments need to catch up with developments in the engineering department. These devices are evidence of anything but a lack of planning and fulfil an important function in allowing the parties to move towards a more detailed and formal agreement. Collins (1999) suggests that such 'gentlemen's agreements' are not usually enforceable on the basis that the intention appears to be to rely on each other's good faith and honour until a formal contract is made. Drawing on a socio-legal analysis, he also points to the importance of past dealings and the non-legal sanctions which might also be available to bind the parties to these preliminary agreements. Neoclassical doctrine tends to pay much greater heed to certainty than to flexibility in contracts. The use of letters of intent in *RTS v Müller*, where a long-term relationship was not anticipated, bought the parties time and built into their commercial dealings the type of flexibility appreciated in empirical studies and the works of relational contract theorists.

Standard form contracts

The classical contract model developed at a time when most negotiations were conducted face-to-face by two parties. Doctrines associated with this model and its neoclassical offshoot continue to influence the modern law of contract despite the fact that a considerable number of legal agreements are now standard form contracts containing express written terms prepared in advance of negotiations and exchange by people who have not met. Standard form contracts probably account for the bulk of inter-business agreements and bring a number of benefits to businesses, most notably the avoidance of repetitive negotiations about a standard term or common procedures. *RTS v Müller* involved a particularly important standard form contract known as the MF/1 contract produced by the IET and widely used in the engineering industry. Engineering contracts can be among the most complex and demanding that are put in place, and often require input from a range of specialists, including engineers, scientists and project managers. The importance of this standard form contract in framing expectations was accepted by Lord Clarke of Stone-Cum-Ebony in the Supreme Court when he opined:

> It is important to note the references to MF/I terms both in the letter of intent and in the judge's conclusions. It seems to us to be *almost inconceivable* that the parties would have entered into an agreement for the performance of the whole project which was not based on detailed terms. (p. 759, emphasis added)

The IET produces several model contracts and commentaries which are designed for use in home and overseas contracts for mechanical and electrical plant, goods and consultancy. The forms are produced by a joint negotiating committee whose members represent the various professions and trades in the electrical and mechanical engineering industries. These model contracts cover such issues as patents, assignment and sub-contracting, site conditions, variation orders, access to premises for inspection of plant, liquidated damages, currency of payment, dispute resolution procedures and confidentiality. The basic object of contracts governed by such terms is to enable the purchaser at an agreed date to take over and operate the plant which has been completed and tested in accordance with the technical specification that forms part of the contract. In practice, the contracts are highly technical and the time required for completion may be lengthy as plant is tested and re-tested to ensure it is fit for purpose. Because of the unique technical specifications needed for each new deal, there is a greater need for the contracts to be tailor-made whilst being modelled on the general conditions. In contrast to practice in other industries, such as construction, it is common for large-scale operators to produce their own 'in-house' models which follow the appropriate recommended model. These contracts become customized only after a careful process of incorporation, variation and addition of terms to suit the parties' project. While RTS was familiar with the industry model forms used in this way on a regular basis, Müller was not. This explains why Müller did not immediately accept the example of a previously customized contract that RTS offered as a model for its contract with Müller.

The incorporation of terms relating to the limitation of liability were at the heart of the dispute in *RTS v Müller* and this issue is an important subject for debate within the industry. Mechanical engineering is a high-tech world where very expensive capital equipment is designed and installed, often using state-of-the-art technology. Unlike a number of standard form contracts which might be offered on a take-it-or-leave-it basis, there is a need for engineering contracts of the type in *RTS v Müller* to be governed by a bespoke technical specification and adapted contracts modelled on the general conditions. These contracts become bespoke only by a careful process of incorporation, variation and addition of terms to suit the parties' particular project. This explains why RTS and Müller were in negotiations for so long before and after the letter of intent was issued and why the contractual negotiations proved to be so complicated.

The losses caused by indirect and consequential damages can also be crippling where production is held up as a result of poorly designed or installed goods. Despite the potential losses for the purchaser, engineers have traditionally claimed the necessity to limit their liability in contracts because the alternative would be that they would have to increase their price significantly to cover the increased cost of insurance. It has been argued by the IET that it is more convenient for the purchaser to take out the level of insurance required because the contractor has no control over the purchaser's investment decisions, the use to which the machine is put or the anticipated return. While the company commissioning the plant has years to recover its investment, the contractor has just one opportunity to do so in the contract price. It has been claimed that the expectation that the insurance burden will be carried by the purchaser rather than the engineer has reached the status of a 'universal philosophy worldwide' in the electrical and engineering plant industry (Gaitskill, 1997, p. 263). It follows that the industry is extremely sensitive to challenges to this order of things.

Assessment in a socio-legal contract module

Assessment in contract law, like most common law modules on the under-graduate degree, is traditionally tied to the fact-pattern test. A module that uses socio-legal materials risks failing to capture a review of the facts within that form of assessment. Once labelled as a secondary concern within assessment, such materials risk falling into the dreaded category of 'additional reading'. The attraction of using *RTS v Müller* is precisely that it might open up new avenues for assessment. It is situated within an industry standard form about which, despite the plethora of such contractual structures in the commercial world, it seems that law students can still graduate barely knowing of their existence and function. There may be a passing recognition that such contracts played a role in cases such as *Phillips v Hyland* (1984) but no real understanding of the significance of the court's interventionist stance in striking down a term within a negotiated industry standard contract as failing the reasonableness test under the Unfair Contract Terms Act (UCTA) 1977.

A contract drafting and planning assessment would encourage students to see Macneil's discrete and relational scenarios as existing on a spectrum rather than as different transactions and to view a contract as a linear journey navigating a path between the expectations of the two parties (Macneil, 2001). Within this type of assessment, students can be asked to suggest a number of clauses that should go into a contract, give their reasons for selecting those clauses and then draft those clauses. The clause selection and explanation is tied to what empirical studies tell them about contract planning and operation. The drafting of those clauses tests both commercial awareness of issues such as risk assignment and insurance availability and also knowledge of doctrinal issues such as UCTA 1977 and the doctrine of frustration. One of the authors was using an assessment similar to the one described here in the hot-bed of radicalism that was the Keele Law School of the 1990s. It withered on the vine in subsequent progression to more conventional establishments. At Keele, this assessment included a briefing on the task from local industries and practitioners. This gave students the opportunity to consider how to deal with particular issues that were cited by the prospective users of the contract as important to them. In the current educational policy climate this seems once again an ideal opportunity for employer engagement with the law school curriculum.

Conclusion

Research into the pursuit of civil litigation has consistently shown that very few cases that enter the civil litigation system ever get to trial. Although it has long been recognized that the cases that get to court are atypical of disputes generally, socio-legal research has recently demonstrated that a lower proportion of litigated cases than ever before are reaching the courts. This instantly renders *RTS v Müller* an unusual case in which the issues at stake appear greater to the parties than the financial or reputational costs and time lost by the parties in the pursuit of the legal issues. Even when contract disputes are pursued to law, the parties generally opt for commercial arbitration rather than adjudication. The Technology and Construction Court remains highly sensitive to the need to compete with arbitration for speedy and effective adjudication, but however much it reforms itself the lure of privacy in arbitral proceedings is likely to trump attempts to bring cases with important legal issues to a public forum. This raises important questions for the development of precedent in the common law and suggests that much of the rethinking of contract doctrine called for by socio-legal and relational scholars will be slow, if it happens at all. This brings with it a danger that doctrine will become even more divorced from practice.

Certain aspects of this case remain a mystery. For many socio-legal scholars this would naturally lead to further empirical inquiry into the dynamics of the disputes. It could be argued that this would allow us to determine the extent to which aspects of the party's claim were transformed as the case progressed through the legal system or the success of the courts and doctrine in meeting the party's needs. Though we have hinted at some of the motivations that might be imputed to the parties above, one of the most perplexing issues raised by *RTS v Müller* is why, having conducted such lengthy negotiations, the parties did not formalize their agreement as originally intended. Was it just laziness? Were the parties so confident of the profits to be made by both sides that they considered the formalization of the contract unnecessary? Were they confident that agreement had been reached? Were non-legal sanctions such as blacklisting or damage to reputation available to secure performance? Was Müller simply too preoccupied with meeting the supermarket order to worry about formal closure of its deal with RTS? When we fail to completely understand what has motivated the parties, it is to a socio-legal approach that many scholars can usefully turn.

Cases cited

Baird Textile Holdings Ltd v Marks & Spencer plc [2001] EWCA Civ 274
Butler Machine Tool Co. Ltd v Ex-Cell-O Corp. [1979] 1 WLR 401

Gibson v Manchester Council [1979] 1 All ER 972

Phillips Products Ltd v Hyland and Hamstead Plant Hire Co. Ltd [1984] EWCA Civ 5

RTS Flexible Systems Ltd v Molkerei Alois Müller GmbH & Co. KG [2008] EWHC 1087 (TCC)

RTS Flexible Systems Ltd v Molkerei Alois Müller GmbH & Co. KG [2009] EWCA Civ 26; [2009] 2 All ER (Comm) 542; [2009] BLR 181; 123 Con LR 130; official transcript

RTS Flexible Systems Ltd v Molkerei Alois Müller GmbH & Co. KG [2010] UKSC 14; [2010] 1 WLR 753

References

Atiyah, P S (1989) *An Introduction to the Law of Contract* 4th edn (Oxford: Oxford University Press)

Beale, H and T Dugdale (1975) 'Contracts between businessmen: planning and the use of contractual remedies' 2 *British Journal of Law and Society* 45–60

Bernstein, L (1992) 'Opting out of the legal system: extralegal contractual relations in the diamond industry' 21(1) *Journal of Legal Studies* 115–57.

Collins, H (1999) *Regulating Contracts* (Oxford: Oxford University Press)

Gaitskill, R (1997) 'Legal update: limitation clauses – a dispatch from the battle front' 7(6) (December) *Engineering Management Journal* 263–4

Hunter, R, C McGlynn and E Rackley (eds) (2010) *Feminist Judgments: From Theory to Practice* (Oxford: Hart Publishing)

Lewis, R (1982) 'Contracts between businessmen: reform of the law of firm offers and an empirical study of tendering practices in the building industry' 9(2) *Journal of Law and Society* 153–75

Macaulay, S (2003) 'The real and the paper deal' in D Campbell, H Collins and J Wightman (eds) *Implicit Dimensions of Contract* (Oxford: Hart Publishing)

Macaulay, S (1963) 'Non contractual relations in business – a preliminary study' 28 *American Sociological Review* 55

Macneil, I (2001) 'Exchange and co-operation' in D Campbell (ed.) *The Relational Theory of Contract: Selected Works of Ian Macneil* (London: Sweet and Maxwell), ch. 4, pp. 89–124

Further reading

Badawi, A (2009) 'Relational governance and contract damages: evidence from franchising', http://ssrn.com/abstract=1443515

Deakin, S, C Lane and F Wilkinson (1997) 'Contract law, trust relations and incentives for co-operation: a comparative study' in S Deakin and J Michie (eds) *Contracts, Co-operation, and Competition* (Oxford: Oxford University Press)

Mouzas, S and D Ford (2006) 'Managing relationships in showery weather: the role of umbrella agreements' 59 *Journal of Business Research* 1248–56

7

Tort Law: How Should Tort be Taught? Utilizing Expertise and Telling Tales in an Innovative Law Curriculum

Karen Devine

Introduction

The effects of widened participation in Higher Education (HE) in the UK are plain to see. The governmental response to a need for greater social justice and economic competitiveness has led to an influx of students from non-traditional backgrounds and under-represented social and cultural groups, with a growing trend of students entering universities from state schools, low participation neighbourhoods and lower socio-economic backgrounds (DFEE, 1998). Indeed, facilitation of the widening participation (WP) initiative (see Public Accounts Committee, 2008–2009) by law schools in the UK has witnessed increased access to law degree programmes by a much wider cross-section of the population with the removal of barriers to HE overcoming the elitism and exclusion of the past. With such radical changes to the make-up of the student body, law schools must re-assess who their students are, what academic skills they are likely to possess on commencement of their studies, how best to equip them with the requisite academic and legal skills to success-fully navigate a law degree, and in what ways delivery of the curriculum can best serve a cohort of students who enter law schools from a wide variety of educational and intellectual vantage points.

This chapter takes Kent Law School's (KLS) approach to the teaching of tort law as an exemplar model that combines innovative modes of delivery with responsiveness to the learning needs of its diverse range of students. The law degree programme within KLS, which includes tort law as a core module for a qualifying law degree (QLD), has been revamped via a curriculum review with the prioritization of research-led teaching (Carr and Horsey, 2010, p. 8) embedding student learning, even in the 'traditional' or core modules. The need for such an overhaul of the curriculum was acknowledged and developed by the KLS learning and teaching team as a direct response to the changing face of the modern-day law student. Rather than focusing totally upon teaching techniques as the main tool with which to impart knowledge and to inspire and develop student understanding, emphasis has been placed upon new forms of legal education. In the delivery of tort law, legal content has been re-evaluated with the disparity of students in mind – this, in addition to capitalizing upon the rich, intellectual expertise of KLS tort law academics – has engendered a tort programme that incorporates three new innovative forms of teaching, namely; presenting case law as 'stories'; the delivery of case classes; and the introduction of 'special studies'.

Students are first introduced to tort law in the Introduction to Obligations module in one term of their first year. During this module, students engage with rudiments of tortious legal harm, debate issues of a so-called compensation culture, and study in detail the legal principles and concepts that define trespass to the person torts before also exploring two elements of contract law – breach of contract and potential remedies. Core texts include Horsey and Rackley's (2011) *Tort Law* and Chen-Wishart's (2010) *Contract Law*, which are supplemented by selected readings made available to students in the form of a readings pack. The module is charged via the curriculum review with teaching aspects of common law development, the historical foundations of legal obligations, the doctrine of precedent and the skill of reading cases, and thus initially explores the key differences between private and public law, civil and criminal law, and tort and contract law. In the second year, students study the Law of Obligations module, which is taught over two terms and similarly encompasses elements of both tort and contract. The tort law section of the Law of Obligations course examines the intricate and complex issues involved in the tort of negligence, occupiers' liability and the land torts before individual students select a tort or contract-based special study. The special study pedagogy was adopted by KLS in its revised curriculum in order to inject research-led teaching into intensive, specialized subject areas and to allow academic experts scope to introduce students to aspects of socio-legal studies associated with their field of expertise.

'Cases as stories': a tale to be told – from boats to snails and from 'Boyle to Royal'

At KLS, new (stage one) students are exposed to the notion that, contrary to most people's idea of law being a 'book of rules',[1] case law – and therefore most of private law – in fact derives from stories that the law got involved in, which were then recorded in the law reports, subsequently becoming legal authority, or 'law'. From the outset, students are introduced to this concept

---

1 The KLS obligations team is indebted to the pro-active teaching approach of now retired senior lecturer, Mr Alan Thomson, for the introduction of this innovative form of teaching and for the provision of a 'mock-up prop' currently used by teaching staff to visually emulate the 'rule book' conception of law.

using a series of cases during an introductory lecture given by the obligations team in induction week. The tone of the lecture is light-hearted but exudes a serious underpinning: the objective is to instil the idea that legal stories invariably have precursors and sequels, and how theorists such as Ronald Dworkin (1998, pp. 228–38) have likened the application of case law to a chain novel – each author (or judge) bringing something new to the work, whilst each must fit with what's gone before. By encouraging students to locate and map cases within a timeline, the ability to unpack and then chart the process of legal precedent within a given area of law is fostered and, as a result, students begin to appreciate the analogies between points of law and fact within preceding cases. Acknowledging that students are receptive to popular culture, the notion of teams of screen-writers writing episodes for a soap opera, such as *Eastenders* and *Hollyoaks*, is used to exemplify this point before introducing some actual case examples.

Using visual aids as lecture-theatre backdrops, students are led through a timeline of case law in a storybook fashion – we begin with the criminal case of *R v Dudley and Stevens* (1884) to create an atmosphere of drama and tension in the lecture theatre, telling tales of the horror that unfolded as three men stranded in a boat sacrificed the defenceless cabin boy in order to preserve their own lives, but with the purpose of illustrating how the defence of necessity can permeate the courts. The story is depicted, not as an isolated event arising from a unique set of circumstances, but as part of a larger story in which, before and after *Dudley*, the courts had to explore in other particular circumstances the boundaries of the defence of necessity as part of legal precedent. Similarly, the facts of *McCutcheon v MacBrayne* (1964) are explored in an attempt to demonstrate how a claimant need not be bound by his previous commercial dealings with the defendant, not because 'the book of rules' stated such a fact, but because of the way the courts had dealt with analogous situations involving signatures on contracts in the past – and how this story then formed part of a wider story involving tickets (*Thornton v Shoe Lane Parking* [1971]), the signing (or not) of documents (*L'Estrange v Graucob* [1934]) and personal injury sustained by ticket-holders (*Thompson v London Midland & Scottish Railway* [1930]), merging into the wider story involving tickets.

In order to introduce the concept of mental injury as an emerging legal harm in tort, *McLoughlin v O'Brian* [1982] is used and serves a dual purpose: not only does the heroine of the story emerge triumphant in her claim against those who caused her to suffer psychiatric injury by their negligence – and providing lecturers with the means by which to elucidate mental harm as a 'new' form of compensable damage – but the case provides the opportunity to illustrate the doctrine of precedent in full force. And of course, no 'tort story' would be complete without the seminal case of *Donoghue v Stevenson* [1932] and within the module KLS's programme pays homage to its importance. Complete with portraits of this story's key actors and photographs of the Well-Meadow Café – as it was then and how the site currently looks, continuing the concept of a timeline – Mae Donoghue and the alleged snail that changed the law of the land are brought to life, before expounding her story's implications for law today.

It is without apology that such care and attention to detail are afforded these pivotal cases of the past. But with so many important cases to choose from, we instil in our students that this is merely a tiny insight into of some of the cases that they will study over the course of their degree. As Caron (2003, p. 4) suggests, students should be encouraged to use their own senses and schema in order to build on knowledge, and:

> [A]s a result, we should not sacrifice depth of coverage at the altar of scope of coverage; rather than rush through the signature cases in our subject in order to get to the latest hot topic or fashionable theory, we should savour the opportunity to unpack with our students what it is that makes these cases central to a deep understanding of the field.

In our experience, the 'hook' of telling tales to teach case method has proved exceedingly popular and effective with first-year students who, as a result, appear to be much more engaged with the reading of cases than demonstrated by previous student cohorts, and appear less reticent (or perhaps better equipped) to locate cases within a legal (or other) timeframe. Such a learning strategy is central in that it provides a framework upon which students can then contextualize the social, political and economic importance of the case under discussion and lends them to nurture their critical thinking skills, an essential tool for studying law. Furthermore, by introducing the parties of a legal action as 'characters', their story becomes personalized and humanized, making it much easier for students to grasp the idea of relationships, responsibilities and legal obligations between individuals in a duty situation. But the adoption of this form of pedagogy does not end there – having extolled the importance of the past, we then invite students to look to the future and, over the previous two years, we have introduced a familiar story to which any law student could not fail to have been exposed – the 'story' of the pervasiveness of reality TV, and particularly of Susan Boyle and *Britain's Got Talent* (BGT).

In direct contrast to examining historical case law, students are catapulted into the modern-day phenomenon of celebrity culture and reality TV, and the 2009 and 2010 cohorts were asked to consider whether the international singing sensation, Susan Boyle, suffered a legally recognized harm following her appearance on BGT, and if so, whom she could have sued. Seminar discussions centred upon the vulnerable mental state that Boyle demonstrated at her first audition in April 2009 and BGT's perceived lack of welfare and concern for her mental well-being. From this follows consideration of whether a duty of care should be owed to contestants on these types of show – particularly the vulnerable, infirm and minors – and by whom – and also the moral and legal role that parents and carers should play. Questions of legal obligations arising from assumed responsibility, standards of care, foreseeability of harm, the complexities of a claim for mental harm and privacy rights are probed before exploring the issue of a claimant's mental capacity and its relevance to the doctrine of informed consent, in an attempt to contextualize Boyle's situation with key elements of tort law, though this is juxtaposed with her individual success as a recording artist.

Having located the legal parameters of Boyle's story, students also explored the socio-cultural contexts within which it played out, such as societal preconceptions of physical attractiveness and personal presentation, and feminist critiques of women's treatment within celebrity culture. Students are encouraged to track the timeline of events that unfolded, from the reaction and treatment that was meted out by judges and audience alike to the actions of the media (see e.g. Revior and Simpson, 2009) in the aftermath of the programme being aired (which arguably contributed to her mental breakdown). Students were encouraged to develop their research skills by considering how different sources can present a story in contrasting ways, and to engage with the collated empirical evidence. By tracing the 'sequel' to Boyle, students began to unravel the legal consequences of the events that took place: despite the fact that Boyle never commenced legal proceedings, the effects of the Susan Boyle story become clear. In the same way that judges use precedent to determine the outcome of cases, students were awakened to the idea that Boyle indicates how past occurrences can shape future behaviour. Through their research, students unpacked the impact and influence that Boyle has had; for example, how production company policies have now been amended to reflect the potential implications of a lack of care. Post-Boyle, the health and well-being of contestants accepted for shows such as BGT and *The X Factor* are now afforded greater priority, including the provision of compulsory psychological testing, and greater monitoring and assistance are given to those who demonstrate signs of becoming overwhelmed by their overnight fame and/or notoriety (Thomas, 2009). In terms of privacy law, students revealed during class discussions how the media were reminded – and are now more mindful – of their responsibilities towards the rights of subjects under the Press Code of Practice (Brook, 2009).

By adopting this methodology, tort law students quickly acknowledge how the future is often determined by the past and how an appreciation of prior events can serve as a potential litigation avoidance strategy. Clearly, this form of case method, combined with independent student research and evidence gathering, provides an effective method by which to stimulate the

acquisition of legal knowledge and understanding in a lively and culturally relevant manner. With the need to capitalize upon popular culture and
up-to-date events to retain student engagement and the maintenance of a
fresh approach to the learning of law, the 2011–2012 first-year cohort at KLS
encountered a new story – that of the marriage of Prince William to Kate
Middleton in April 2011. Moving from 'Boyle to Royal', students were invited
to accept the notion that the ideology of cases as stories can have a usefulness in the study of law even where legal harm has not actualized. Moreover,
this pedagogical approach can illustrate that stories do not have to have a
legal outcome in order to demonstrate their potential legal consequences.

The Royal Wedding story proved to be an innovative and topical way to
extrapolate certain elements of tort and contract law, helped largely (as with
Boyle) by students' familiarity with the topic – even those from overseas.
The use of YouTube clips introduced the concept of negligence and personal
injury by bringing the students' attention to certain events that played
out during the occasion, such as the Royal Horseguard who was thrown
by a spooked horse, which then galloped unseated through the wedding
procession, illustrating potential harm (both physical and mental) to the
demounted rider, the crowd and the royal couple. In addition, students
explored potentially tortious issues associated with crowd control and street
parties and celebrations, as well as public body liability, public nuisance,
the duties of local authorities, and anti-royal protests which *could* – and in
some cases *did* (Press Association, 2011) – include elements of trespass to the
person torts in assault, battery and false imprisonment (including 'kettling')
and issues regarding the right to assembly and freedom of speech. Associated
areas of law such as an action for breach of confidence in relation to the
secrecy agreements surrounding the identity of the designers, makers and
dress design of Kate Middleton's wedding dress were also discussed before
students were introduced to the interplay between tort and contract in
the context of Royal Wedding merchandise. Issues of contractual obligations and product liability were analysed whilst drawing upon existing case
law to contextualize the potential for litigation arising from defective or
sub-standard goods. Analogies were made between the ability to purchase
'royal condoms' (by drawing comparisons to the condom product liability
case *Richardson* v *LRC Products* [2000]) and the re-introduction of *Donoghue*
v *Stevenson* to students by discussing the sale of Papa John's 'William
and Kate' pizza, with the legal implications of *Donoghue* demonstrating
how the presence of an alleged snail back in 1932 allows consumers legal
protection today.

As part of KLS's curriculum review, a 'skills matrix' was created in order to
'spiral' new-found skills from one module to other, reinforcing and building
upon attained legal knowledge and tool acquisition. The spiralling of skills

in this manner has been described as, 'a complex map of the teaching of skills and their repetition and progression across not only the core modules but also the optional modules and is gradually and continually being built, added to and developed' (Carr and Horsey, 2010, p. 5). In the spirit of the skills spiral, tort law students are encouraged at stage two to develop understanding of and reflect further upon the issues raised by the stories discussed in stage one and to use that legal knowledge as a springboard for a student-led debate concerning the socio-legal aspects of compensation culture, accident compensation, claims management companies and the role of insurance. One of the central features of the skills matrix is critical reading[2] and it is with this skill in mind that the Obligations modules in stage one and two further embed the skill of case law reading by way of case classes.

Case classes: injecting socio-legal research into the reading of cases

Comprised of groups totalling approximately 30 to 35 students, four case classes are delivered throughout the stage one Introduction to Obligations module – two classes based on tort and two on contract. The case class mode of delivery was adopted with the aim of continuing the enthusiasm for case reading developed via teaching case method and storytelling to help students to explicitly master elements of legal process whilst developing their critical reading skills. Indeed, the case classes foster a clear engagement with the legal doctrine, court structure, court proceedings, counsels' submissions, the doctrine of precedent and the skill of legal argument. Hard copies of the cases are disseminated to students a week prior to class and a selection of 'thinking points' are suggested such as how the cases under discussion fit into the law of tort, how one case builds upon the other, the legal issues involved and reasons given for the decisions, as well as whether students agree with the case outcome. This provides ample time for students to read and reflect upon the issues in detail and to develop questions and points of discussion that they bring – with some enthusiasm, as both teachers and students have noted – to class. As one student commented on completion of the module:

> First, case classes allow a deeper look into cases relevant to a principle of law without the time constraints present in seminars. This should provide a stronger grasp of case law within the relevant area. Secondly, the cases studied as applications of the core cases involved in the relevant area of law show a practical example of the application of precedents. This, when coupled with the

---

2   KLS includes six key skills in its skills matrix: effective learning, academic writing, research and information handling, critical reading, problem solving and oral skills.

> knowledge of the core cases from the seminar, provides a stronger
> foundation of case law for students to take into exams.[3]

The cases chosen for study in the case classes are selected to complement the research interests of the law lecturers delivering the module. For example, this author's research is broadly situated within the area of legal obligations, with a particular emphasis on the tort of negligence within healthcare provision, and more specifically on the collection of bodily materials and the role of informed consent. The first set of tort cases that students were exposed to was carefully selected with consent to medical treatment in mind. *St George's Healthcare NHS Trust v S, Regina v Collins and Others, Ex parte S* [1999] and *The NHS Trust v Ms T* [2004] concerned the refusal of consent to medical treatment. The first case illustrates this in the context of a 36-week-pregnant woman presenting at hospital with pre-eclampsia who was given a caesarean section against her will, and the second in relation to the administering of a blood transfusion to a patient following repeated episodes of self-harm, again without her consent – indeed, against her express and seemingly lucid wishes. As an expert in the field of consent to medical treatment, this author was able to facilitate a lively discussion and debate concerning these case studies and, drawing upon individual research, including substantive publications in this area (Devine, 2010a; 2010b) was subsequently able to introduce the students to other theorists and scholars in this field. The doctrine of informed consent and the law on risk disclosure was explored in detail by highlighting the way in which health professionals can be open to litigation if they fail to communicate the risks and benefits involved in a proposed medical procedure, therefore rendering invalid their patient's consent to the treatment. This author's research into the potential legal liability of health professionals who procure cord-blood stem cells at the request of pregnant women was used to illustrate this point. This discussion included an explanation of an empirical study carried out in 2006–2007 (Devine, forthcoming 2012) to determine how consent procedures for the collection of cord blood were being conducted within National Health Service (NHS) maternity units in England – the results of which demonstrated a clear disparity between NHS hospitals with regard to information provision. Such empirical research provided a clear example to KLS law students of how healthcare professionals can be at risk of clinical negligence if consent is deemed invalid by a court of law.

Similarly, other tort law teaching staff have injected elements of their own research and expertise into the second tort case class – which examines

---

3 Introduction to Obligations (LW315) anonymous student evaluation form, academic year 2010–2011. This student observation is particularly interesting because this module does not have an exam as part of its assessment, which means that the skills are, as the obligations team had hoped, cross-modular and cross-stage.

the *Wainwright* cases (*Wainwright* v *Home Office* [2003] and *Wainwright* v *UK* (2007)) – such as those with a particular interest in the field of bodily integrity, autonomy, trespass to person torts and the intentional infliction of indirect harm, as well as human rights and the protection of a person's privacy. Socio-legal aspects of these cases focus upon the increasing legal and societal acceptance of a greater need to protect privacy rights in modern-day society, a violation of which has potentially damaging effects on the victims and their families (*Campbell* v *Mirror Group Newspapers Ltd* [2004] and *Mosley* v *News Group Newspapers* [2008]), and on the judicial response to some of the identified gender inequalities of the trespass to the person torts, as seen particularly in the law's response to the issue of stalking (*R* v *Ireland* [1998] and *Khorasandjian* v *Bush* [1993]). Student reaction to this form of research-led teaching was indeed a positive one, and it could be said that arousing interest amongst students perhaps depends, 'less on technique (but) more upon having something of interest and importance to say' (Carr, 2009). Having encountered case classes in the introductory Obligations module in stage one, students studying Law of Obligations in stage two, where concepts and ideas become steadily more difficult, had a strong background of case reading and were able to build on this in a further six case classes.

Over both stages of study, case classes have replaced some of the traditional expository lectures in Obligations and were designed to address in part the perceived legal skills deficit within our law students and to engage students with law in a more interesting and pro-active way. The motivation for this type of teaching was borne from the realization that it is not enough to 'tell' students about how law works in a mechanical, ritualistic manner, but to intellectually stimulate them through engagement with dialogue rather than mere 'coverage' (Carr and Horsey, 2010). Students are supported in their study by repeating the format of the case class each week (with a new case(s) under discussion) to ensure that their understanding from the previous week's class remains in place before introducing new skills and legal concepts to build on their prior knowledge. This form of pedagogy takes the traditional teaching methods – seminars and lectures – to a new level. It embeds the advantages of each into a class that emulates the interactiveness of seminars combined with the directional guidance of lectures, but with the added 'twist' of allowing a larger number of students to be exposed to academics researching in a particular field of expertise whilst in a supportive atmosphere, less intimidating than a large lecture theatre. Ostensibly, case classes fall midway between a seminar and lecture, but are designed to allow discussion beyond the doctrinal – indeed, the theoretical, historical, socio-legal, economic and political context within which the selected case law is located, and a critical engagement of the key issues and concepts is actively encouraged and fostered by teaching staff. An example of this can be demonstrated with reference to the case classes on consent: these cases provoked discussions regarding the changing nature of the doctor–patient relationship, which has witnessed a shift in recent years from a prudent-doctor standard in tort law ('the doctor knows best') to a prioritization of patient autonomy as seen in cases such as *Chester v Afshar* (2004). Furthermore, gender inequalities associated with the perceived power imbalances within healthcare, particularly in other pregnancy-related cases (*Parkinson v St James and Seacroft University Hospital* [2001] and *Rees v Darlington Memorial Hospital NHS Trust* [2002]) are teased out, as well as accenting the political sway towards litigation avoidance strategies (such as informed consent to treatment provides) within a risk-averse society.

There appears to be a direct correlation between the rationale for case classes and the expectations of those currently studying law. Research into learning and teaching, in particular the student learning experience of those attending law school, was explored in a study carried out in 2008 and reported at the Association of Law Teachers conference in 2009 (Bone, 2009). Analysis of the findings revealed that the provision of seminars and lectures was rated highly by students, compared to knowledge that they purportedly gained from other educational mediums such as law textbooks and online resource materials. Of the 1428 responses to a questionnaire, 81 per cent agreed or strongly agreed with the statement that 'lectures are the most important part of my learning experience at University' and a staggering 93 per cent agreed or strongly agreed with the statement: 'Seminars are an effective means of improving my understanding.' Given that case classes mirror in an advanced form the techniques used in both the traditional modes of educational delivery, it may be deduced that the teaching methods used in case classes would have been met favourably by a large proportion of students who participated in the study. Although the use of this innovative form of teaching is in its infancy, initial reactions from KLS students via their anonymized student evaluation forms appear to suggest that interactive pedagogy is accepted as being particularly conducive to learning and the understanding of law. Student comments generally exude an overwhelmingly positive response. For example, one stage-two student said:

> Last year, during the week leading up to a case class, groups of people were forming in order to work through the case and participate in the class. The questions that were provided with the case were thought-provoking and a sensible way to ensure the students were understanding the case. I have always been a huge supporter of case classes and think that they are an excellent way to learn. We had four last year for obligations, however, when it came to exam period it was clear that case classes would have

helped across the board, especially in public law and criminal law where the cases almost formed the lion's share of the exam itself.

Furthermore, student attendance rates at case classes in the first year of the degree programme have been overwhelmingly good when compared to the diminishing number of students attending live lectures at KLS.

The use of case classes also fulfils one of the main requirements set down by the UK Professional Standards Framework (Higher Education Academy, n.d.), the standards set to ensure targets for professionalism in teaching and supportive learning are met within HE. The implementation of the framework acknowledges the distinctive nature of HE, and in particular it provides 'a means by which professional approaches to supporting student learning can be fostered through creativity, innovation and continual development' (Higher Education Academy, n.d.). Indeed, case classes fulfil all these criteria in the sense that they are in themselves a creative and innovative form of teaching within KLS that inspire and stimulate students. The materials and legal concepts studied during the case class are then reintroduced for discussion in seminars (further demonstrating the spiralling of skills) and then fed into coursework assignments upon which students are assessed and receive written and oral feedback (as well as, in stage two, the final exam paper). This ensures that the learner understands the legal concepts to which they have been introduced, that the learning outcomes for the module have been achieved, and that they can then take those newly found skills into the second year of their study of Obligations.

If we locate this type of teaching within the context of theories of knowledge as advocated by Neumann et al. (2002), it may be argued that case class teaching responds to the fact that legal knowledge is multifarious in nature and law teachers must respond by using a variety of techniques and methods with which to deliver the curriculum. In other words, learning law requires the use of a combination of teaching methods to reflect the fact that law consists of both 'pure hard' knowledge (arguably best taught instructionally by mass lectures and problem-based seminars) and 'pure soft' knowledge (which is purported to be holistic and qualitative in nature and best facilitated by class meetings that encourage discussions and debates) (Linddlom-Ylanne et al., 2006). Clearly, the case class encompasses both ideals and perhaps explains its apparent success with first-year law students who often find learning law difficult enough in and of itself (Carr et al., 2009, p. 2). Furthermore, its success may also be attributed to the notion that a case class fosters a greater opportunity for students to 'participate' within the class discourse and, as such, the learner becomes more involved in the exchange of ideas within the group, which ultimately promotes a sense of group belonging and social integration for the individual. As Sfard (1998, p. 6) observes:

> [L]earning a subject is now conceived of as a process of becoming a member of a certain community. This entails, above all, the ability to communicate in the language of this community and act according to its particular norms ... [F]rom a lone entrepreneur, the learner turns into an integral part of the team.

How then do these academic practices contribute to student-centric learning? Participation in research-led teaching demonstrates an element of evidence and logic to the content of our curriculum delivery and by actively engaging in the 'spirit of enquiry' (Westergaard, 1991) one can contribute to the students' learning experiences and help them to achieve their educational goals. Furthermore, professional values can equally be demonstrated via other forms of professional practice such as ensuring that law students follow appropriate academic guidelines, referencing procedures, and develop individually as members of the professional bodies within which they enrol post-graduation, such as the Bar Council and the Law Society. Indeed, academic rigour in addition to the personal development of our law students can both be viewed as aspects of professionalism (Brew, 2006).

Over and above the cases-as-stories approach backed up by the use and development of case classes, and in further recognition of the need to embed socio-legal research into the curriculum (Nuffield Inquiry, 2006) and of the benefits of utilizing the expertise of our tort law academics, students carry out independent research in a focused study of a particular area of tort law at the end of stage two via a special study in the Law of Obligations module.

Special studies: utilizing special knowledge and developing legal researchers

In line with the skills matrix, stage-two Obligations students are exposed to the special study pedagogy, which draws upon the introductory research skills developed at stage one in Introduction to Obligations, as well as a piece of individually conducted research in Public Law 2 (a one-term module completed at the beginning of stage two), but to an enhanced and more intensive level. This mode of legal education serves a dual function: first it is designed specifically to nurture individual legal researchers within the supportive framework of guided learning by academics with specialist expertise; and, second, it develops legal writing skills – in particular, presenting and holding an argument throughout an extended essay – an essential tool for the successful completion of coursework essays in other modules and in the exam, as well as preparation for larger projects such as dissertations. Through the facilitation of these aims, students deepen their understanding of the nature of tort law and of the way that obligations are determined, controlled and limited by the law.

The special study is undertaken in the final four weeks of the course and differs from the special study regime experienced in their Public Law module in that students are able to choose (subject to numerical limits and on a first-come-first-served basis) from a number of tort or contract-based topics, rather than being restricted to one set area of law. Whilst the Public Law special study allows students to conduct guided research in a specialized area of law, it is comparatively more restrictive in the sense that students conduct a special study in the research topic specific to the area of expertise of their allocated seminar leader, whereas Obligations students are offered a choice of academic supervisors. Indeed, they are able to select from a rich, diverse range of socio-legal subject areas within tort which include: public body liability; asbestos/mass tort litigation; privacy law and the media; theories of tort law; civil liability for mental harm; and reproductive harms and obligations.[4]

The public body liability special study is taught by an academic specialist researching specifically in the area of police liability in negligence (Horsey, forthcoming 2012). Students electing for this topic will have encountered the rudiments of tortious liability for public authorities in one of the tort case classes for this module, the *Smith* [2008] and *Van Colle* [2008] litigation, earlier in the year. In addition to police and emergency service liability, students are encouraged to consider how the social services and housing and education authorities may be held to account through private law, how policy justifications can be used by the courts to deny a duty of care, and how this may complement or be at odds with human-rights considerations. Socio-legal aspects of this special study drill down into the accountability of those carrying out a public function and the noticeable change in the public's willingness to question authority, as demonstrated by not only the police and social services cases that have reached the courts, but also in healthcare (the consent cases) and even legal advocacy (*Arthur J S Hall v Simons* [2002]). Furthermore, students are signposted towards a number of policy factors that underpin the general exclusionary rule that operates when a defendant is also a public body.

Similarly, the ability to study privacy law as it relates specifically to the media is offered by an academic with a keen research interest in this area of law. In this special study, students are directed to explore the development of available causes of action (for example, an action for a breach of confidence), recent case law in the UK and the European Court of Human Rights, and media and academic debate that this area of law promulgates, including the controversial use of the super-injunction by celebrities and others in order to

---

4 Students can also elect to take a special study in an area of contract law, namely: consumer rights; feminist perspectives on illegal contracts; or theories of contract law.

keep private information away from the public. Students who have completed this special study have successfully embarked upon research in topics such as the tension between Articles 8 and 10 of the European Convention on Human Rights, the introduction of the Human Rights Act 1998 and its effect on the development of the common law for invasions of privacy, and in discrete areas such as the rights of ex-offenders to a private life, and the in-depth critical assessment of a singular recent Court of Appeal or House of Lords case. Although students generally do not embark upon this special study with any prior knowledge of this area of law, the concept of celebrity and the media will be familiar from the Susan Boyle and Royal Wedding stories explored in the first year, and those studying the Media Law module offered at KLS will also have a grounding in the general legal principles and case law in this area. Students are awakened in this special study to the political implications for recognizing privacy rights, particularly since the introduction of the Human Rights Act 1998 and in an era when members of the public are now very much aware of, and are afforded access to, the ability to vindicate their rights, which has contemporary salience as the recent phone-hacking scandals demonstrate (Leveson Inquiry, 2011).

With its catchy title, 'Brave new harms: reproductive harm and 21st century obligations', another special study explores how new and novel medical and reproductive technologies have allowed us to separate, store and utilize previously inalienable parts of our bodies (sperm, human tissue, embryos, stem cells etc.), adding value for individuals, industry and society, and as a result potentially giving rise to new moral and legal obligations within society. Students are asked to explore and critically assess the varying mechanisms of tort law (and contract) and how they can be employed to regulate the provision of modern-day healthcare and to consider how traditional notions of harm have now been tested by the emergence of 'new' forms of harm, such as the destruction of frozen sperm as a form of property capable of compensation (*Yearworth v North Bristol NHS Trust* [2009]) and the judicial reluctance to recognize 'unwanted' skin colour to sound in a legal claim (*A and B by C (their mother and next friend) v A Health and Social Services Trust* [2011]). This special study is delivered by a member of the teaching team who holds a particular interest in medical ethics, patents and socio-legal approaches to medical technologies. Outside of academia, this member of the teaching team also fulfils the role of legal editor at the registered charity, Progress Educational Trust,[5] publishing a weekly online newsletter, *BioNews*, which provides news and comment on assisted reproduction and related areas. This form of 'external' expertise helps to inject a working knowledge of the co-existence of law, science and medico-healthcare into the special study.

---

5 Progress Educational Trust www.progress.org.uk/home.

Drawing on the theme of mental harm studied at stage one, students are offered a special study in aspects of liability for mental harm (elements of which were studied in Introduction to Obligations at stage one) delivered by a member of the teaching team who is also a KLS Kent Law Clinic solicitor and has many years' experience in practice, dealing in particular with personal injury claims. The student study experience is enhanced by academic professional expertise in the respect that legal principles and themes can be explored with practical, modern-day legal situations in mind and 'live' cases being dealt with in the clinic can be used by way of contrast and analogy. For example, students can consider how different areas of law can be used to address claims for mental distress, and how differing policy-led decisions may drive the inconsistencies in the case law and their underlying rationale. In a socio-legal context, students track the change in judicial attitudes towards a recognition of negligently caused mental harm as capable of sounding in damages, expounded by a greater understanding of the causes of mental injury through advancements in medical knowledge in this area, thus demonstrating a clear interplay between law and medicine. Similarly, the asbestos/mass torts special study is delivered by an academic whose research interests focus upon the difficulties of establishing causation and the concept of risk within asbestos-related claims, and whose practical experience as a barrister working on asbestos litigation cases, combined with substantive publications in this area (Laleng, 2010; 2011), adds both credibility and practicality to student learning. In the same way, the theories of tort law special study is offered by an academic whose field of expertise and doctoral research is located within legal philosophy. Students undertaking this special study are encouraged to question whether the seemingly contradictory values that underpin tort law can be explained by a particular theory or whether they exist simply as a reflection of political pressure brought upon social policy.

Within the four-week special study period, students build upon their research and legal reading and writing skills acquired in Public Law, although they are encouraged throughout the Obligations special study to be more independent of their supervisor in order that organizational skills and the need to discipline one's workload are prioritized. A one-hour class is delivered for each special study, but, in contrast to the normal teaching seminar, the aim of the special study seminar is to explore in general terms the key issues arising from the topic under discussion, and to settle upon a suitable essay working-title, agreed by the supervisor. Such a teaching strategy encourages student ownership, and fosters academic independence and personal development. However, there are certain learning frameworks that need to be put in place before students can begin to develop these skills. To safeguard against student disengagement and to ensure that they do not feel immediately overwhelmed or 'at sea' by the task in hand, suggested readings, materials, online links and/or podcasts are provided prior to class via the KLS online resource site, Moodle. Drop-in sessions are then provided by the special study leader to discuss the student's plan, to iron out any difficulties with the research and to offer guidance and support. Although working more independently, students – in addition to support from their supervisors – are also given bespoke research training by law librarians in groups or via individual drop-in sessions. In order to promote the KLS ethos of student-centric learning, it is essential that students are provided with the appropriate scaffolds with which to gain an insight into their chosen topic and to assist in focusing on relevant information (Brush and Saye, 2000).

Assessment: evaluating skills at stages one and two

The key focus of assessment at stage one in Introduction to Obligations is for students to demonstrate the ability to write a critical case note of 1000 words by the beginning of week seven, drawing on the theories and concepts to which they have been introduced. For example, students in the 2011–2012 cohort were asked to write a case note on *Donachie v CC of Greater Manchester* [2004], a case involving a claim by an on-duty police officer against his employers for mental injury. Students were encouraged to critique the case, drawing upon their new-found knowledge of this area of law and to unpack any policy considerations, such as the difficulties faced by claimants for this relatively new form of harm – especially against a public authority – that may have had a bearing on the outcome of the case. By way of assessing case reading and writing skills, students must demonstrate knowledge of the law, including the procedural history of the case, identification of the *ratio(nes)*, judicial interpretation (including any dissenting judgment), an understanding of its socio-economic and contextual underpinnings and a clear engagement with any policy factors that may have influenced the court, supported by academic commentary and/or empirical research.

At the end of the module, students are also tested on their problem-solving skills by way of a 2000-word complex problem question consisting of the areas of tort and contract studied throughout the course. Confirmation that students have the ability to problem-solve is essential if they are to enter stage two equipped with the necessary skills to proceed to, and to succeed in, the Law of Obligations module, as well as other modules and the exams. The format of assessment is comprised of: 30 per cent for the case note, 60 per cent for the problem question and 10 per cent for seminar participation, based on individual students' verbal contribution to class discussion and debates and a short piece of weekly written-work designed to complement the seminar topic studied each week. It is worth noting that as the Introduction to Obligations module is assessed by 100 per cent coursework (and hence no exam), the assignments set are robust in nature to ensure that students are academically challenged in a meaningful and practical manner.

Problem solving is tested further in stage two in the form of a 1500-word problem question at the end of *both* the contract and tort sections of the Law of Obligations course, but to an even more advanced level than expected in stage one. Indeed, students are encouraged to draw upon the written and verbal feedback received on their problem-solving assessment in Introduction to Obligations to demonstrate improved technique in this latter stage of their legal training. Each problem question attracts 10 per cent each of the overall grade, the special study making up a further 10 per cent, with the exam accounting for 70 per cent. As previously discussed, the special study is designed to assess students' legal reading, writing and research skills and their ability to unpick and elucidate upon the broader contextual socio-legal themes that underpin their research, backed up by relevant legal, social, political or philosophical theories, academic critique and/or empirical evidence.

Conclusion

As part of the Obligations teaching team, this author has been able to partake and involve students in this innovative form of research-led, student-centric teaching since its inception in the newly devised Obligations modules, which began in the academic year 2009–2010. With research-led teaching at the forefront of legal education, it is important that students are led by academics who have a passion not only for teaching, but for their own research interests. The introduction of socio-legal research into the law curriculum has been met with positive responses from both students and academic staff alike. By adopting the skills spiral, research can be fed into legal education whilst enhancing skills-based learning at every stage of the degree programme. Within Obligations, this approach has also been adopted to ensure that legal principles and themes are taught in a lively, creative manner whilst injecting the programme with direct input from a wide variety of researchers in an innovative, yet constructive, way. This has been achieved by engaging students with case law, by presenting them with cases as stories and then focusing in more detail upon case structure and legal principles within case classes, which provide an opportunity to locate the law within its socio-legal, political and economic context. Having been encouraged to research around studied case law, students then spiral those skills into their special studies where new legal research skills are gained and built upon.

By adopting socio-legal research and innovative teaching ideas and techniques into the tort law programme at Kent, legal education has been brought up to speed and with the twenty-first-century law student in mind. Through this type of pedagogy, KLS academics have had the unique opportunity of directly engaging students with aspects of their own fields of expertise whilst engaging them in an inventive and interactive way. For the student learning experience to be an effective one, scholarship and scholastic credibility must be demonstrated. No longer is it enough for educators simply to be good at teaching and managing students or to possess good organizational skills, 'the most significant professional qualification for the education of others may well be that teachers are educated people themselves' (Carr, 2009, p. 12).

Cases cited

A and B by C (Their Mother and Next Friend) v A Health and Social Services Trust [2011] NICA 28

Arthur J S Hall v Simons (2002) 1 AC 615

Campbell v Mirror Group Newspapers Ltd [2004] UKHL 22

Chester v Afshar [2004] 3 UKHL 41

Donachie v CC of Greater Manchester [2004] EWCA Civ 405

Donoghue v Stevenson [1932] AC 562

Khorasandjian v Bush [1993] 3 All ER 669

L'Estrange v Graucob (1934) 2 KB 394

McCutcheon v MacBrayne (1964) 1 WLR 125

McLoughlin v O'Brian [1982] 1 AC 410

Mosley v News Group Newspapers [2008] EWHC 1777 (QB)

Parkinson v St James and Seacroft University Hospital [2001] EWCA Civ 530

R v Dudley and Stevens (1884) 14 QBD 273 DC

R v Ireland [1998] AC 147

Rees v Darlington Memorial Hospital NHS Trust [2002] EWCA Civ 88

Richardson v LRC Products [2000] PIQR P164

St George's Healthcare NHS Trust v S, Regina v Collins and Others, Ex parte S [1999] Fam 26 (CA).

Smith v Chief Constable of Sussex Police [2008] EWCA Civ 39

The NHS Trust v Ms T [2004] EWHC 1279 (Fam)

Thompson v London Midland & Scottish Railway [1930] 1 KB 41 (CA)

Thornton v Shoe Lane Parking [1971] 2 QB 163

Van Colle v Chief Constable of Hertfordshire Constabulary [2008] 3 All ER 977

Wainwright v Home Office [2003] UKHL 53

Wainwright v UK (2007) 44 EHRR 40

Yearworth v North Bristol NHS Trust [2009] EWCA Civ 37

References

Bone, A (2009) 'The twenty-first century law student' 43(3) *Law Teacher* 222–4

Brew, A (2006) 'Conceptions of research and scholarship: implications for higher education, teaching and learning' Institute for Teaching and Learning, University of Sydney, www.aare.edu.au/99pap/bre99364.htm (last accessed 16 December 2011)

Brook, S 'Susan Boyle: press warned to back-off *Britain's Got Talent* star', *The Mail Online*, 3 June 2009, www.guardian.co.uk/media/2009/jun/03/susan-boyle-britains-got-talent-press-warned (last accessed 4 November 2011)

Brush, T and J Saye (2000) 'Implementation and evaluation of a student-centred learning unit – a case study' 48 *Educational Technology Research and Development* 3

Caron, P L (2003) 'Back to the future: teaching law through stories' 71 *University of Cincinnati Law Review* 2

Carr, D (2009) 'Revisiting the liberal and vocational dimensions of university education' 57(1) *British Journal of Educational Studies* 1–17

Carr, H, S Carter and K Horsey (2009) *Skills for Law Students* (Oxford: Oxford University Press)

Carr, H and K Horsey (2010) 'Things aren't what they used to be: collective responses, spiralling skills and re-energising the law curriculum' (2010) Higher Education Academy (unreported), www.ukcle.ac.uk/resources/curriculum-content-and-development/carr/ (last accessed 12 December 2011)

Chen-Wishart, M (2009) *Contract Law* 3rd edn (Oxford: Oxford University Press)

Devine, K (2010a) 'Risky business? The risks and benefits of umbilical cord blood collection' 183 *Medical Law Review* 330–62

Devine, K (2010b) 'Tying the cord around the midwife's neck: the problem with umbilical cord blood collection' 26(2) *Journal of Professional Negligence* 83–95

Devine, K (forthcoming, 2012) 'Ethics and choice in healthcare: the case of public v private cord blood banking' *Ethics, Law and Society* vol. v (Aldershot: Ashgate)

DfEE (Department for Education and Employment) (1998) '*Higher Education for the 21st Century:* response to the Dearing Report', Press Release 581/98, 16 December 1998

Dworkin, R (1998) *Law's Empire* (Oxford: Hart Publishing)

Horsey, D and E Rackley (2011) *Tort Law* 2nd edn (Oxford: Oxford University Press)

Horsey, K (forthcoming, April 2012) 'Trust in the police? Police negligence, invisible immunity and disadvantaged claimants' in J Richardson and E Rackley (eds), *Feminist Perspectives on Tort Law* (Abingdon: Routledge)

Laleng, P (2010) 'Causal responsibility for uncertainty and risk in toxic torts' 18(2) *Tort Law Review* 102

Laleng, P (2011) *'Sienkiewiczv Grief (UK) Ltd and Willmore v Knowsley Metropolitan BC*: a material contribution to uncertainty' 74(5) *Modern Law Review* 777–93

Leveson Inquiry (2011) www.levesoninquiry.org.uk/ (last accessed 12 December 2011)

Linddlom-Ylanne, S, K Trigwell, A Nevgi and P Ashwin (2006) 31(3) 'How approaches to teaching are affected by discipline and teaching context' *Studies in Higher Education* 285–98

Neumann, R, S Parry and T Becher (2002) 'Teaching and learning in their disciplinary context: a conceptual analysis' 4 *Studies in Higher Education* 405–17

Nuffield Inquiry on Empirical Legal Research (2006) *Law in the Real World: Improving Our Understanding of How Law Works* (2006) www.ucl.ac.uk/laws/socio-legal/empirical/docs/inquiry_report.pdf (last accessed 12 December 2011)

Press Association, 'Man shot with Taser at unofficial Royal Wedding street party' *Guardian Online*, 3 May 2011, www.guardian.co.uk/uk/2011/may/03/taser-unofficial-royal-wedding-party (last accessed 12 December 2011)

Revior, P and R Simpson, *'Britain's Got Talent* – the backlash: Priory clinic boss attacks producers as Susan Boyle suffers "breakdown"' *The Mail Online*, 2 June 2009, www.dailymail.co.uk/tvshowbiz/article-1189954/Britains-Got-Talent-backlash-Priory-clinic-boss-attacks-producers-Susan-Boyle-suffers-breakdown.html (accessed 12 December 2011)

Roderick, G and M Stephens (1974) 'Scientific studies and scientific manpower in the English civic universities 1870–1914' 4 *Science Studies* 41–63

Sfard, A (1998) 'On two metaphors for learning and the dangers of choosing just one' 27(2) *Educational Researcher* 4–13

Thomas, L (2009) '*X Factor* contestants to undergo psychological testing after Susan Boyle "meltdown"' *The Mail Online*, 19 August 2009, www.dailymail.co.uk/tvshowbiz/article-1207557/X-Factor-contestants-undergo-psychological-testing-Susan-Boyle-meltdown.html (last accessed 12 December 2011)

Westergaard, J (1991) 'Scholarship, research and teaching: a view from the social sciences' 16(1) *Studies in Higher Education* 23–8

8
Public Law

Simon Halliday

Introduction[1]

One of the challenges of writing about the integration of socio-legal studies into the teaching of the law curriculum is that, as a number of commentators have noted, the definition of 'socio-legal' can be quite hard to pin down (e.g. Harris, 1983; Galligan, 1996; Cotterrell, 2006). The history of socio-legal studies in the UK, perhaps because of its predominant development within the law schools (Thomas, 1997), is best understood as a reaction against the approach to the study of law which had dominated legal scholarship up to the 1960s. In this sense, the socio-legal movement in the UK has a clearer negative identity than a positive one: it is easier to identify what socio-legal is not, rather than what it is. The broad range of disciplinary and theoretical perspectives which can now be accommodated under the banner 'socio-legal' testifies to this. The strapline of the Socio-Legal Studies Association, for example ('where law meets the social sciences and humanities'), is notably inclusive. And the approach to law against which socio-legal defines itself is narrow doctrinal analysis: the exposition of positive law, isolated from its economic, political and cultural contexts. Cotterrell, for example, reflecting on his own experiences, locates the attraction of a socio-legal approach in:

> a set of new perspectives on law to allow a breakout from the claustrophobic world of legal scholarship and education, as previously encountered. Most legal study...at the end of the 1960s seemed to focus on technicality as an end in itself and was unconcerned with fundamental questions about law's nature, sources, and consequences as a social phenomenon or about its moral groundings. (2002, p. 633)

---

1 I am grateful to Jeff King, Tom Mullen, Maurice Sunkin, Robert Thomas and Adam Tomkins for helpful feedback on earlier drafts.

Equally Bradney, has suggested that:

> the essential aridity of doctrinal study has a disabling effect on most of those who are subject to it... [D]octrinal study... forbids the making of connections with the wider questions which lie at the root of human enquiry. (1998: 76)

However, although socio-legal studies was in its origins a minority reactive movement (Thomas 1997), this no longer seems to be the case today. Twining, for example, charts the development of socio-legal studies alongside broader developments within the field of legal education (Twining, 1993). He notes that the socio-legal movement is only a little bit younger than the modern law school in the UK. Prior to the late 1960s, legal education was largely considered to constitute vocational training only. It is only since then that legal education has been viewed as constituting a liberal education in addition to equipping some graduates for the legal profession (Cownie, 2004). It is to be expected, then, that changes in the nature and scale of legal education should prompt developments in the approach to legal scholarship and teaching. Evidence of this can be found in Cownie's survey of UK law teachers (Cownie, 2004). In 2004, she reported that half of law academics described themselves as adopting a socio-legal approach to the study of law, and many of the other half, who described their approach as 'black-letter', also believed in the importance of introducing 'contextual issues' to students. It is likely, then, that the narrow approach to legal study which first prompted the socio-legal studies movement is now largely a 'boutique' offering within the modern legal academy.

Such is certainly the case with public law scholarship. Indeed, it is arguable that public law has never really been part of the 'claustrophobic world' of arid doctrinal study characterized above by Cotterrell and Bradney. The overlap between constitutional doctrine and political theory has been a recurrent feature of public law scholarship (e.g. Robson, 1928; Jennings, 1933; Loughlin, 1992; Allen, 1993). As Harlow and Rawlings note, '[b]ehind every theory of administrative law there lies a theory of the state' (2009, p. 1). Further, the distinction between 'law in the books' and 'law in action' has had much less purchase in relation to public law. Public law has long been concerned with the study of political conventions, customs and practices alongside statutes and case law. The presence of academic lawyers within the founding and continued membership of the Study of Parliament Group is one small example of this.[2] Also, the doctrines of public law have always

---

2 The Study of Parliament Group, comprising lawyers, political scientists and parliamentary officers, has contributed to *Public Law*. See, for example, Study of Parliament Group (1981).

been placed in the context of constitutional history. Even dear old Dicey, the bête noire of public law scholarship, expounded constitutional law through the medium of historical and comparative contextual analysis (Dicey, 1915).

So a principal contention of this chapter is that many aspects of what could easily be called a socio-legal approach have long been integrated into the study of public law in the UK. At one level, then, public law teachers need no guidance about how to approach the subject from socio-legal perspectives. Such has been a long-standing practice within UK law schools. That said, given the eclectic and inclusive character of the socio-legal movement, it is inevitable that some aspects of socio-legal scholarship are more prominent in the study of public law than others. Despite the unavoidably empirical concern with constitutional practice in light of the uncodified nature of our constitution, public law scholarship probably has a closer relationship to political theory than the empirical enquiries of political science. This is, perhaps, due to the essentially normative character of public law's 'big question': what is the appropriate role for law in relation to the state's governing activities? This question is played out, for example, in the differences between normative and functionalist approaches to public law, as Loughlin puts it (Loughlin, 1992), or between red light and green light theories, as Harlow and Rawlings put it (Harlow and Rawlings, 2009), and also in debates about the proper balance between legal and political constitutionalism (Tomkins, 2005). It is reflected too in doctrinal tensions between judicial control and agency autonomy and between individual and agency interests (Halliday, 2004). Nonetheless, notwithstanding the particular intimacy between public law scholarship and political theory, this chapter argues that another aspect of socio-legal studies – empirical legal research (Cane and Kritzer, 2010) – similarly has long been present in public law scholarship and, of course, feeds into the normative debates of public law. Empirical legal research in public law has not, perhaps, always been recognized as such and it may at times have been something of a poor relation to political theory. However, contrary to scepticism about the general role of empirical legal research in the law curriculum (Bradney, 2010), it is well established as a core feature of the study of public law.

Overview of the chapter

The aim of this chapter is twofold. First, I aim to document some of the existing contributions of empirical legal research to the mainstream study of public law. This, it is hoped, will have a dual benefit. Socio-legal scholars should be able to see that 'orthodox' legal scholarship has a great deal of the socio-legal in it. In return, orthodox lawyers should be able to see that so-called socio-legal scholarship has long been a core element of the public law field. This is an important message. It should help us move beyond unhelpful distinctions such as that between socio-legal and black-letter approaches to law – a distinction that risks obscuring more than it reveals.

The second aim of the chapter is to explore additional examples of empirical legal research which have, to an extent, been overlooked thus far within the public law canon. The objective here is to build on the existing use of empirical public law research and show how the additional examples might shape the study of public law further. Once we acknowledge the fact that empirical work is a core feature of orthodox public law scholarship, we should follow the mandate to approach public law empirically to the full.

The above two aims are achieved in tandem by setting out the different ways in which empirical legal research does and can enrich the teaching of public law. The suggestion is that there are three key themes within public law to which empirical work contributes: first, it offers knowledge about the structure of our constitutional arrangements – it maps out, in other words, the offices and organizations, which either exercise public power or render those exercises of power accountable; second, it reveals the ways public bodies actually operate, offering insights into what our constitutional values are and how and why these change over time; and third, it helps us examine the use and effectiveness of accountability mechanisms. Each of these contributions is considered in turn.

The empirical study of public law

Mapping the constitutional landscape

In terms of mapping out our constitutional landscape, it is important to recognize that public law scholarship has always had to do this. The exposition of public law in the textbooks is inevitably premised on an empirical claim about the identity of the major landmarks on the map, traditionally noted as the Crown, the Houses of Parliament, Ministers of the Crown and the courts. So the contribution here of empirical legal research does not represent a new enterprise, as such, for public law. Rather, its contribution is continually to update the field with new data, systematically obtained, which can help us refine our sense of the contours of the map. Our constitution is, after all, a dynamic entity (Jowell and Oliver, 2007). By surveying our constitutional landscape, empirical legal research can offer fresh accounts of what our constitutional map looks like and thereby develop our sense of what is essential or desirable knowledge for students of public law.

Many such public law developments have been so manifest in public life that they have been easily observed by scholars and included within public law analyses without the need for systematic data collection as such. For example, entities such as local government authorities, ombudsmen, the institutions of the European Union, and devolved parliaments and executives have effortlessly become part of the canon of public law textbooks.

Other important developments such as the 'contraction' of government, as Galligan (1996) has put it, in an era of new public management (Hood, 1991; Gamble and Thomas, 2010) and the rise of the regulatory state (Loughlin and Scott, 1997; Prosser, 2007) have also been observed and are now becoming the focus of a few textbook writers (e.g. Craig, 2008; Harlow and Rawlings, 2009).

Some public law developments, however, have been less immediately visible and have required empirical enquiry by way of a systematic review of institutional developments in order to reveal their scale and constitutional significance. An early example of such work would be Robson's *Justice and Administrative Law* (1928) where the growth of administrative tribunals was charted and its constitutional significance considered. A more recent example of work whose findings similarly challenge orthodoxy is that of Hood et al. (1999) who shed important new light on the regulation of government by public regulators. As Hood et al. noted in relation to regulation inside government:

> [o]nly a minority of constitutional lawyers and political scientists have recognized regulation inside government as a key part of accountability regimes, and none has explored it systematically. Yet regulation in government merits attention as a matter of some political and constitutional significance. It is conventionally argued that the orthodox constitutional checks on executive government – the courts and elected members of the legislature – face inbuilt dilemmas and limitations as control and checking mechanisms... Regulation inside government, coming somewhere between these two orthodox 'separation of powers' checking devices, accordingly has a quasi-constitutional importance... [I]t is only beginning to be discussed as an overall system. (1999, p. 4)

Given the scale and importance of this system of public accountability, should we not be teaching our students more about it, alongside discussions of tribunals, ombudsmen, parliamentary debates and questions, the select committee system, judicial review, internal complaints systems and so forth?

Research such as that of Robson (1928) and Hood et al. (1999), which inter alia catalogues the scale of institutional developments, can also perform a related task which builds on this descriptive work. Through their findings, they can challenge some of the imagery that we use to describe our constitution. One such image still used in some public law textbooks to capture the architecture of our constitution is that of its three branches (the legislature, the executive and the judiciary), usually alongside a discussion of the separation of powers (e.g. Barendt, 1998). However, as work such as Robson's (1928) and Hood et al.'s (1999) suggests, a systematic examination of the various offices and organisations that populate our constitutional landscape undermines the usefulness of such imagery. Indeed, such is the complexity of our constitutional landscape that such imagery may obscure much more than it reveals (Jennings, 1933).

In addition to those already mentioned, we might also point to a number of accountability systems which cannot be accommodated easily within the imagery of three branches. These would include, for example, the various species of inquiries (e.g. Tomkins, 1998), human rights commissions (e.g. Langer, 2007), information commissioners (e.g. Austin, 2007; John, 2009) and public auditors (e.g. White and Hollingsworth, 1999; Lapsley and Lonsdale, 2010). We might also focus on specific entities such as the Committee on Standards in Public Life (Leopold, 2007) and the Administrative Justice and Tribunals Council (Thompson, 2010). All of these perform important roles of holding governmental power to account, but do not sit easily within the tripartite division of legislature, executive and judiciary.

Similarly, debates around legal and political constitutionalism (Griffiths 1979; Loughlin, 2000) are often cast as a question of the extent to which the courts, as opposed to Parliament, should have a role in holding government to account (e.g. Tomkins, 2005). Although the appropriate role of the courts in controlling governmental power is a central question for public law, the debate needs to place the courts in opposition not just to Parliament but also in opposition to the various non-parliamentary offices and entities which perform accountability roles.

In short, the imagery that is sometimes used to describe our constitution does not serve it well given what we know empirically about its increasing complexity. It is for this reason that Rubin (2005) has suggested we abandon the image of three branches and replace it with the image of a network (see also Buck et al., 2011). Although Rubin's thought experiment focuses on the USA, the suggestion is equally useful in relation to the UK. The benefit of a network image is threefold. First, it helps us visualize the complexity of our constitutional arrangements – all of the difficult-to-categorize entities and systems above with various investigatory, regulatory, executive and adjudicatory functions simply become locations or nodes on the constitutional network. Second, the image of a network is well equipped to accommodate changes in our dynamic constitution. As new institutions and bodies are created or abolished, they can simply be added to or deleted from the overall network. Third, there are various vantage points from which we might view a network. We can zoom in and zoom out, in other words. We may zoom in to identify and locate local bodies such as the Scottish Human Rights Commission or Information Commissioner. But we may also zoom out to locate the Westminster Parliament in a regional and international network where we may also identify other locations of power such as the European Parliament, the European Commission, the World

Trade Organization, the United Nations Security Council, and so forth. Public lawyers already talk in terms of a multi-layered constitution (e.g. Bamforth and Leyland, 2003; Gamble and Thomas, 2010), thus capturing the vertical dimension of our constitutional arrangements. The image of a network accommodates both vertical and horizontal dimensions and is better equipped to subsume ongoing empirical findings about the UK's constitutional map.

Revealing the practices of public entities

The second contribution of empirical legal research to the study of public law is to reveal the actual operations of public bodies and offices. At first glance, this may seem like a superfluous endeavour for public lawyers to embark upon. As noted in the introduction to this chapter, by virtue of the uncodified nature of our constitution, public law scholars have an unavoidable empirical interest in constitutional practice. Given the importance of conventions to the UK constitution, public lawyers must concern themselves with political practices around issues such as the exercise of prerogative powers, the accountability of Ministers to Parliament, and so forth. Much of these data are routinely placed in the public domain, do not require empirical enquiry as such and are, accordingly, very familiar terrain for the textbook writers. Equally, research aimed at revealing the practices of public entities may seem redundant given that it appears to mirror the basic function of the constitution itself. The complex and varied public accountability systems noted in the previous section are all geared towards revealing the realities of how public bodies operate. Everything from parliamentary debates and questions, to the select committee system, to ombudsmen investigations, to certain forms of inquiry, to public audit, to regulatory oversight, to freedom of information regimes, all share the task, inter alia, of opening up the operations of various constitutional actors to public scrutiny. Public lawyers have made great use of such data to assess and critique constitutional relations and governmental action (e.g. Tomkins, 1998). Why should we additionally go beyond these readily available sources of data and use the research techniques of the social sciences to obtain even more data about the workings of public bodies?

The answer is twofold. First, notwithstanding the complex ways in which we hold public power to account, there is still a great deal about the workings of public bodies that we do not understand. The data produced by accountability mechanisms often give only a limited picture of a more complex empirical reality, particularly where they emerge from dispute resolution forums (Halliday and Scott, 2010). It is not just our systems of accountability that have grown in an attempt to match the increased expansion and complexity of state activity during the last century. Our ignorance of governmental operations similarly and inevitably tracks the expansion of government in all its forms. A great deal of the 'public life' of our constitution still takes place in the dark. Yet, the critique and assessment of our constitution – a very familiar and important aspect of public law scholarship – need a solid empirical understanding of constitutional operations as their foundation (Daintith and Page, 1999).

Second, public lawyers have justifiably been curious about the use and effectiveness of the accountability mechanisms that exist: to what extent are the accountability mechanisms that are available for use by citizens actually put into action? In what ways do accountability mechanisms make a difference to the ways in which public bodies work? Such questions are not only of intrinsic interest. They also relate to normative and doctrinal questions – the bread and butter of public law scholarship. For example, some questions of impact, such as the potential effects on public service delivery of damages payments in tort or human rights cases, are doctrinally relevant (King, 2007). Equally, normative debates in public law, such as the appropriateness of state liability in tort law (e.g. Harlow, 2004; Halliday et al., 2011) or about changes in the heads of review in administrative law (King, 2010), can and should draw on questions of impact (Richardson and Sunkin, 1996). Much of public law debate rests on explicit or implicit empirical assumptions about constitutional operations. Legal research that reveals the practices of public entities, accordingly, has a general importance.

Some empirical legal researchers have sought to reveal the realities of primary and secondary legislative processes (e.g. Griffiths, 1974; Page, 2001), though much more research on legislative process would be welcome. Equally, the operations of accountability mechanisms themselves have been a focus of enquiry including work on the courts (e.g. Paterson, 1982), tribunals (e.g. Baldwin et al., 1992; Thomas, 2011), ombudsmen (e.g. Buck et al., 2011), administrative review schemes (e.g. Buck, 1998; Sunkin and Pick, 2001; Cowan and Halliday, 2003) and complaints systems (e.g. Mulcahy, 2003). Other empirical legal research under this heading can be understood as a response to emerging forms of governance and represent attempts to understand their operation and significance. For example, a number of UK scholars have explored the increased role of contracts within governmental operations (e.g. Davies, 2001; Vincent-Jones, 2006). Relatedly, but more broadly, the rise of the regulatory state has brought with it the rise of regulation scholarship. The study of governance through regulation is much too extensive to capture well in this chapter. Some helpful introductory and law-related texts are available (e.g. Baldwin and McCrudden, 1987; Baldwin et al., 1998; Morgan and Yeung, 2007; Harlow and Rawlings, 2009). It is sufficient to note for the purposes of this section that a great deal of this research has sought to reveal the ways in which various regulators operate (e.g. Hawkins, 1984 and 2002; Baldwin, 1995; Black, 1997; Hall et al., 2000). Comparatively much less research has sought to reveal how public bodies respond *to* regulation (e.g. Hood et al., 1999; Bevan and Hood, 2006).

Other research projects constitute attempts to understand and explain more general areas of government activity that have not previously been well understood. A classic example of this approach would be Daintith and Page's *The Executive in the Constitution* (1999). They explain the importance and value of this kind of empirical legal research:

> our objection is only to reliance on values and principles to underpin a *positive* theory of the constitution, a theory of what it is as opposed to what it ought to be. Our preferred approach ... is to address ourselves directly to the task of finding empirical evidence of constitutional rules. In the sphere of the executive ... such rules may as often be informal, or based on established practice, as formal ... Broadly speaking, therefore, we view our task as expository of the constitution in an area hitherto little studied and leave to others the task of suggesting improvements or reforms in the light of preferred principles or values. (1999, pp. 20–1)

Daintith and Page's point is that there is a level at which questions of constitutional value are empirical rather than normative. In order to answer the question 'how *does* the constitution function?' rather than the question 'how *should* it function?', values must be discovered by observing constitutional practice. Indeed, such an approach to questions of constitutional value has a long pedigree, particularly when focusing on why constitutional values have changed over time. Much of this work is historical in nature and is a very familiar feature of public law scholarship and textbook writing. A classic example would be the account of the political struggles in seventeenth-century England and the ultimate supremacy of Parliament over the Crown. Another example would be a description of the early twentieth-century tensions between the Commons and the Lords and the enactment of the Parliament Act 1911. Historical work might also shed important light on the nature and operation of our constitutional conventions. Tomkins' analysis (2003) of the Crichel Down papers as a means of unpacking the convention of ministerial responsibility is an excellent example of this approach.

It is important to recognize that this familiar historical work is, similarly, a contribution of empirical legal research to our understanding of public law. As one historian has noted, '[h]istory is the empirical study of the past' (Trevor-Roper, 1969). Even though much of this aspect of public law scholarship relies on secondary data sources, historical constitutional work is an account of the way things were and of how and why they changed over time and is ultimately grounded in standard social scientific research methods.

The examination of government or official papers, for example, is no more than an exercise in documentary analysis or archival research, a familiar and common research technique within law and society scholarship (e.g. Friedman and Percival, 1981; Greenhouse, 1986; Rosenberg, 1991).

The affinity between historical and empirical legal research can be illustrated by comparing two recent books that have explored bills of rights (though in very different senses of that term). The first, Tomkins' *Our Republican Constitution* (2005), is an historical work which examines the establishment of the Bill of Rights in seventeenth-century England as part of his broader thesis about the republican nature of the British constitution. The second, Erdos' *Delegating Rights Protections* (2010), is a political science examination of the development of bills of rights in the Westminster world, including the enactment of the Human Rights Act 1998 in the UK. Tomkins draws heavily on historical research about the relations between the Crown, the Commons and the courts to advance his argument that, empirically, the constitutional settlement of the seventeenth century was a victory won by the House of Commons rather than the common law courts and was driven by republican ideals. Erdos, in a standard political science approach, relies on primary data collection – interviews and documentary analysis – to advance his thesis about the conditions under which bills of rights will emerge in Westminster political systems. Tomkins and Erdos are, of course, examining different periods of British history. They also have different research questions. Whereas Tomkins is looking to the past to understand what values underpinned constitutional change, Erdos has one eye to the future in terms of predicting when bills of rights are likely to emerge. But both, essentially, are in the same business of using or drawing from empirical research methods to answer their respective questions. And in both cases, their questions relate to how and why basic constitutional values have changed – the supremacy of Parliament over Crown in Tomkins' study, the protection of human rights in Erdos' study.

On a much smaller scale, other public law scholars have conducted empirical research with a view to revealing narrow aspects of public administration, such as local authority housing departments (Loveland, 1995), criminal justice social workers (Halliday et al., 2009) or the child support agency (Davis et al., 1998), and their underpinning values. This focus on what is often called 'street-level bureaucracy' (Lipsky, 1980) presents a counter-intuitive image of the implementation of law where it is generated as much, perhaps more, from the bottom up rather than the top down and where the street-level bureaucrats are as concerned with the implementation of cultural morality as they are with legal rules and principles (Halliday et al., 2008).

The effectiveness of accountability mechanisms

There are two aspects to the issue of the effectiveness of accountability mechanisms: first, their effectiveness as a way of influencing public administration; and second, their use and effectiveness as a means of redress.

Effectiveness as a way of influencing public administration

This research agenda has a particular resonance for public law scholarship because it connects so well with the image of public law as a control mechanism over government – a theme which has been sufficiently prevalent in public law thinking that it seems fundamental to the subject (Loughlin, 1992; 2003). However, while so much of public law scholarship places a stress on (and implicitly puts its faith in) the external control of government by various constitutional actors, empirical work about the operation of public bodies and the effectiveness of accountability mechanisms draws our attention to the significance of *self-control* in our constitution (Daintith and Page, 1999). Much of this body of work demonstrates the considerable barriers that external control mechanisms face in changing internal behaviour.[3]

Although research in this vein is quite varied in focus, the most obvious body of work here is probably that relating to the impact of judicial review on government administration. Quite a lot of empirical research on this issue has now been conducted and is explored in some public law textbooks (e.g. Cane 2004; Harlow and Rawlings, 2009; Elliott and Thomas, 2011). The UK research on judicial impact has also been helpfully reviewed by Richardson (2004), though subsequent important work has also been published (Platt et al., 2010). Other accountability mechanisms such as tribunals (Baldwin et al., 1992), ombudsmen (Hertogh, 2001; Gill, 2010), internal review schemes (Cowan et al., 2006) and compensation claims (Halliday et al., 2011)[4] have also been analysed empirically in terms of their impact on public bodies.

Use and effectiveness as a means of redress

The second dimension of effectiveness shifts our attention away from public bodies and towards those seeking redress for governmental action. It examines issues of access to accountability mechanisms, the extent of their use and individuals' experiences of these processes. This research, conducted by social policy scholars as well as empirical legal researchers, has looked mainly at tribunals and judicial review.

---

3 For a more optimistic account, however, see Platt et al. (2010).
4 In a comparative study looking mainly at the USA, Epp (2009) also considers the effects of tort litigation on British police.

In terms of citizens' decisions about whether actually to use accountability mechanisms, the obvious point here is that we should be sceptical about the effectiveness of an accountability mechanism if citizens have difficulties in using them or are reluctant to do so. Adler and Gulland (2003) have helpfully conducted a review of research which has explored such barriers in relation to tribunals. More generally, we can usefully distinguish 'practical' barriers such as cost, physical accessibility, lack of general awareness and procedural complexity, from the 'attitudinal' barriers on the part of potential users, such as scepticism, fatigue, faith in the rectitude of rules, and satisfaction (Cowan and Halliday, 2003).

Closely related to issues of access, a number of researchers have examined patterns of use of accountability mechanisms. Sunkin, with various colleagues, has developed a considerable body of empirical work on the use of judicial review. Some of this work, which has been replicated in Scotland (Mullen et al., 1996) and Northern Ireland (Hadfield and Weaver, 1995), examined patterns of judicial review applications (Sunkin, 1987; Bridges et al., 1996; Sunkin et al., 2007). Whilst a general increase in applications for judicial review has been detected over the years, this finding has been qualified in a number of important respects. A dense concentration of activity in the south-east of England – in London in particular – skews that general finding. So, although judicial review litigation is now a routine experience for some public bodies, for most it remains a rarity (Sunkin et al., 2007). Equally, the judicial review case load is generally dominated by a very small number of policy areas, such as immigration, asylum and homelessness (Bridges et al., 1996; Mullen et al., 1996). Further, although applications for judicial review have been rising, the number of applications that get beyond the permission stage in England and Wales has been dropping (Sunkin and Bondy, 2008). In this sense, full judicial review hearings have *not* been on the rise. There is also evidence of considerable disparity of practice between individual judges in relation to permission decision-making (Sunkin and Bondy, 2008). Inevitably, in light of such findings, the empirical focus has turned to settlement practices in judicial review. In a recent study, Sunkin and Bondy (2009) suggest that, while applicants now face greater barriers in being granted permission to pursue judicial review, a greater number of claims are being settled in claimants' favour prior to the permission stage.

The third strand of research in this area has been to examine the experiences of those who manage to use accountability mechanisms. Some of this has explored quite specific questions such as how users respond to delays, formality of process and self-representation (e.g. Baldwin et al., 1992). Larger data sets have also been obtained to permit broad comparisons of perceptions and experiences between various groups of users. Genn et al. (2006), for example, have done so with a view to comparing white, black and minority ethnic citizens' experiences of tribunals. Among a broad range of findings, they note, for example, that South Asian and some other non-European users were consistently more negative than other ethnic groups in their assessments of tribunal hearings, but were less likely to be so if the tribunal panel is ethnically diverse. Such findings are important and can be set against the policy ambitions of various tribunal reforms. A repeated finding regarding the routine operation of accountability mechanisms (e.g. Genn, 1994) is that some kind of expert representation of citizens significantly increases their chances of success before tribunals and other accountability forums (Halliday and Scott, 2010).[5] In combination with the research above, such findings may cause us to question the extent to which the Franks (1957) and Leggatt (2001) ambitions of accessibility, freedom from technicality and user-friendliness have been achieved in the tribunals system.

Conclusion

The label 'socio-legal' does not denote a particular disciplinary approach or ideological position. It is an umbrella term which embraces a multiplicity of disciplinary and theoretical approaches. Indeed, given the breadth and inclusivity of the label, and given the broader developments within UK legal education, there does not seem to be all that much left to separate the 'legal' from the 'socio-legal'. Perhaps it is time to recognize law as an academic field that invites a broad range of disciplinary perspectives and so treat it as a focus of study rather than as a discipline in its own right, or, as David Downes once said of criminology,[6] to see it as a 'rendezvous subject'. The methodological challenge for public law – and indeed for law more generally – is to take account of, and take part in, long-standing debates about the nature of the social world (including law and governance), about how we might adequately investigate it, about the validity of empirical data and about the cogency of normative critique. Such is the staple diet of the social sciences and the humanities and, of course, produces a very wide variety of views, approaches and ideological positions.

Within the study of public law, there is plenty of scope for debate about the underlying methods used by public law scholars of various hues to advance particular positive and normative arguments about our constitution. Further, there is considerable room for a greater variety of textbooks, both in terms of methodological approach and subject matter. And, of course, as a body of

5 Adler's recent research, however, presents a more optimistic account of self-representation (Adler, 2010).
6 Attributed to Downes by Paul Rock in Rock (1994, p. xii).

scholars we should continue to draw on the methods and insights of history, philosophy, sociology, political science, and so forth, to challenge constantly the assumptions and propositions that we find in public law scholarship and to deepen our knowledge of governance and the role of law within it.[7] This chapter has set out how empirical legal research contributes to this endeavour and can enrich the teaching of public law to our students. On the basis of the review of research set out in this chapter, a course in Public Law which enthusiastically embraces the contribution of empirical legal research should be underpinned by three basic convictions:

1 When describing the UK's constitutional map – setting out the range of constitutional actors or institutions about which students need to learn – the focus should be broad. The implications of this are, first, that our focus on accountability mechanisms needs to move beyond discussions only of Parliament and the courts, and, second, that the image of the branches of government should be abandoned in favour of a constitutional network.

2 The approach to constitutional principles or values should recognize that, at one level, this is an empirical question about how public power is exercised and constrained. This means that we need to think about constitutional values from the bottom up, as well as from the top down. In others words, a sole focus on constitutional doctrine and political theory is likely to give a skewed image of what our constitutional values are, as opposed to what they should be.

3 Discussions of accountability mechanisms need to take account – so far as empirical data are available – of their significance for the routine business of government. Equally, discussions of citizen redress against government action should take account of how such mechanisms are used and the barriers to use experienced by citizens.

Nonetheless, it seems clear from the scholarship reviewed in this chapter that, so far as embedding socio-legal studies into the LLB curriculum, public law scholarship is in a reasonably healthy state. Indeed, much of the empirical work referred to in this chapter has been published in *Public Law*, the main UK journal in the field. Ultimately, the breadth of the socio-legal studies movement encourages considerable variation in the ways in which teachers of public law may approach the subject. The main argument made here is that public law scholarship has for some time displayed many of the fine qualities that socio-legal studies brings to the study and teaching of law. It begs an interesting question of whether the socio-legal studies movement has

---

7 Empirical work influenced by a law and economics approach is not yet present within the UK canon of public law scholarship, though such is generally the case with UK socio-legal research.

been successful in integrating the socio-legal into the study of public law, or whether public law scholarship has been successful in demonstrating how law might be studied from various socio-legal perspectives.

References

Adler, M (2010) 'Social security and social welfare' in P Cane and H Kritzer (eds) *The Oxford Handbook of Empirical Legal Research* (Oxford: Oxford University Press)

Adler, M and J Gulland (2003) *Tribunal Users' Experiences, Perceptions and Expectations: A Literature Review* (London: Council on Tribunals)

Allen, T R S (1993) *Law, Liberty and Justice: The Legal Foundations of British Constitutionalism* (Oxford: Oxford University Press)

Austin, R (2007) 'The Freedom of Information Act 2000: a sheep in wolf's clothing?' in J Jowell and D Oliver (eds) *The Changing Constitution* 6th edn (Oxford: Oxford University Press)

Baldwin, J, N Wikeley and R Young (1992) *Judging Social Security: The Adjudication of Claims for Benefit in Britain* (Oxford: Oxford University Press)

Baldwin, R (1995) *Rules and Government* (Oxford: Oxford University Press)

Baldwin, R and C McCrudden (eds) (1987) *Regulation and Public Law* (London: Weidenfield & Nicolson)

Baldwin, R, C Hood and C Scott (eds) (1998) *Reader on Regulation* (Oxford: Oxford University Press)

Bamforth, N and P Leyland (2003) *Public Law in a Multi-Layered Constitution* (Oxford: Hart Publishing)

Barendt, E (1998) *An Introduction to Constitutional Law* (Oxford: Oxford University Press)

Barnett, H (2011) *Constitutional and Administrative Law* 8th edn (Abingdon: Routledge)

Bevan, G and C Hood (2006) 'What's measured is what matters: targets and gaming in the English public health care system' 84(3) *Public Administration* 517–38

Black, J (1997) *Rules and Regulators* (Oxford: Oxford University Press)

Bradley, A and K Ewing (2010) *Constitutional and Administrative Law* 15th edn (Harlow: Pearson Education)

Bradney, A (1998) 'Law as a parasitic discipline' 25(1) *Journal of Law and Society* 71–84

Bradney, A (2010) 'The place of empirical legal research in the law school curriculum' in P Cane and H Kritzer (eds) *The Oxford Handbook of Empirical Legal Research* (Oxford: Oxford University Press)

Bridges, L, G Mezsaros and M Sunkin (1996) *Judicial Review in Perspective* 2nd edn (London: Cavendish)

Buck, T (1998) 'Judicial review and the discretionary social fund' in T Buck (ed.) *Judicial Review and Social Welfare* (London: Pinter)

Buck, T, R Kirkham and B Thompson (2011) *The Ombudsman Enterprise and Administrative Justice* (Aldershot: Ashgate)

Cane, P (2004) *Administrative Law* (Oxford: Oxford University Press)

Cane, P and H Kritzer (eds) (2010) *The Oxford Handbook of Empirical Legal Research* (Oxford: Oxford University Press)

Craig, P (2008) *Administrative Law* 6th edn (London: Sweet & Maxwell)

Cotterrell, R (2006) *Law Culture and Society: Legal Ideas in the Mirror of Social Theory* (Aldershot: Ashgate)

Cowan, D and S Halliday (2003) *The Appeal of Internal Review: Law, Administrative Justice and the (Non-)Emergence of Disputes* (Oxford: Hart Publishing)

Cowan, D, S Halliday and C Hunter (2006) 'Adjudicating the implementation of homelessness law: the promise of socio-legal studies' 21(3) *Housing Studies* 381–400

Davis, G, N Wikeley and R Young (1998) *Child Support in Action* (Oxford: Hart Publishing)

Cownie, F (2004) *Legal Academics: Cultures and Identities* (Oxford: Hart Publishing)

Daintith, T and A Page (1999) *The Executive in the Constitution: Structure, Autonomy, and Internal Control* (Oxford: Oxford University Press)

Davies, A C L (2001) *Accountability: A Public Law Analysis of Government by Contract* (Oxford: Oxford University Press)

Dicey, A V (1915) *Introduction to the Study of the Law of the Constitution* (London: Macmillan)

Elliott, M and R Thomas (2011) *Public Law* (Oxford: Oxford University Press)

Epp, C (2009) *Making Rights Real: Activists, Bureaucrats and the Creation of the Legalistic State* (Chicago: Chicago University Press)

Erdos, D (2010) *Delegating Rights Protections: The Rise of Bills of Rights in the Westminster World* (Oxford: Oxford University Press)

Franks, O (1957) *Report of the Committee on Administrative Tribunals and Enquiries* Cmnd 218 (London: HMSO)

Friedman, L and R V Percival (1981) *The Roots of Justice: Crime and Punishment in Alameda County, California, 1870–1910* (Chapel Hill NC: University of North Carolina Press)

Galligan, D J (1996) 'Introduction' in D J Galligan (ed.) *A Reader on Administrative Law* (Oxford: Oxford University Press)

Gamble, A and R Thomas (2010) 'The changing context of governance' in M Adler (ed.) *Administrative Justice in Context* (Oxford: Hart Publishing)

Genn, H (1994) 'Tribunal review of administrative decision-making' in G Richardson and H Genn (eds) *Administrative Law and Government Action* (Oxford: Oxford University Press)

Genn, H, B Lever and L Gray (2006) *Tribunals for Diverse Users* (London: Department for Constitutional Affairs)

Gill, C (2010) 'Researching impact' 39 *The Ombudsman* 12

Greenhouse, C (1986) *Praying for Justice: Faith, Order and Community in an American Town* (Ithaca: Cornell University Press)

Griffiths, J A G (1974) *Parliamentary Scrutiny of Government Bills* (London: Allen & Unwin)

Griffiths, J A G (1979) 'The political constitution' 42 *Modern Law Review* 1–21

Hadfield, B and E Weaver (1995) 'Judicial review in perspective: an investigation of trends in the use and operation of judicial review in Northern Ireland' 46 *Northern Ireland Legal Quarterly* 113–45

Hall, C, C Hood and C Scott (2000) *Telecommunications Regulation: Culture, Chaos and Inter-dependence inside the Regulatory Process* (London: Routledge)

Halliday, S (2004) *Judicial Review and Compliance with Administrative Law* (Oxford: Hart)

Halliday, S, N Burns, N Hutton, F McNeill and C Tata (2008) 'Shadow writing and participant observation: a study of criminal justice social work around sentencing' 35(1) *Journal of Law and Society* 189–213

Halliday, S, N Burns, N Hutton, F McNeill and C Tata (2009) 'Street-level bureaucracy, interprofessional relations and coping mechanisms: a study of criminal justice social workers in the sentencing process' 31(4) *Law and Policy* 405–28

Halliday, S, J Ilan and C Scott (2011) 'The public management of liability risks' 31(3) *Oxford Journal of Legal Studies* 527–50

Halliday, S and C Scott (2010) 'Administrative justice' in P Cane and H Kritzer (eds) *The Oxford Handbook of Empirical Legal Research* (Oxford: Oxford University Press)

Harlow, C (2004) *State Liability: Tort Law and Beyond* (Oxford: Oxford University Press)

Harlow, C and R Rawlings (2009) *Law and Administration* 3rd edn (Cambridge: Cambridge University Press)

Harris, D (1983) 'The development of socio-legal studies in the United Kingdom' 3 *Legal Studies* 315–33

Hawkins, K (1984) *Environment and Enforcement: Regulation and the Social Definition of Pollution* (Oxford: Oxford University Press)

Hawkins, K (2002) *Law as Last Resort: Prosecution Decision-Making in a Regulatory Agency* (Oxford: Oxford University Press)

Hertogh, M (2001) 'Coercion, co-operation and control: understanding the policy impact of administrative courts and the ombudsman in the Netherlands' 23 *Law and Policy* 47–67

Hood, C (1991) 'A public management for all seasons' 69 *Public Administration* 3–19

Hood, C, C Scott, O James, G Jones and T Travers (1999) *Regulation Inside Government: Waste-Watchers, Quality Police, and Sleaze-Busters* (Oxford: Oxford University Press)

Jennings, W I (1933) *The Law and the Constitution* (London: University of London Press)

John, G (2009) *Relations that Unite and Divide: A Study of Freedom of Information Legislation and Transparency in Scotland* (PhD thesis, University of St Andrews)

Jowell, J and D Oliver (eds) (2007) *The Changing Constitution* (Oxford: Oxford University Press)

King, J (2007) 'The justiciability of resource allocation' 70(2) *Modern Law Review* 197–224

King, J (2010) 'Proportionality: a halfway house' *New Zealand Law Review* 327–67

Langer, R L (2007) *Defining Rights and Wrongs: Bureaucracy, Human Rights and Public Accountability* (Vancouver: UBC Press)

Lapsley, I and J Lonsdale (2010) 'The audit society: helping to develop or undermine trust in government?' in M Adler (ed.) *Administrative Justice in Context* (Oxford: Hart Publishing)

Leggatt, A (2001) *Tribunals for Users: One System, One Service* (London: Lord Chancellor's Department)

Leopold, P (2007) 'Standards of conduct in public life' in J Jowell and D Oliver (eds) *The Changing Constitution* 6th edn (Oxford: Oxford University Press)

Lipsky, M (1980) *Street-Level Bureaucracy: Dilemmas of the Individual in Public Services* (New York: Russell Sage Foundation)

Loveland, I (1995) *Housing Homeless Persons: Administrative Law and Process* (Oxford: Oxford University Press)

Loughlin, M (1992) *Public Law and Political Theory* (Oxford: Oxford University Press)

Loughlin, M (2000) *Sword and Scales: An Examination of the Relationship Between Law and Politics* (Oxford: Hart Publishing)

Loughlin, M (2003) *The Idea of Public Law* (Oxford: Oxford University Press)

Loughlin, M and C Scott (1997) 'The regulatory state' in P Dunleavy, A Gamble, I Holliday and G Peele (eds) *Developments in British Politics 5* (Basingstoke: MacMillan)

Morgan, B and K Yeung (2007) *An Introduction to Law and Regulation* (Cambridge: Cambridge University Press)

Mulcahy, L (2003) *Disputing Doctors: The Socio-Legal Dynamics of Complaints about Medical Care* (Buckingham: Open University Press)

Mullen, T, K Pick and T Prosser (1996) *Judicial Review in Scotland* (Chichester: Wiley)

Page, E (2001) *Governing by Numbers: Delegated Legislation and Everyday Policy Making* (Oxford: Hart Publishing)

Paterson, A A (1982) *The Law Lords* (London: MacMillan)

Platt, L, M Sunkin and K Calvo (2010) 'Judicial review litigation as an incentive to change in local authority public services in England and Wales' 20 (suppl. 2) *Journal of Public Administration Theory and Research* 243–60

Prosser, T (2007) 'Regulation, markets and legitimacy' in D Oliver and J Jowell (eds) *The Changing Constitution* (Oxford: Oxford University Press)

Richardson, G (2004) 'Impact studies in the UK' in M Hertogh and S Halliday (eds) *Judicial Review and Bureaucratic Impact: International and Interdisciplinary Perspectives* (Cambridge: Cambridge University Press)

Richardson, G and M Sunkin (1996) 'Judicial review: questions of impact' *Public Law* 79–103

Robson, W A (1928) *Justice and Administrative Law* (London: Macmillan)

Rock, P (1994) (ed.) *The History of Criminology* (Aldershot: Dartmouth)

Rosenberg, G (1991) *The Hollow Hope: Can Courts Bring About Social Change?* (Chicago: Chicago University Press)

Rubin, E (2005) *Beyond Camelot: Rethinking Politics and Law for the Modern State* (Princeton: Princeton University Press)

Study of Parliament Group (1981) 'Private Bill procedure: a case for reform' *Public Law* 206–27

Sunkin, M (1987) 'What is happening to applications for judicial review?' 50 *Modern Law Review* 432–67

Sunkin, M and K Pick (2001) 'The changing impact of judicial review: the independent review service of the social fund' *Public Law* 753–62

Sunkin, M and V Bondy (2008) 'Accessing judicial review proceedings' *Public Law* 647–67

Sunkin, M and V Bondy (2009) 'Settlement in judicial review proceedings' *Public Law* 237–59

Sunkin, M, K Calvo, L Platt and T Landman (2007) 'Mapping the use of judicial review to challenge local authorities in England and Wales' *Public Law* 545–67

Thomas, P (1997) 'Socio-legal studies: the case of disappearing fleas and bustards' in P Thomas (ed.) *Socio-Legal Studies* (Aldershot: Dartmouth)

Thomas, R (2011) *Administrative Justice and Asylum Appeals: A Study of Tribunal Adjudication* (Oxford: Hart Publishing)

Thompson, B (2010) 'Current developments in the UK: system building – from tribunals to administrative justice' in M Adler (ed.) *Administrative Justice in Context* (Oxford: Hart Publishing)

Tomkins, A (1998) *The Constitution after Scott: Government Unwrapped* (Oxford: Oxford University Press)

Tomkins, A (2003) *Public Law* (Oxford: Oxford University Press)

Tomkins, A (2005) *Our Republican Constitution* (Oxford: Hart Publishing)

Trevor-Roper, H R (1969) 'The past and the present: history and sociology' 42(1) *Past and Present* 3–17

Twining, W (1993) 'Remembering 1972: the Oxford Centre in the context of developments in higher education and the discipline of law' 22 *Journal of Law and Society*, Special Issue 35–49

Vincent-Jones, P (2006) *The New Public Contracting: Regulation, Responsiveness, Relationality* (Oxford: Oxford University Press)

White, F and K Hollingsworth (1999) *Audit, Accountability and Government* (Oxford: Oxford University Press)

9
Criminal Law: Thinking about Criminal Law from a Trial Perspective

Matthew Weait

> ...trial by jury is more than an instrument of justice and more than one wheel of the constitution: it is the lamp that shows that freedom lives. Patrick Devlin (1956, p. 164)

Introduction

Although it is necessarily a rough-and-ready distinction, research and scholarship in socio-legal studies typically distinguishes itself from its criminological cousins by focusing on civil and public law. While there are shared concerns (the legal enforcement process, the lived experience of participants and stakeholders, the resolution of disputes, policy implementation issues, regulation etc.), it is probably fair to say that many if not most scholars who identify as 'socio-legal' would not consider themselves to be criminologists (and vice versa). This distinction is not, in itself, significant. It does, however, raise questions as to what might constitute a socio-legal approach to the study of criminal law that wasn't simply another name for a 'criminal justice' approach, and caused me difficulties when it came to thinking about the focus for this chapter. One option was to provide a critical survey of the literature on the use of empirical research in Criminal Law courses, but that (I soon found) would not only have made for an extremely short contribution, it would not have been particularly useful. Another would have been a more general and speculative piece about how socio-legal studies might inform the curriculum, but this too seemed fraught with difficulties – precisely because I was conscious that this would simply end up arguing for greater use of the excellent criminal justice texts and research that already exist. Instead, it seemed more fruitful to focus on the legal and pedagogical expertise of those who typically teach criminal law, and of the expectations and interests of those who are studying it, and to suggest one specific way in which we might bring the lived experience of criminal law into the classroom. That is what this chapter seeks to do.

I take as my starting point the fact that most, if not all, Criminal Law courses at undergraduate level in England and Wales focus on teaching the fundamental principles of criminal law (often referred to as 'the general part', and including matters such as *actus reus* and *mens rea*, causation and defences) and a number of specific offences such as murder, assault, theft and rape categorized within 'the special part' as exemplars of fatal and non-fatal offences against the person, property offences and sexual offences. This focus reflects, first, the division of legal education and training in this jurisdiction into the 'academic' and 'vocational' stages, with the academic stage being traditionally concerned with providing students of law with the knowledge and understanding of criminal law they need before going on to learn more practical skills. Second, it reflects an emphasis on what might alternatively be called a conceptual, principled or philosophical approach in traditional criminal law student texts – an approach which tends to mean that the enforcement and application of criminal law by police, prosecutors and trial judges tend to be addressed cursorily, if at all, and when they are as introductory matters to be disposed of as briefly and succinctly as possible.[1] Third, it is a focus that reflects the disaggregation of substantive criminal law from evidence and procedure. Evidence is not a foundation subject for the purposes of a qualifying law degree (and where it is taught on such degree courses generally incorporates civil evidence too), and criminal procedure is rarely taught as a separate subject, relegated to being studied as an element of courses on criminal justice or criminology.

From one perspective, this approach to undergraduate criminal legal education is both explicable and defensible. It is explicable on practical grounds (the substantive law has to be taught at some point, and it makes sense to do so before addressing its more practical aspects) and pragmatic ones (there are only so many hours' teaching available); it is defensible, one might argue, on the intellectual grounds that understanding the core principles and conceptual architecture, or grammar, of criminal law and criminal offences is essential to an appreciation of its operation in the real world of criminal justice institutions.

Whatever the strengths and weaknesses of these arguments (see e.g. Farmer, 1995), it would be fair to conclude that most law students complete their study of criminal law without engaging with the way in which that law plays out in practice in the trial courts. This means that their understanding of the law is limited (and here I deploy that term neutrally) to the

---

1   There are, of course, notable exceptions, exemplary among which is Lacey et al.'s *Reconstructing Criminal Law* (2010).

interpretation of legislation by, and common law developments in, the criminal appeal courts. This is regrettable for a number of reasons (Maranville, 2001). One is that it gives a misleading impression of the operation of criminal law in practice: that it is concerned with the finding of facts rather than the interpretation of statute; that the majority of defendants plead guilty and that there is no trial; that most people are convicted of relatively minor and/or common offences and of those which are less frequently covered in the syllabus because they are too complex, or fail to exemplify the principles of the general part (such as offences relating to drug possession, health and safety and public order). Another is that it results in what one might call a deadening, or muffling, of the issues that have given rise to these relatively abstract principles.

That is not to suggest that the stories as recounted by appellate judges are not compelling or are lacking in human interest; rather it is that in their appellate editing, which necessarily reduces dialogue to monologue, and contestation to resolution, the vibrancy of dispute and the complex interrelationship between procedure, evidence and substantive law are lost. It is in the criminal trial process that we are able to see most vividly the interaction between legal principle and lived experience. It is in the language that is used, the questions that are asked, the answers that are given, the assumptions that are made, the implications that are drawn, and in the verdicts that are reached, that we may come to understand the way events in the world are translated into a set of discrete legal problems to which a legal resolution (and only a legal resolution) is reached.

The point I hope to make is this. Appellate judgments provide a vital and irreplaceable source of knowledge for those who wish to understand the criminal law, and they provide legal theorists and textbook writers with the raw material they need to explain, analyse and criticize 'the law', but they cannot, by definition, provide a comprehensive account of how or why that decision was reached. The arguments, counter-arguments and evidence that provide the foundation for the development of legal principle in a particular area of law are buried deep and (typically) unexcavated.

In this chapter I want to suggest that active engagement with the trial provides those teaching and studying criminal law in the undergraduate curriculum with the opportunity not only to gain a richer understanding of the law in action (a central concern of socio-legal studies) but also of the appellate cases that constitute its core. In the context of this latter aim – the more ambitious – I want to suggest that it is through considering the trials that lead to these appellate decisions that we may provoke and promote a critically reflective stance on these decisions and so increase learners' appreciation of what appellate law actually is: a distillation, reduction and abstraction of a much more complex process.

The material I use to explore these issues is drawn from the trial of Feston
Konzani, and the subsequent Court of Appeal decision (*R v Konzani* [2005]). I
have explored this case and its doctrinal implications more extensively elsewhere (Weait, 2005a; 2007). It is, however, a good case to use in the context
of the aims of this collection of essays and the particular aims of this chapter.
Not only is it one that most students of criminal law will be familiar with
(it is referred to in most undergraduate texts), it is one that illustrates in a
particularly vivid way the issues that I have identified above. I show this in
the following way. First, I describe and summarize the appeal decision in the
form that most readers will find familiar. Second, I explore the trial, using
transcript material to illustrate the issues that gave rise to, and informed, the
appeal. Finally, I provide some reflections on the relationship between the
trial and the appeal with a focus on what this can provide for those with an
interest in the socio-legal dimensions of criminal law.

Consent and HIV transmission in the Court of Appeal: *R v Konzani*

The case of *R v Konzani* was the second English HIV transmission case to be
heard by the Court of Appeal and has to be read against the first. In *R v Dica*
[2004] the court ordered a retrial on appeal against a conviction under s. 20
of the Offences Against the Person Act 1861 (OAPA). Mr Dica had appealed
on the basis that the trial judge had been wrong as a matter of law when he
refused to allow his defence (that his partners had consented to the risk of
transmission) to be considered by the jury. Mr Dica did not deny that he
had failed to disclose his HIV status to those partners. The Court of Appeal
held that a distinction had to be drawn between consenting to the deliberate infliction of actual or serious bodily harm (which may not operate as
a defence, other than in certain limited contexts such as recognized contact
sports), and consenting to the risk of such harm (which may be raised as a
defence). In so concluding, the court indicated that risk-taking of this kind
was not something that it could, or should, outlaw – and that if it was felt
appropriate to change the law this was a matter for Parliament.

It was the fact that the Court in *Dica* had accepted the principle of consent
operating as a defence to the risk of transmission (without elaborating on
what this might mean) that provided Feston Konzani with his ground of
appeal against conviction. Mr Konzani, a Malawian national living in the UK,
had been imprisoned for ten years in May 2004 after being found guilty of
recklessly transmitting HIV to three female sexual partners. At trial he had
sought to argue that his partners' consent to unprotected sex equated to
consent to the risk of HIV transmission. He brought his appeal on the ground
that the trial judge had misdirected the jury as to the proper meaning of

consent. The Court of Appeal upheld his conviction. It concurred with the trial judge's finding that there was a difference between merely running a risk and consenting to a risk. The latter, if it was to operate as a defence recognized at law, had to be 'willing' and 'conscious'. The strength of the court's position on this point is clear:

> If an individual who knows that he is suffering from the HIV virus conceals this stark fact from his sexual partner, the principle of her personal autonomy is not enhanced if he is exculpated when he recklessly transmits the HIV virus to her through consensual sexual intercourse. On any view, the concealment of this fact from her almost inevitably means that she is deceived. Her consent is not properly informed, and she cannot give an informed consent to something of which she is ignorant.[2]

In the absence of disclosure of diagnosed HIV status it was extremely unlikely (although not impossible) that a person would consent to the risk of transmission, and difficult for a defendant to argue that he *honestly believed* in the existence of such consent – which may also operate as a defence – because the absence of disclosure was incongruous with, or undermined the credibility of any claim of, honest belief.

Put in these simple terms, *R v Konzani* deserves the attention it generally receives in texts on the criminal law – a short discussion or footnoted reference. It provides authority for a relatively straightforward, if novel and contentious, proposition of English law that consent to the risk of serious harm in the context of non-fatal offences against the person will only operate as a defence to a charge under s. 20 of the OAPA where it is willing and conscious (i.e. that there was an awareness of the specific risk(s) at the relevant time), and that an honest but mistaken belief in consent based on an assertion that the victim in fact ran the risk is insufficient.

The background to the decision, however, in the form of the trial that preceded it, provides additional material that contextualizes, complicates and illuminates the reason for upholding of the conviction and this is what I turn to now, concentrating on the way in which prosecution, defence and judge engaged with the question of consent.

Consent: prosecution and defence strategy

Before turning to prosecuting counsel's approach to disproving the existence of consent, it is important to note that Konzani's admission that he in fact caused the complainants' infections and that he had been reckless (i.e. aware

---

2 *R v Konzani* [2005] at [42].

of the risk of transmission) meant that, in strictly legal terms, his conduct and
fault were not in question. Despite this, prosecuting counsel was concerned to
show the jury that Konzani was a man who had behaved in such a way that it
was absurd to conclude that he could reasonably have believed the complainants to have consented to the risk of infection. Put another way, the prosecution strategy was to emphasize that the risk of infection was something to
which *he* exposed them, rather than something to which *they* exposed themselves: that he was the active agent in bringing about the physical harm they
had suffered.

This strategy is apparent in the following extracts from the examination-
in-chief of one of the complainants in the case. Complainant A was 15 years
old at the time she and the defendant met, and testified that prior to intercourse with him she had never had sex:[3]

Q: Did he [Konzani] know how old you were?
A: Yeah, I told him.
Q: And what was his reaction?
A: He wasn't very much bothered.
Q: I think you have said that you had sex with Feston?
A: Yeah.
Q: How often did that take place?
A: Er, when I moved in with him it was every night.
Q: And how did you find that?
A: Me, I was all right with it at first but then I just, I didn't like it no more.
Q: Why didn't you like it?
A: Because he was going too hard and it was hurting.
Q: Did anything happen as a result of it hurting?
A: Erm, I started bleeding.
Q: Did you tell Feston about that?
A: Yeah.
Q: Now, at this time when you were living with Feston did you have sex with
   anyone else?
A: No.
Q: And the sex that you had with Feston, did he use protection?
A: No.
Q: Do you understand what I mean by that?

---

3   This extract and all the other quoted extracts used in this chapter are taken from the official
    transcript of the trial of Feston Konzani in the Crown Court at Teesside, 6–14 May 2004
    (ref: T20037605). The abbreviations I use to denote the source of the extracts are as follows:
    E:A (evidence of complainant A); P:CS (prosecution closing speech); D:CS (defence closing
    speech); S (submissions prior to swearing-in of the jury); R:SU (recorder's summing-up). The
    page numbers after the abbreviations refer to the page numbers of the different documents
    in which the various quoted extracts are to be found.

A: Yeah.
Q: Did he wear a condom?
A: No.
Q: And when you had sex did he ejaculate inside you?
A: Yeah.
Q: Did you worry about becoming pregnant?
A: Not at first, no.
Q: Did you have any discussion about any other risks?
A: No. (E:A pp. 3–4)

These questions are designed to elicit an account of a man willing to have sex with an under-age woman, focused on fulfilling his own sexual pleasure at her expense, oblivious to (or actively ignoring) the fact that her experience was unpleasurable and painful, and who failed to use protection that would have minimized the risk of pregnancy and the transmission of disease. Disproving Konzani's defence is undertaken through painting a picture of someone of appalling moral character – someone it would be impossible for a jury to believe or find sympathetic. To counter this, the defence strategy (the only one realistically available) was focused on trying to convince the jury that the complainants were, irrespective of any moral fault on Konzani's part, aware of the risk they were taking. In so doing, counsel hoped to show that despite his failure to disclose his HIV status, they had – in effect – consented: not to the transmission of HIV itself (a defence that, in light of the House of Lords' earlier decision in *R v Brown* [1994],[4] was not legally available), but simply to the risk of its transmission. Because there had been no disclosure by Konzani, the only realistic strategy was to focus on the complainants' knowledge of the risks associated with having unprotected sex with someone about whose HIV status they were ignorant. Consider the cross-examination of complainant A:

Q: ...did you get sex education classes at school?
A: Yeah.
Q: It's a long time ago now but do you remember them?
A: Sort of, yeah.
Q: Did they teach you about contraception?
A: Yeah.
Q: About how to practise safer sex?
A: Yeah.
Q: Did they tell you about sexual infections?

---

4 It was in this case that the House of Lords held (3:2) that consent could not – other than in a number of established contexts – operate as a defence to the deliberate infliction of actual or serious bodily harm.

A: Yeah.

Q: And were you aware that if condoms are worn it reduces the risk of spreading a sexual infection?

A: Yeah.

Q: Did they tell you anything about HIV? Did you know anything about AIDS?

A: No.

Q: Either from those lessons at school or from what you heard on the news?

A: Er, well, they told us about it in school but I still didn't get to grips with what it was about. (E:A p. 6.)

Counsel has established, here, the general extent of A's risk-awareness – which does not (inconveniently, but perfectly understandably given the level of knowledge among many young people) extend to HIV. He thus changes tack slightly and focuses on the extent to which she was conscious of the risks associated with having unprotected sex with this particular man, whom she did not know very well before she agreed to have sex with him:

Q: What did you know about [Feston Konzani] at that stage?

A: Not much.

Q: But what had you asked him about himself?

A: Well, I asked him where he was from.

Q: And where did you understand him to be from?

A: Well, he said 'Africa', so I just...

Q: And were you aware that there is an AIDS problem in Africa?

A: Not really, no.

Q: Did you think about that?

A: No.

Q: Did you ask him about his previous sexual partners, whether he had had any girlfriends before?

A: No...

Q: What did you know about him before you agreed to have sex with him?

A: Not much.

Q: Why did you have unprotected sex with him when you had been taught about the safety of using a condom at school?

A: I don't know.

Q: Did you realise you were taking a risk of becoming pregnant?

A: Yeah.

Q: Were you prepared to take that risk?

A: Yeah.

Q: Did you realise you were taking a risk of catching a disease?

A: Yeah.

Q: And were you prepared to take that risk?

A: (No reply)

Q: Are you able to answer that question, please, [name of witness]?
A: Yeah.
Q: What is your answer?
A: Yes, I was, yeah.
Q: You knew you were taking a risk?
A: Yeah. (E:A pp. 7–8)

Counsel has now established A's awareness of the risk of catching a sexually transmitted infection (STI) by having unprotected sex, and so seeks to
consolidate the impression of a risk-taking person. He does this by exploring
her sexual relationship with P, another – subsequent – partner who (albeit on
a purely probabilistic and epidemiological basis) was at greater risk of being
HIV positive or having an STI.

Q: Did you know that people who inject drugs are at greater risk of having
   HIV?
A: Yeah.
Q: Because of sharing needles.
A: Yeah, I know.
Q: So why did you have a relationship with somebody who you knew was
injecting drugs and might have...
A: Well, I didn't know at first. When I first got with him he wasn't injecting.
[...]
Q: ...but you came to know that he was injecting, didn't you?
A: Yeah, I found him in the bedroom injecting.
Q: How soon after you had started going out with him was that?
A: About two month.
Q: But you were going out with him for three months, weren't you?
A: Yeah.
Q: So is it true, [complainant's name], that you carried on having sex with
   him knowing that he was an injecting drug user?
A: Yeah.
Q: So what risk did you know you were taking doing that with P?
A: I knew it was a big risk.
Q: You also told [the complainant's doctor] that P might be gay or bi-sexual?
A: Yeah.
Q: Do you know what risk there is of HIV in people who are gay or
   bi-sexual?
A: Yeah.
Q: Is it a greater risk or a smaller risk than people who are heterosexual?
A: I don't know, I only know it's a risk.
Q: So P was both an injecting drug user and gay or bi-sexual.
A: (No reply). (E:A pp. 8–9)

This cross-examination will, it is suggested, have created for the jury a compli-cated impression of A's understanding of HIV risk. As a young woman, not long out of school, she demonstrates only partial comprehension about the risks associated with unprotected sex. There is awareness of an increased HIV risk associated with having such sex with those who inject drugs, and with men who have sex with men, but a lack of understanding as to the magni-tude of that risk as compared with unprotected sex with men who do not fall into those categories. Armed with that limited knowledge she is presented as someone willing to take a chance.

Persuading the jury

On the day the *Konzani* trial started, the Court of Appeal delivered its deci-sion in *R v Dica* [2004] (Weait, 2005b). This resulted in extended discussions between counsel and the recorder as to its implications. The prosecution sought to persuade the recorder to adopt a restrictive interpretation, so that the defence of consent to risk should mean consent to the risk of HIV or another serious STI *only*, while the defence attempted to persuade him of the merits of a more expansive approach, so that it would be a defence if there was consent to the risk of *any* STI (including those that are less serious). The reason for these arguments over interpretation was that it would be easier for the prosecution to prove to the criminal standard that a person infected by a partner had not consented to the risk of *that* consequence. On the other hand, it would be to the defence's advantage if agreeing to unprotected sex implied consent on the part of the complainants to the risk of catching *any* disease that might result. The recorder was not persuaded by the defence argument, which in his judgment failed to reflect the fact that the charge was s. 20 of OAPA (an allegation of inflicting serious bodily harm), and in consequence the prosecution sought to show how the defendant's appear-ance and demeanour gave the complainants no grounds for suspecting that he might be HIV positive, emphasizing Konzani's active and conscious deception towards them, and his failure to engage in safer sex (and so limit the risk of transmission) by using condoms consistently. This enabled counsel to suggest that it was inconceivable that consent existed. For the defence, the ruling meant that the only viable approach was to concen-trate his cross-examination on the complainants' awareness of the range of risks associated with unprotected sex – something with which (as we have seen with complainant A) he had some success. This at least enabled him to invite the jury in his closing submission to interpret this awareness as amounting (in effect) to consent to the risk of HIV transmission. In doing so, this provided him with an opportunity to suggest that the prosecution had in some sense misled the jury as to what really matters:

> Time and time again in his closing speech for the Prosecution you were told that none of these women would have had sex with him if they had known. That is utterly irrelevant. It has no bearing on any legal principle here involved. It supports no aspect of any charge which is legally laid against Mr Konzani. It only serves to promote your moral censure of Mr Konzani, which is utterly beside the point, and to confuse two issues. We are not concerned with whether there was consent to sexual intercourse.
>
> They have said, 'These women wouldn't have consented to having sex if they had known'. That is not an ingredient of any charge faced by Mr Konzani. We are concerned not with his knowledge of his condition, that is utterly beside the point. So we are not concerned with consent to sexual intercourse, we are not concerned with knowledge of his condition, we are not concerned with re-writing the criminal law and making it an offence to have sexual relations without disclosing an infectious disease. That is not the law, and we are not in this case about the business of re-writing the law. You could make a moral argument for re-writing the law. This is not Parliament. We are here to do justice according to what the law is and the only issue which you are here to decide is whether in each specific case of the three women with whom you are concerned the specific facts in each case show that she may have consented to the risk of being infected with HIV, consent to the risk, not consent to being given the disease – two wholly different concepts. (D:CS pp. 12–13)

Here we can see that the defence, faced both with an unhelpful ruling from the judge and a deeply unsympathetic defendant, seeks to reduce the question it has to answer to a morally neutral, technical, legal one. Undoubtedly conscious of the effect which the complainants' evidence may have had on the jury's sympathies, and of the risk that the jury's prejudices and moral response could impact on their interpretation of the testimony, counsel tries over and over again to deny the relevance of these. In the process of reducing and abstracting the facts of the case to a set of discrete legal issues he attempts to ensure that their focus in deliberations is not on the risks that others expose us to, but those to which we willingly expose ourselves:

> No-one wants HIV. No one wants lung cancer, but how many people risk those conditions? On the way up to court I picked

up a packet of cigarettes that had been discarded. 'Smoking seriously harms you and others around you'. You can stand outside this court at lunch time and look at all the cigarette ends on the ground and if you trace the trail you will find groups of smokers puffing vigorously outside. They all have packets like this that tell them that smoking seriously harms them and people round them, people they love, their children, their wives, there is a serious health risk and yet these are sold all over the town in shops [sic] which say, 'Smoking kills you'. You go up to one of those smokers, you say, 'Do you consent to getting lung cancer?' They'll say, 'I'm more likely to get run over by the number 99 bus', 'My grandfather, Dave, lived till he was 99 and he smoked 20 Woodbine a day'. That's what they will say, I guarantee it. They are taking an obvious risk of serious harm to their health and deaths from smoking in this country are more significant a health factor than deaths from HIV.

That shows you that people do take risks with their health and if you ask them whether they consent to taking the risk of lung cancer they will say 'No', but the question which they are actually answering is, 'Do you want lung cancer?' isn't it? That is what they are saying, 'I don't want it'.

No-one wants HIV, no-one wants lung cancer, but the way people rationalise these risks is if they want something enough they are prepared to put those risks to the back of their mind. It does not mean when they go to the doctor they look at the x-rays and they are shown to have lung cancer that they have not consented to that risk.(D:CS p. 13)

There are, it is clear, difficulties with this line of reasoning. It is not obvious, for example, how cigarette smoking (the result of a nicotine addiction that can cause smokers to ignore advice about health risks) can be compared to the desire for unprotected sex. Even if it were the case that the complainants desired this to such an extent that they were willing to ignore potential harm, a clear distinction exists between consenting to a risk in situations where the source of that risk can act so as to minimize it, and consenting to a risk with respect to which the potential 'victim' alone has control. The defence argument is arguably more persuasive and better taken when he focuses on the precautions we may reasonably be expected to, and do in fact, take in other non-addictive contexts (for example, the precautions that were taken during the scares about salmonella in eggs, mad cow disease and foot and mouth in the 1980s and 1990s). Counsel is also more persuasive when he points out that boxers and others involved in dangerous sports may suppress their awareness of the risks associated with those sports, but such suppression does not mean that they are not consenting to those risks. Counsel develops this theme when suggesting that the evidence of character and behaviour adduced by the prosecution to emphasize the defendant's culpability and the complainants' blamelessness tends towards establishing the converse:

> All that evidence perhaps helps you to understand is how many, many different women of different ages and from different origins seem to have had an immediate attraction for Mr Konzani. It shows in the history of some three or four years that we have looked at how women would meet him on the street and come to his house and be in bed with him, knowing almost nothing about him.
>
> No careful courtships in evidence here before entering into sexual relations. It just shows the speed with which these relationships started and helps to demonstrate how little thought is given by either party to engaging in sexual activity, because you will know from your experience of life that when people hit it off and they are strongly attracted and there is passion, reason goes out of the window. That does not mean that those people are not taking risks with their sexual health or as to whether they become pregnant or not. Because someone is overcome by passion and emotion and has unprotected sex, they can't say, 'Well, I didn't consent to the risk of becoming pregnant and having a baby'. They have consented to that risk. They have taken that risk. Of course, it was not in the forefront of their mind at the time and, of course, they didn't want it to happen but they took the risk. (D:CS p. 17)

It should be evident that there is a damaging paradox here. In the course of attempting to draw a line between the affective and emotional dimensions of the case and the technical question of whether consent to risk existed, counsel suggests that people use common sense and general knowledge as the basis for behavioural change. However, the rationality which is supposed to provide the basis for that change – the rationality that justifies criticizing and describing as blameworthy those who fail to take care when they are in a position to be able to do so – is frequently lacking when behaviour is the consequence of, or affected by, passion. He wants, needs indeed, the jury to conclude that at the relevant time(s) the complainants were thinking clearly and exercising a voluntary, willing, consent; but the converse may be true precisely because of the emotional, passionate, uncontrolled context in which unprotected sex occurred. It is similarly difficult for him to assert convincingly that even if they were not aware, they should have been:

> What this also demonstrates, doesn't it, and this is relevant because you have to consider what thought these young women gave to the risk, if he was prepared to sleep with them so easily, surely it must have been apparent to them that he must have slept with others in that way and that if he is someone who is therefore involved in casual sexual relationships he is someone who it is more risky to have unprotected sex with. Is that not a fair point?
>
> If he is in bed with woman A after 36 hours of knowing her is it not reasonable for her to think, 'Well, I wonder if he does this often? I wonder if he's married. I wonder if he's got a string of girls. I wonder if he'll come back next week'. If he has with them struck up such a passionate relationship leading to intimacy so quickly ought they not be on guard that he might be someone who is at higher risk of transmitting sexual diseases? Is that not obvious? (D:CS p. 17)

What is most notable here (and students of criminal law may find this a particularly illuminating example of the way in which courtroom advocacy is impacted by the principles that constrain it) is how counsel deals with the legal test for consent to risk. This depends upon persuading the jury about the existence of such consent as matter of fact, but here – in this context – demands avoidance of any reference to the complainants' actual states of mind when they were having sex with Konzani. Rather, he is obliged to focus instead on the *normative* question of what they ought to have been thinking. The prosecution has had the opportunity to suggest that there was no consent to risk because they had no knowledge of that risk (or at least no knowledge deriving from disclosure by Konzani) and this requires defence counsel to suggest that there *was* consent because there *ought* to have been knowledge. The strategy is to try and persuade the jury that Konzani's sexual partners were in a position to make willed, rational, decisions and that their failure to do so makes *them* the (ir)responsible parties.

Summing up and directing the jury

The summing up in this, as in any criminal case, was critical. It is at this point that the judge explained the law, drew together the evidence that had been presented, indicated the weight that the jury might wish to give to that evidence, suggested the credibility to which they should give the testimony of particular witnesses and explained the relevance and significance of Konzani's failure to testify. The fact that this case explored a relatively new area of legal liability, had provoked significant media interest, and involved issues both of sexual ethics and serious disease meant that the way in which the recorder directed the jury was especially important and had to be handled very carefully. There is no question that he took pains to explain that they needed to reach verdicts on the three counts with which Konzani was charged using their innate common sense and reason, and not influenced by moral sentiment:

> Can I just say this, and it is an important matter? In drawing any inference be reasonable, be fair, be logical, use your common sense and your knowledge of the world. The subject matter of this case is a very human matter, isn't it? You will need to get to grips with people as they were behaving and as they were thinking – and that is an important element – some years ago now, so draw inferences that you think to be right and fair and proper but be fair in doing so...
>
> You twelve people come from different walks of life, different life experiences and most importantly in a case like this you can apply your accumulated wisdom – if you will forgive the word, it is a bit of a pompous one – but do you see what I mean? You apply your experience of life to the questions that arise in this case. Do not shrink from drawing such inference as you might think right to draw but be careful not to jump to conclusions, illogical and unfair ones.
>
> I have said, 'Use your common sense and your knowledge of the world and of people'. Make sure that emotion does not enter into your judgment in this exercise that you must embark upon. There is an old saying that, 'When emotion comes in, sense moves out'. Emotion has its place, of course, but it can mislead judgment. (R:SU p. 5)

There is some irony, perhaps, in the warning that emotion may impact inappropriately on the jury's evaluation of the facts, when – critically – they are being requested to determine in a dispassionate way the impact of emotion on the complainants' judgment. Put another way, their obligation was objectively to determine the presence or otherwise of consent, the existence of which depended on rational thought and whose non-existence could be explained by the effects of irrational passion. This complex contradiction led the recorder to take care when explaining the legal and evidential burden on the prosecution:

> the Prosecution must make you sure that at the time of being so infected with the virus the young woman in question, whichever

it was, did not willingly consent to the risk of suffering that infection. Note that I use the phrase 'to the risk of suffering that infection' and not merely just to suffering it. That is an important point which [defence counsel] rightly drew to your attention in his speech to you this morning. He put it this way, it is whether she consented to that risk, not consented to being given the disease which is, as he put it graphically, a mile away from the former.

That is right, but note that I use the word 'willingly' in the phrase 'willingly consent' and I did that to highlight that the sort of consent I am talking about means consciously, that is to say thinking about the matter at the time as opposed to either not giving it any thought at all or having a theoretical or general awareness of life's risks. (R:SU pp. 9–10)

It is arguable that, notwithstanding both the painstaking review both of the complainants' evidence and their credibility and the clear and accurate direction as to the inferences the jury were entitled to draw from Konzani's decision not to give evidence, that a conviction was assured. The recorder was especially keen to squash defence counsel's suggestion that the ignorance of the complainants about Konzani's HIV status had no bearing on whether there was consent:

One very significant matter...would be whether or not the young woman in question knew Mr Konzani was HIV positive at the time and here [defence counsel] was wrong to tell you that 'it is utterly irrelevant' – that is his phrase – that such a young woman would not have had sex with Mr Konzani if she had known he was HIV positive; it is relevant, for if she did know of his infection and in that knowledge had unprotected intercourse with him, one may well think she would have been prepared to run the risk.

Of course, the uncontradicted evidence here in each case is that she did not know he was HIV positive, so although the two things, knowledge on the one hand and consent on the other, are inevitably linked in the way I have just demonstrated, the ultimate question for you is not any knowledge on her part of his infection or the lack of such knowledge on her part but her consent to running the risk of being infected with the HIV virus.

I would add only that although it is a matter entirely for you, you may think that unless she was consciously prepared to take whatever risk of sexually transmitted infection there may be, in other words have deliberately and completely abandoned care for her own safety, it is unlikely she would have consented to a risk of major consequent illness if she was ignorant of his having the virus, but I stress that is a matter for you. (R:SU pp. 10–11)

The defence had sought to argue that the central issue in the case was consent to risk, not to sex, and that such consent could exist in the absence of knowledge about the defendant's HIV status. Although a jury could have concluded, had they been given a more general direction, that there was such consent, it was to all intents and purposes impossible for them to do so after receiving the direction the recorder did give. And it is, I suggest with respect, a confusing and somewhat contradictory direction. Note that the recorder emphasizes that the central question to which the jury must address themselves is consent to the risk of infection (which could, theoretically and in fact exist despite knowing a particular sexual partner's HIV positive status). At the same time there is the suggestion that the complainants' knowledge is both relevant *and* irrelevant: relevant because its presence might lead one to conclude that there *had* been consent (even though these are not the facts before the jury), and irrelevant because knowledge is not a necessary pre-condition for the availability of the defence. Drawing on the reasoning of the Court of Appeal in *R v Dica*, the recorder, advising properly that it is a matter for the jury to decide, suggests how one might reasonably doubt consent to the risk of infection *unless* the complainants had deliberately chosen to behave incautiously and *if* they were ignorant of Konzani's status. The use of two conditionals ('if' and 'unless'), which if met *may* lead to a particular conclusion will – one suspects – have caused the jury at least some pause for thought. The recorder too appears to recognize the potential difficulty and, having referred back to defence counsel's arguments about consent to risk during health scares and in the context of contact sports, provides further assistance:

> You give these arguments such weight as you think appropriate, but I am going to give you this one which is the best help that I can give you. Note the very clear and important distinction between running a risk on the one hand and consenting to run that risk on the other.
>
> You may not be willing to run the risk of falling through the ice on a frozen pond and drowning, you may believe it will support your weight, you may be wrong and go through because it may not be as thick as you believe or even hope. You are running that risk, but you have not consented to it just because everyone knows that such accidents happen.
>
> If, on the other hand, the farmer has put up a sign, 'Danger – thin ice' which you read but think you know better or at least are a good enough skater to whiz across unscathed, then that

would be an example of your consenting to run the risk of falling
through thin ice. Why? Because it has been drawn to your attention by the farmer's sign. (R:SU pp. 12–13)

One might question the extent to which this clarifies matters. The jury has
already been advised that their verdict turns on the presence or absence of
consent, not on knowledge *per se*. The recorder affirms and emphasizes this
using the thin ice analogy, but this – it is suggested – adds further compli-
cation. First, he suggests that our general understanding of the risks associated with certain activities does not necessarily imply consent to run those
risks. Second, he contrasts such situations with those where one actively,
consciously and willingly consents to risk because, in advance of taking it,
the person with relevant knowledge has warned one about that particular
risk. Put another way, the recorder would seem to be indicating that it is
only the existence of a warning from the person in a position to give that
warning that distinguishes consensual risk-taking (where a defence will be
available) from the running of risks (where it will not be). Put bluntly, there
is the strongest possible indication that there can be no legally recognized
consent without knowledge of risk gained as a consequence of disclosure –
the very position he had earlier sought to explain was not the case.

That the jury were somewhat confused is evidenced by a note from one of
their number and which was read in court:

My teenage children regularly accept lifts in other people's cars
from friends or taxi drivers. They willingly or knowingly consent
to the very low risk of being involved in a serious accident.

If the driver was obviously drunk, smelling of alcohol, slurred
speech, et cetera, the likelihood of accident would be very much
higher and I would expect my children to refuse the lift. If they
accepted the lift and were okay I would say they were foolish and
lucky; if they regularly accepted such lifts I would say they were
irresponsible and very lucky. They were consenting to increased
risk of injury or death.

What if the driver was high risk but did not show any outward
signs of being so, for example he might be a recreational drug
user or an epileptic who has been told by his doctor not to drive
or he may have been banned from driving? I could not reasonably expect my children to ask the driver to take a drugs test and
to show his driving licence and his medical records. Unless the
driver volunteers the information my children are not willingly
and knowingly consenting to any increased risks.

In any of the above situations if an accident did lead to serious
injury or death I would expect the law to take action but maybe

the seriousness of the punishment would reflect the specific circumstances.

In summary, I suggest the HIV positive person who engages in unsafe sex is analogous to the persistently drunken and/or dangerous driver. He might get away with this behaviour many times but eventually he will cause serious harm to some innocent party. The law needs to punish this behaviour as a deterrent to others. (R:SU pp. 48–9)

This note illustrates clearly the confusion provoked by the application of legal principle on these particular facts. In it we can see how complicated the exact relationship between knowledge and common sense is to lay people, and how a common-sense understanding of the world leads to the conclusion that people who consciously take risks may be thought to have consented to them. However, the person with HIV is at the same time identified as deserving a guilty verdict, essentially on the basis of unjustifiable risk-taking. It is a note that provides an excellent example of the way the distinction between *liability* (Are all the offence elements present? Is there a valid defence?) and *culpability* (Is the defendant morally blameworthy?) is capable of easy elision in the trier of fact, and – significantly – how the finding of guilt on the evidence presented is capable of being influenced by normative considerations.

No doubt conscious of the significance of the misunderstandings manifest in the note, the recorder reminded the jury that there was in English law no positive obligation for a person to disclose his diagnosed HIV to a sexual partner, that their function was simply to apply the law as he had directed, not on the basis of what they believed the law ought to be. He also refers back to the thin-ice analogy, noting that they 'kindly nod' when reminded of the distinction between running risks and consenting to them. Before concluding, he provides one further image which he hopes will assist them in their deliberations:

I leave you with this acid test which you may find of practical use. If a little bird had whispered in [the particular complainant's] ear as she was about to have unprotected sexual intercourse with Feston Konzani, 'Would you be doing this if you knew he was HIV infected?' and that little bird had gone on to describe what that meant... would she reply, 'No, I wouldn't' or would she reply, 'It doesn't matter, I'll be all right'?

If you are sure she would say, 'No, I wouldn't', then that would lead you to a guilty verdict. If it is your judgment that she would have said or may have said, 'It doesn't matter', then he is not guilty. (R:SU p. 53)

An acid test indeed, one might think. The jury decided that with such knowledge (which the complainants did not possess, and which seems to be described as determinative of the presence or absence of their consent) there would have been no agreement on their part to unprotected sex with the defendant. The trial lasted two weeks and involved testimony of 16 witnesses. Despite this, and a direction that they should reflect on all the evidence they had heard, the jury returned a unanimous guilty verdict on all counts in less than four hours.

Conclusion

All criminal appeal cases have their origins in the trial courts. All legal principles developed by the appellate courts have their origins in things that have happened to and between real people living in the real world. Despite the accurate and often vivid accounts that appeal court judges provide of the facts that have given rise to appeals, these accounts will necessarily be partial and monologic. Because appellate judges are concerned with those matters that give rise to appeals (such as misdirections as to the law by trial judges), they will necessarily and inevitably focus on matter that is material to the question they are asked to address and discard the flotsam and jetsam irrelevant to that question. For the undergraduate student who merely wishes to 'know what the law is', there is no need to be concerned with the trial. But for the one who wishes to understand what the law involves, engaging with the human origins of that law is, I suggest, a valuable thing. Not only does it provide a fuller picture that can help explain, in an exciting and engaging way, the basis for the development of legal principle, it has an important pedagogical effect – one discussed in the context of medical education by Martin Johnson (2002). In a fascinating essay, Johnson discusses male medical students' attitudes to examining the male body – something which, in the context of intimate examination, many find difficult. One cause of this, Johnson suggests, is the fact that medical students' approach to living bodies is profoundly influenced by the fact that their first confrontation is with dead ones. Johnson speculates about the way in which there may be parallels (and similarly negative consequences) in legal education:

> In education generally, and professional education such as medicine and law in particular, there has perhaps been too little emphasis on the role that emotions can play in conditioning intellectual and behavioural activities. Thus, the expression of emotion professionally is generally disapproved of, and this disapproval has translated somewhat illogically into training and educational regimes that encourage suppression of emotion and thereby denial of its importance. (Johnson, 2002, pp. 99–100)

I think Johnson is right, and I think that by teaching law primarily through legal cadavers (the decided case), we contribute to the distancing of students from the affective dimensions of the subject. For some, no doubt, this will be thought right and proper; but I do think there is scope for at least exploring the 'living law' in parallel, for at least part of the study of criminal law.

The law has to confront a range of problems when dealing with human relationships, especially sexual relationships. Consent as a defence to a charge under s. 20 of OAPA is a technical, legal question but one that has developed through cases, such as *R v Konzani*, where we are witness (if we engage critically with the evidence at trial) to a number of important matters: the (mis)communication that can exist between sexual partners, the source and causes of false and harmful assumptions about risk and potential harm, the ways in which physical desire can result in the repression and denial of danger, the way conscious participation in risky behaviours increases with growing intimacy, how trust is developed and undermined, and the way the dynamics of specific, meaningful relationships can cause people to ignore risks of which they are conscious in general terms.

Trial transcripts give us, as students and teachers of law, an opportunity to reflect on the way human passions, sentiments, behaviours and expectations are, through the reductive lens of the criminal law, understood as problems capable of legal resolution. Lived experience is rendered into a set of discrete resolvable questions, organized and framed by the elements of the offence to be proven, which are possible (and necessary) to answer. That answer (the reaching of a verdict) is achieved by the asking of questions which must of necessity occlude the inconclusiveness and complexity of experience. The difficulty is that it is not possible to exclude fully from such questions the complexity, the relevance of which they attempt to deny. The reductive process is porous, impossible to seal completely. There is, it would appear, an intuitive sense that knowledge matters – that it is important in establishing the presence or absence of consent (in this case illustrated by the idea that a person consciously aware of a partner's HIV positive status might reasonably be thought to have consented). In this sense the importance of knowledge is affirmed. At the same time it is *denied* (because there is no legal obligation – unlike, for example, in Canada – to disclose such status). Of more concern, perhaps, is the fact that all this lived experience – what happened in the real world, in real time, to real people – can be reduced to imagining, hypothetically, the effect on the complainants' decision-making of information provided via the surreptitious whispers of a fictive, talking bird.

The trial of Feston Konzani provides us with a valuable insight into the ways in which concepts and categories, typically articulated and explored merely as legal principles open to intellectual analysis and clarification within the comparatively sterile surroundings of the criminal appeal courts, have a vibrant and contested life, meaning and application in the real world of trial courts. We can continue to ignore this, or we can embrace it. I would suggest that the latter has the potential to make the study of criminal law more relevant, more exciting and more *real*.

Note on accessing and using court transcripts

Find the court the person was tried in (their name, the name of the presiding judge, the part of the hearing you want and the date(s) of the trial). For example, Joe Bloggs, Giggleswick Crown Court, Judge Tom Cobbly, sentencing remarks, 30 November 2011. Each case has an individual indictment number beginning with a T, e.g. T20101685, which may be found for recent cases at www.thelawpages.com. If you know this number, use it in all correspondence.

Contact the court (to find out which company provides its transcription service). If you are not a party to the case you may need the permission of the court in order to be allowed a transcript of the case. Court permission to see a transcript is given by the judge of the case and is normal practice for cases involving sexual crimes, where reporting restrictions have been imposed and sometimes if the witnesses were vulnerable people (minors, adults with learning disabilities). You should also provide a reason for wanting the transcript, legal research is generally an acceptable reason. Transcribers will generally request a copy of the written permission of the court. You contact the court with the above case details and ask for permission for the transcript. You will need to provide the transcribing firm with the same case details because the court will not do this for you. A specific form exists for obtaining transcripts (EX107) but the system is more confusing than writing direct to court and transcriber. Usually only law firms ask for transcriptions and the system is designed around these requests and so others asking are an unusual occurrence for courts and transcribers. Often the process is simple and quick but you may need to be patient and persistent, contacting court or transcribers more than once.

Although transcripts will sometimes have the names of complainants redacted, this is not always the case. It is vital that if redaction has not occurred, and/or where there have been reporting restrictions, material is appropriately anonymized.

Cases cited

R v Brown [1994] 1 AC 212
R v Dica [2004] 2 Cr App R 28
R v Konzani [2005] 2 Cr App R 198

References

Devlin, P (1956) *Trial by Jury* (London: Stevens & Co.)

Farmer, L (1995) 'Bringing Cinderella to the ball: teaching criminal law in context' 58(5) *Modern Law Review* 756–66

Johnson, M (2002) 'Male medical students and the male body' in A Bainham et al. (eds) *Body Lore and Laws* (Oxford and Portland OR: Hart Publishing)

Lacey, N, C Wells and O Quick (2010) *Reconstructing Criminal Law* 4th edn (Cambridge: Cambridge University Press)

Maranville, D (2001) 'Infusing passion and context into the traditional law curriculum through experiential learning' 51(1) *Journal of Legal Education* 51–74

Weait, M (2005a) 'Knowledge, autonomy and consent: *R v Konzani*' (October) *Criminal Law Review* 163–72

Weait, M (2005b) 'Criminal law and the sexual transmission of HIV: *R v Dica*' 68(1) *Modern Law Review* 120–33

Weait, M (2007) *Intimacy and Responsibility: the Criminalization of HIV Transmission* (Abingdon: Routledge-Cavendish)

Note

The commentary on the court extracts in this chapter has been adapted from material contained in chapter 2 of Weait, M (2007) as above.

10

European Union Law

Charlotte O'Brien

European Union (EU) law is a perfect site for asking big socio-legal questions. The origins and organs of law are garishly on display, and explicit legal power dynamics dispense with the myth of objectivity and blast aside fig leaves of rationality. There is something nakedly functional about a legal system to serve ideological ends, and something sociologically compelling about the existential war for the heart of Europe: the market or the polity. Add to this the rapid, contemporary shifts in the law, and we face territory richly fertile for cultivating a range of interdisciplinary approaches, and especially for drawing upon socio-legal theory, materials and learning activities.

And yet... EU law often manifests in curricula as dry, alienating and, most bizarrely of all, dusty – modules often seem to go through the motions as set down years ago, becoming an unpleasant but necessary rite of passage for students wishing to get qualifying law degrees. Students are expected to trawl through a lot of institutional information – disregarding not only socio-legal, but also legal analytical skills, with an emphasis on description that would not be entertained in a history syllabus at primary school level. While the EU has abandoned its clunky pillars, we still think in terms of three modular pillars – 'institutions', 'principles' and 'substantive law'. And when we get to the law, there is barely room for theoretically questioning some heavy, abstract doctrinalism, because of case-cramming. Because it is all important, we feel we have to teach it all. But it is an entire multi-national legal system, a vast array of subjects, and only one module.

We are, perhaps naturally, dynastically attached to module structures we have encountered ourselves. But the 'traditional' approach to EU was always going to be problematic for us at York Law School (YLS) because core course content is delivered through problem-based learning (PBL). PBL involves students taking charge of their own learning, as a group addressing simulated client cases and identifying key research questions, setting learning objectives and then seeking to meet them in time for a feedback session (Fitzpatrick and Hunter, 2011). We have had to approach EU law in a different way. Excavating the PBL-ability and practical impact of EU law is tied up with thinking about the social influences on and social impact of the EU. Bringing a socio-legal approach to the undergraduate study of EU is thus not a question of simply adding more stuff into an already over-stuffed syllabus; it is about a different way of learning – more thinking, less memorizing – and it is increasingly vital if we want students to gain any meaningful understanding of EU law.

This chapter is a collection as much of colleagues' ideas as of examples in practice. In outlining problems and possibilities, I draw upon the detailed and extremely useful UK Centre for Legal Education (UKCLE) report on the teaching of EU (Ball and Dadamo, 2010). Lots of people are thinking about what to do about EU; the 'teach everything' model inherited down through the years is becoming more clearly unsustainable the larger 'everything' gets. But not many are yet in the position to overhaul it, so I have collected views from academics from a number of institutions[1] as well as York – as a springboard for future discussion, since our general consensus seems to be that we would like to do more to integrate socio-legal approaches. This is not a survey, and so not at all meant to be an example of socio-legal research itself, any more than is your average essay which harvests a number of interesting ideas from better-informed sources. The results are arranged in four sections: first, a 'big picture' sketch – an exploration of whether we are really deciding up-front what we want students to know; second a summary of possible challenges in adopting socio-legal methods; third, a look at the socio-legal potential of EU law due to its inherently interdisciplinary nature and themes, which could replace the subject's three pillars of institutions, principles and law; and fourth, a review of suggestions for different learning activities, and how they might tie to themes and assessment.

Please approach this as a collection of thoughts to feed into the discussion many of us are already having. Hopefully, sharing some experiences from the YLS module might, on some basic level, back up a couple of the preliminary points made in the first section – that it is possible, legitimate, and arguably desirable, to try to lose some of our self-imposed disciplinary shackles. It is, however, a work-in-progress, and not presented as a 'model'.

The big picture: the purpose of learning EU law

What do we want students to get from an EU module? It is difficult to shake the sense that there is an objective list of facts and topics that make a module robust, and that departure from this list would set students at a disadvantage (a) with regard to the requirements of regulatory bodies and (b) as compared to those studying elsewhere. If we address (a), it is clear from the responses gathered in the UKCLE survey that perceived professional body requirements

---

1 Thanks are due to Jess Guth at Bradford, Dagmar Schiek at Leeds, Samantha Currie at Liverpool and Tammy Hervey at Sheffield.

were the most influential factor in determining course contents (rated by 26 institutions as crucial or determinative, and by 14 as of considerable importance) (Ball and Dadomo, 2010, p. 44). The study notes this to be 'somewhat surprising', which indeed it is, given the extremely free reign the regulatory bodies allow universities. An EU Law module, according to the 1999 *Joint Statement* of the Law Society and the Bar Council, should cover 'the key elements and general principles' of EU law (Law Society and General Council of the Bar (1999), Schedule 2). This is not very prescriptive. Actually, by trying to cram in too much, we might even be contravening the one rule set – we are not taking responsibility for identifying what is 'key'.

It is possible that in deferring to tradition and/or submitting to non-existent restrictions, we are not really deciding what it is we think students need to know and why. If we think about the consideration at (b) above, the concern about comparative disadvantage, the question surely arises as to context – in practice lawyers are unlikely to be quizzed on intricate details of European Commission rotation, and there are not all that many facts that need be cerebrally imprinted in an age of quick information retrieval. So we should identify the career advantages created by studying EU law. In practice, for instance, we would like graduates to be able to identify and engage with EU-based legal arguments in the course of UK cases, and to be able to follow topical EU legal developments and to understand their effects on the UK legal landscape. In terms of academic outcomes, it is probably fair to say that we would like students to engage critically with the issues raised by the 'fact' of EU law, and with the themes that emerge from its content. None of which requires intense and minute detail.

We should probably ask ourselves honestly how well current EU modules equip future lawyers with the skills to spot, use and contest points of EU law and to engage with social research to effectively use appropriate evidence (for instance, indirect discrimination claims may depend on statistical evidence). If we get caught up with a desire to convey huge swathes of information, we might lose accessibility and relevance. Similarly, potentially controversial and intellectually stimulating concepts can get obscured by the shadow cast by towering reading lists. The whole of EU law can no more be taught in one module than the 'whole law' of any other jurisdiction; so it is necessary to be explicitly – and perhaps radically – selective, in order to attain some intelligent simplicity – or as Meyers and Nulty paraphrase Biggs' mission, to capitalize 'on things within our control to get students to use higher order cognitive processes' (Meyers and Nulty, 2009, p. 567). This is of course necessary for us at York, to fit with the PBL mandate, whereby core learning happens around a few central problems, and assessment should be directed at content covered in this way. It is a considerable challenge (covered also below in the final section on learning activities) to relinquish chunks of detail – not only for course designers, but for students too. They can find being catapulted into the unknown, with the need to select and research background detail as they go along, a bit of a shock to the system. I have not yet got the balance right for catching those who struggle at that first deep-end plunge; we are working on some transition activities so students approach the rest of the course with some familiarity with the EU. However, the initial shock aside, many adapt well and quickly, because the up-front issues are instantly accessible. By directing the focus of the course onto problems and concepts, it is possible to make room for thinking differently and to recognize the central role of socio-legal studies.

Assessment should, of course, target the same learning objectives pursued by the course if we think in terms of 'constructive alignment' (Biggs, 1996), which although described as an idealized 'technical, rational model' of curriculum design divorced from the messy social, political and historical processes we undergo (Oliver, 2002) has nevertheless proved highly influential in informing curriculum design principles (Meyers and Nulty, 2009). If what we want students to get from EU is an ability to draw upon EU law practically, and an ability to engage critically with themes and issues, then we should be careful to ask whether the traditional forms of assessment are appropriate in format and in content. 'Traditional' being the operative word; essays and exams apparently dominate EU assessments and the UKCLE survey produced 'resounding' evidence that 'EU Law lecturers appear to be highly conservative in their utilisation of more innovative forms of assessment'. Of course, here we face issues of resources and time, but we should think about whether the exams and essays we set measure the things we wish students to learn – the ability to think creatively about social implications of aspects of EU law, to reflect on the impact of topical developments, and to spot and back up EU legal argument. It may be that different forms of assessment do the job rather more naturally – dissertations, simulations, portfolios etc. It seems that many institutions provide imaginative formative activities, and it may be possible to extend those into summative processes; for instance, the law school at Bradford has had very positive experiences of using online competitive games and quizzes during the course. Or, it could be that we should draw upon assessment methods we have felt more comfortable introducing in optional modules; in Sheffield, for instance, the optional Current Issues in EU Law module is adventurous in its delivery and assessment with 15 per cent based on a group presentation of results. The students must devise a suitable mode of presentation – past examples include websites, videos and a group portfolio. We could also 'borrow' from assessment methods at postgraduate level; in Bradford, masters students are assessed on a 'press diary' in which they must comment throughout the year on EU issues.

Having established that socio-legal approaches are necessary for a deep understanding of EU law, it is necessary to think about how they might feed into assessments. Portfolios have worked well for this in YLS, allowing students to frame their work around their own experiences and observations. It worked especially well for students who had also taken the clinic module, allowing for some fruitful cross-fertilization, e.g. thinking about public understanding of EU law. A new innovation at Liverpool – a compulsory Law and Social Justice module – could allow for similar joined-up learning. Students follow one of four pathways, which include a practical streetlaw pathway, and may include the putting together of a Citizens' Initiative – an EU construct that emerged from the Lisbon Treaty. EU modules could tap into the imaginative work and assessment conducted in such modules. A socio-legal approach can provide us with a 'reality check', making us address the purpose of studying EU law, and could lead to rather different-looking modules. Admittedly, teaching EU already comes with its own challenges, so I should make the case that a socio-legal approach helps to tackle, rather than serves to multiply, those challenges.

Challenges and 'fit'

Attempts to make the teaching and learning of EU law more socio-legal may face some module-specific challenges. First, there is the problem of the systemic strangeness of the EU, stemming from lack of prior knowledge of what the EU is or does, and a socio-legal approach would leave less space for detail and institutional knowledge to familiarize students with the systems and processes of EU law. Second, the basic concepts in EU law are unfamiliar in a way that terms such as 'provocation' and 'consideration' generally are not. Rather than play with ways of thinking about EU law, the supposed strangeness of it all leads us to think students just want to be taught rather than to learn. Experiences at Leeds University, where some students reacted negatively to a focus on 'economic, social and political perspectives' of integration theory suggests that in some cases a socio-legal approach may serve to further abstract the subject from territory with which students are familiar and comfortable. Third, EU law is often unpopular, possibly related to negative or non-existent media coverage; lack of public engagement means that ways into thinking about the EU and society are not obvious. Shared student experiences also feed this distaste – teaching EU in the third year at YLS means many of our students have 'been warned' by their peers in other institutions who have studied it in the second year. EU is already perceived as 'different enough', so maybe a socio-legal reformulation not echoed elsewhere in the curriculum would be alienating.

When it comes to meeting these challenges, socio-legal methods offer the opportunity to normalize some of the 'strange' aspects of EU law – by looking to real life impacts and accessible studies. Requirements for large amounts of information absorption can be avoided partly through following a themes-led approach, explored in the next section; reducing space for detail can be a positive thing, making more space for thinking. Rather than falling into spoon-feeding teacher-centredness to take the pressure off confused students, that potential confusion is all the more reason to find ways of active learning to aid comprehension. And the EU is not as low profile as we might think – and is certainly media-present enough for students to accept its treatment as a social force/actor/series of actors.

So much for the premise – but the challenges of implementation remain. As the Kingston respondent in the UKCLE survey put it, 'You have to start with the institutions, which is boring', pointing out that 'Everything is novel' to students at the start of the course (Ball and Dadomo, 2010, p. 79). I suppose here is the point where I ask a quick question and dive for cover – *why* do we have to start with the institutions? It surely makes sense to try and crystallize exactly what it is about the institutions that we think is necessary to know in order to feed into the learning objectives of engaging critically with EU law, and to differentiate 'key' from 'background' or analytical from descriptive. Having done that, it is worth thinking about the order – whether those analytical points are the first things students should encounter – or whether we take them 'into' EU law through a more familiar route. As will be seen below, I argue for dismantling the institutions/principles/law pillars of traditional modules, but, even adopting an integrated approach, it is necessary to think honestly about how much 'framework' information is needed to begin with. Some of that framework could potentially be relocated to other modules – basic consciousness of EU institutions feeding easily into English legal systems and public/constitutional and administrative law. This could give a little more freedom to play with the module's style of opening, plus, adopting a touch of EU jargon, it 'mainstreams' the EU, or adopting a more cynical metaphor, inoculates students to avoid significant adverse reactions when exposed to higher dosages later.

Crossing modules has to be done carefully of course, keeping an eye on what is being assessed in each, especially as professional bodies do require us to assess modules separately. But that should not stop us from placing content appropriately. Of particular interest over the next few years will be the developing Graduate Diploma in Law course at Sheffield, in which the EU content is to be divided up and delivered entirely through other modules. It is a bold move with a clear message about the role and place of EU law as bound up with, rather than packaged up separately from, national law. However, the suggestion here is to retain the space a module gives for EU-related socio-legal issues, while setting the thematic scene a bit earlier, and normalizing basic structures and principles, through introduction/mentions within other modules. At York we have as much as possible linked up the teaching of EU with Public Law 2, as we find that it is much easier to set authentic problems when they involve integrated modules. It has made clear the inter-related nature of the European and domestic legal systems and also stressed common themes about state responsibility and subjecthood/citizenship.

The belief that institutions are incompatible with socio-legal approaches should seem all the more misguided when we consider how amenable to socio-legalism the study of UK institutions has proven – whether considering judicial perspectives through feminist drafting exercises (Hunter et al., 2010), or critiquing balances of power by analysing immigration policy debates, or assessing the responsibilities of the state through a review of qualitative studies of applicants declaring themselves homeless (Fitzpatrick, 2000). We can invite students to look behind EU judgments and legislation in similar ways – all the more so as it is a continually growing and relatively weakly harvested field. There is plenty of inspiration from existing academic work in, for example, the role of nationality-related interests, or apparent personal ideological preferences amongst advocates-general and judges (Cohen, 2008), but there remain genuine opportunities for undergraduates to demonstrate original insight. There is no reason not to adopt similar methods in the context of EU institutions – investigating the relationship between national influence and gross domestic product for instance; considering the possible effects of the gender imbalance of, for example, the European Commission (which has now had 11 presidents, all male) on its work – such study could draw upon Kenney's work with regard to the gender imbalance in the European Court of Justice (ECJ) (Kenney, 2002), who applied the social/legal policy concept of gender mainstreaming to the processes of judicial selection. It is also possible to explore questions of power balance by tracking discrim-ination policy debates; Beger's application of queer theory to two key ECJ cases provides an example of the Europeanization of law-based socio-political theory (Beger, 2000).

Negative or absent media coverage – though arguably exaggerated as a problem – can be an obstacle to tapping into students' socio-legal imagina-tions; it contributes to a sense of 'distance' from the subject and a predis-position to beware impenetrable, bureaucratic law. Explicitly negative media coverage is always a good springboard in itself for discussion, so it is really the absence of coverage that creates the biggest barrier, impacting upon possible activities and materials, because there is a reported 'paucity of televisual resources' (Ball and Dadomo, 2010) that lecturers might otherwise use to draw students in. However, many stories with explicit or implicit EU aspects make it into the news, and it is worth catching them and flagging them up. Bradford law school has started having a special session with students in which they must bring along cuttings of stories that they think have EU law implications, which they must talk about and relate to the themes of the course – a session that is described as a bit challenging because of the unpredictable nature of the content. However, the courage to 'let go' of control over the content of the session yielded productive and germane discussion, and it was felt that it would be good to have more detail on each person's piece, and to have this feed more directly into assessment. On the point of student-directed learning, it is worth noting the approach of the Sheffield optional Current Issues in EU Law module, which requires the student group to identify at the outset the current issues on which they wish to focus.

At YLS we started an 'EU in the news' blog, but this foundered because it was not written by students. Anecdotal feedback suggests I chose too cumbersome a VLE (virtual learning environment) blog tool, as it required students to go through a large number of pages to get to it, the interface was poor, and the 'public' nature, meaning all students on the course had access, was too intimidating for would-be contributors. We are experimenting with getting something more quickly accessible up, with separate group blogs, and flagging up early on how, and if, using it might contribute down the line to assessment. It should still help to bring to the fore topical and controversial debates in which EU law plays a part.

EU law is no more impervious to socio-legal methods than other branches of law. Not only is it entirely possible to learn new things and think about them at the same time, such thought and analysis is the only way to really learn, as opposed to passively imbibe. The lofty technicality of modules can be scaled down, and we can embrace that which makes EU law particularly ripe for socio-legalism – its inherent interdisciplinarity.

Replacing pillars with themes and problems

One of the first things colleagues from other institutions seize upon when thinking about the presence of the socio-legal in the EU curriculum is its openness to a variety of disciplinary influences – including political philosophy, political economy and social policy – but this openness tends to be postponed for postgraduate study. In assuming there is some theory-free bare bones of EU that needs to be studied first at undergraduate level, we accidentally treat one account – typically a doctrinally influenced pro-market account – as 'objective'. Instead, it is worth using these interdisciplinary influences to introduce different ways of thinking about EU law early on.

EU law is an amalgam of social and political sciences and law: we are forced to confront law as an instrumental product of economic, political and social objectives, so offering strong and current criticisms of 'ideal' theories such as natural law and moral absolutism (Aggestam, 2008, p. 8). It combines such a variety of perspectives, and its legitimacy bears such different interpretations as to create problems for legal positivists (as argued by Obradovic, 1996, p. 197) and for social, political, psychological and ethnographic theories on the nation state, such as Durkheim's 'organic solidarity' (Durkheim, 1984), Hobbes's requirement of sovereign coercion (Hobbes, 2008), Gellner's 'single conceptual currency' (Gellner, 1983, pp. 32–4) and Hegel's shared national destiny (Hegel, 1991). We also get a different view of emerging constitutionalism than we might otherwise in the UK alone – the dynamic and fluid nature of a constitution being rather easier to comprehend in a young and growing polity (Pernice, 1999; Besselink, 2007).

Possible interdisciplinary themes running throughout EU law include democracy, legitimacy and citizenship, migration, inter-governmental and supra-national power relations, capitalism, public understanding of the EU, liberalism, solidarity and human rights protection. And each of these themes is tied up with *law* procedurally and substantively. A themes-led approach requires the integration of institutions with substantive law, not only from a practical point of view (to understand the factors at play in decision and case-law making) but also from a theoretical point of view, to question the purpose and nature of the substantive law. By bringing institutions, principles and substantive law together, it should be possible to think about the forces feeding into the shape of the law in the UK, for instance thinking about the role of law as an international bartering tool/product of compromise, and thinking about the attitudinal factors underpinning EU judicial decision-making – are the judges really 'inter-judicial' rather than national?

The nature of our course is such that the traditional three-pillar module simply would not work. The module is divided into blocks and each block has to be driven by problems or simulated cases, so a division between substantive/non-substantive is not an option. But I hope that is a good thing; encouraging us to shake off some of the positivism that leads us to trot out lots of legal 'facts' – slotted into institution/principle/law pillars.

Analytical themes draw the institutional and the substantive together. The challenge for us at YLS is to create problems that lead students into asking those deeper questions beyond the applicable substantive law – to use arguments relating to institutions and principles in critiquing that law. For non-PBL syllabi, it should be possible to be a bit more directional and explicit about what the themes entail, and what research is required to engage in a more than superficial way with the law in question. An example theme from the above list and also used at York is legitimacy, which as a socio-legal question combines substantive and institutional components. To tackle this, we recently presented an area of law in which EU developments – ideally in terms of legislation and case law – have had significant impacts upon parallel UK law, and also raises bigger questions about morality and law, such as discrimination law. On questioning the nature and purpose of discrimination law, we moved on to the political element of the law, and the relationship, and sometimes differences of pace, between social developments and changes to the law. In looking at particular cases (e.g. *Coleman* [2008]), we asked students to think about whether there were differences between the principles of judicial interpretation in the ECJ and in domestic courts, and to think about international judicial activism and the role of the ECJ as the 'true' interpreter of European legislation. Then we turned to that legislation itself and thought about the social conditions that led to its creation, and the different inputs different institutions had, and specifically the different inputs the UK had within those institutions, and invited students to assess whether the balance was fair and/or democratic, and then to seriously question what we mean by democratic input. Finally, it all tied back to the subject matter, by questioning whether the area of law is one in which the EU was a legitimate actor.

The problem we used to delve into the democratic deficit question and related legitimacy issues was partly a market access problem, to introduce the concept of and important case law pertaining to the internal market; it involved an outraged Member of the European Parliament (MEP), whose imprecations about the EU in general were used as a trigger to look behind, and question the validity of, the law. It also raised questions about another theme – public understanding of the EU, on which subject students could be invited to find evidence.

Eurostat (European Commission statistics database) and Eurobarometer (European Commission Public Opinion surveys) are very helpful for developing a public-understanding theme – as explored in learning activities below; but so are the students' own opinions (encouraging a bit of reflection and low-level empirical investigation), and the materials they can readily gather from mainstream media. We also encourage students to look at and question the various presentations of reality made by national politicians, and to compare and contrast with positions taken by UK representatives within EU fora. When discussing the political controversy generated by according social rights to migrants, it is possible to draw students towards a variety of qualitative studies on experiences of vulnerable workers (Citizens Advice 2005; Trades Union Congress, 2008), studies on asylum-seeker experiences (Refugee Action, 2006), non-governmental organisations' (NGO) analyses of welfare reform (Citizens Advice, 2008; Shelter, 2011), and quantitative studies into homelessness and nationality (Department for Communities and Local Government, 2008). There are plenty of small-scale investigations students can undertake themselves, for instance, examining European Parliament (EP) debate texts. In the context of discrimination law, if students have seriously considered issues of legitimacy, legitimate objectives, and ideological capture, and other possible arguments for and against EU involvement, it is then interesting – and I daresay disillusioning – to look at EP debates to examine the reasons given by those voting. For instance, Polish MEP (Konrad Szymanski) declared in an EP debate that the proposed measures on extending the framework Equal Treatment Directive to cover services were the product of a European left 'obsessed with pushing through the latest homosexual demands by any possible means' (EP debate, 2009, [14]).

The issue of ideological tension is something that we have only touched upon tangentially at York, but judging by student interest – and given its sheer centrality – it is something we should think about developing more clearly as a theme. Students were very receptive to related materials, and a considerable majority took up the opportunity to do an optional learning activity contrasting Marxist (Peebles, 1997), liberal (Majone, 1993) and 'responsible capitalist' (Maduro, 1999) explanations for the EU's development – and they showed a higher degree of political engagement and social awareness than that with which law students are typically credited (*Legal Week*, 2011).[2] We could think about engaging more with the 'heart of Europe' debate, possibly teaching competition law and social law together, using social-theoretical studies of competition law (Snyder, 1989).

Learning activities

Having set some big-picture outcomes for the module, and replaced the institutional/principle/law pillars with learning-driven themes, it is necessary to explore the mechanics of that learning – things students can actually do, beyond reading/attending passive contact opportunities. Here it is worth thinking about what theories of curriculum design say about tasks. Meyers and Nulty develop five principles of activity design, suggesting that learning activities should be: (a) authentic, real-world and relevant; (b) constructive, sequential and interlinked; (c) engaging students with progressively higher order cognitive processes; (d) aligned with each other and the desired learning outcomes; and (e) challenging, interesting and motivating (Meyers and Nulty, 2009, p. 567).

From these starting-points, it is clear that it would be inadvisable to drop in a couple of token empirical tasks into an otherwise traditional module – to do so would jar with student expectations and raise questions about fit, purpose and assessment. Colleagues at different institutions have tried to adopt some disciplinary diversity in terms of the materials called upon – to use appropriate statistical and policy documents. At York we

---

2　The Law Student survey 2010 on reasons for studying law and influences on choice of firm found that out of 18 factors salary was the most important.

bring Eurostat and Eurobarometer materials and media commentary into plenaries (interactive lectures) early on, to encourage students to think in terms of evidence. For example, we run through the questions used in a Eurobarometer survey on citizenship and identity (European Commission, 2004; 2011), surveying the room and comparing the results with those recorded for different Member States. This also gives us the opportunity to question the nature and validity of the survey, which involves a bit of methodological insight. This also creates a way into thinking about empirical work, as we (perhaps wrongly) do not expect students to have thought about questionnaire formulation, survey sample sizes and issues of self-selecting respondents.

One possible development would be to open up the concept of the survey more explicitly, to ask what sorts of evidence, apart from opinions or popularity, can be gathered when testing areas of EU law. This, of course, requires asking what we would be testing for, opening up questions about effective implementation, margins of discretion, and also effective communication and degrees of agreement between different legal systems. It is possible then to hone in on an example case – such as *Horvath* [2009], in which the legitimacy of the UK maintaining different systems as between Scotland and England was raised (see Cardwell and Hunt, 2010), or *Omega* [2004] in which the differences in cultural salience between Member States of 'dignity' as a human right was at issue (see Nic Shuibhne, 2009) – and to ask what sorts of evidence were, and might have been, compiled. We could also focus on a particular legal issue, such as the status of children in the EU or child migration (Stalford, 2010), and look at how researchers have backed up their suggestions. And, finally, we can look at areas of clear national cultural divergence, such as fundamental rights, or citizenship requirements, or the use of medical criteria in recruitment, and find out what research has been conducted to shed light on them, and why (EU Network of Independent Experts on Disability Discrimination, 2004).

The notion of judicial friction can be explored through methodically examining cases 'as data'. At Bradford, a sample case is used for students to scrutinize the differences in reasoning – and expression – of the court and the advocate-general. It might be possible to go both deeper and broader by also bringing in to play the reasoning of the domestic court and the containment of the issue through careful preliminary reference drafting, and to look at different methods of analysis (e.g. content analysis). Related commentaries could be similarly systematically analysed: Schepel and Wesseling performed a quantitative study on journal articles to argue that European lawyers and commentators contributed to the creation of a formalism in EU law and to identify the norms of that community and the characteristics of the 'legal field' (Schepel and Wesseling, 1997, adapting the legal field concept from Bourdieu, 1994).

Jess Guth of Bradford University suggested that we think about devoting more time to fewer cases to allow more deep thinking; for example, by constructing some of our contact time, such as lectures, around one case each. This could tie into the module objective of being able to use EU law practically, because understanding how domestic courts frame questions is key to persuading them to make the reference in the first place. With a suitably designed case it is then possible to ask students to draft arguments to a domestic court for making a reference, and to produce a draft set of questions, which we do towards the end of the year at York. This also requires them to think about the nature of a preliminary reference, the role of the ECJ, and to do the leg work of actually following the court's guidance on drafting a reference.

Thinking about making references – or just about constructing arguments in a domestic dispute – requires us to emphasize the relevance, rather than the abstraction, of EU law. It can be useful to stress the omnipresence of EU influences, and in this regard an activity which could model as good practice is the earlier mentioned 'bring along a cutting' session at Bradford. Such an activity might take more of a central role in the module, for example, through setting certain stories that the group must then follow during the year, or through allowing students to construct bundles of evidence for and against certain points of view. However, any course that requires empirical data collection to be conducted needs to factor in methods training/self-training. Tammy Hervey noted that in Sheffield's Current Issues in EU Law module many of the students who set themselves empirical projects ended up changing their minds, or failing to put together something convincing, because their projects were too ambitious, or poorly time-scaled. This could be an argument for integrating more empirical work into the curriculum generally and early on (such as activities that encourage desk-based evidence gathering) so that students have more than a passing acquaintance with data collection and analysis and are in a better position to conduct more strongly empirically flavoured work later.

Socio-legal approaches are essential for a deeper, more sophisticated engagement with the practical, as well as the academic, aspects of EU law, and they make the subject infinitely more palatable to students who fear turgid, boring texts. On touching on the role of the EU in employment law, at YLS we try to emphasize social context. An activity about the construction of the concept of pregnancy discrimination steers students to think about surrounding national social norms, to question who was involved in defining them, and to finally go behind the judicial curtain to see whether there was any scientific/well-evidenced reasoning for the limitations attached to the concept. As an exercise in gathering appropriate sociological evidence to back up legal arguments, we invited students individually to assume the role of one of the European Commission's social partners and to draft a response to a real consultation. On reflection, we did not give students enough guidance, they were not provided with a model, and for some it turned more into a creative writing task. It might have worked better as a group exercise, with instructions to first of all explain which social partner was chosen and why, and to include evidence to explain why they felt the partner would adopt the position given. However, as to the actual content, many students showed a degree of investigative prowess in producing evidence supporting the argument presented.

Simulation in general, not just in written exercises, is a useful avenue for placing the legal into social context. PBL has some of that effect on a small scale. But bigger simulations can work. We have explored some different simulations, including a mock judicial review (inviting the drafting of preliminary references) and constitutional debates. Samantha Currie at Liverpool suggested that students could demonstrate understanding of the relevance and impact of EU law through some form of communication/dissemination exercise, whereby the target audience could be a national NGO. This could build on an idea already trialled at Liverpool – a piece of coursework that invited students to choose one of seven scenarios on which to write a memo about an EU law issue. The memo task apparently stirred up concern and confusion. To avoid that, the activity would be group-based, possibly drawing upon authentic situations and identifying real interested parties, and in a PBL-like way ensure that research objectives were set and divided up.

A large simulation exercise has been used and documented (Zeff, 2003) in the US for teaching about the EU, with a view to giving students some insight into the different social variables influencing individual actors/Member State representatives. It is described as a simulated European Council, with different students adopting the position of different Member States. This general premise is interesting and could be developed in a number of ways. Rather than devoting the course or a substantial chunk of it to the simulation itself (which is the case in the original, with the participants presented with a particular scenario and invited to debate/negotiate on it), it could form a background, or something drawn into the course at various points, through following real EU news and asking for comments from appropriate representatives during plenaries/lectures. Students might from the start be individually, or in groups, assigned to represent a particular country, or institution, or Directorate General (of the European Commission). Having allocated interests, it would then be possible to require students to address given tasks or issues with that interest in mind, as individuals or as united groups, or to ask them to interact with other representatives in negotiation scenarios, or to have their role as representative to be more of a lens to aid any reflective or own-initiative tasks.

The interactive element is pretty seductive, implying as it does an element of competition. Another trend noted in Bradford was for enthusiasm for certain online, non-assessed formative tasks, because of their competitive element. It risks being resource-heavy and would need careful managing to avoid it losing direction, or sprawling across available contact time. In systems that allow for regular small group work, such as PBL, it might be possible to carve out sections of those sessions for reviews and updates on the simulation; it is of course worth considering whether some form of rotation of roles to allow students to adopt different perspectives is worthwhile. If there were some element of work-swapping or interaction, then the nature of the task would need closer control than simply following the latest real news, so that there was some common background task. Jess Guth suggested that this could be broken into clear stages – stepping stones – of smaller tasks or pieces of information released online. The UKCLE survey and my discussions with colleagues point to some untapped potential with regard to electronic resources, which have typically been exploited by EU teachers for optional 'extra' non-assessed elements, but which could be used to a greater extent in terms of delivering course content/providing the means for assessed work. Colleagues have shown an interest in the idea of incrementally releasing the details of a problem or task, with students having to complete each level before the next details are released. There is an element of this idea in the Sheffield curriculum, which sets an umbrella problem at the outset of the course, with students being invited to work on it during the year as different aspects are covered. It is possible to borrow the creative drive of that practice, and build on it, using technology to tie the release of related information to work performed, and creating online group work space. Given timetable constraints, it could be that the best way to enable group interaction is to do it online. In terms of what the overall background task/issue might be, an ideal subject might be a pending accession from a new Member State – tapping into all the right big-picture questions.

Conclusion

EU law is essentially a very socio-legal subject. As Cohen puts it, 'European integration is an acid test for the sociology of law' (Cohen, 2008, 'Introduction'). Rather than defensively assert its law credentials through heavy doctrinal, case-dense courses, we should embrace its interdisciplinary nature in the interests of meaningful study of case law, of giving students a way in to fascinating academic studies, and of helping students handle EU law practically as lawyers. For students who have not had much empirical exposure, it offers an ideal opportunity to think about social context, to handle empirical data (survey results, demographic data, electoral trends etc), to engage with studies that employ a variety of methodologies, and to take informed positions on issues subject to speculative rhetoric. It just does not make sense for such a socially charged subject to be distilled into a highly concentrated concoction of facts. Instead, this piece has argued for the dismantling of the three-pillar module, while recognizing the challenges this creates in terms of onus upon students to fill in the gaps if we are not explaining everything, and admitting that perhaps they need a bit more support than we have yet managed. A theme-led module allows for the consideration of fused institutional, principle-based and substantive elements, and, depending on the themes chosen, allows for an emphasis on important socio-legal questions. Learning activities will ideally help develop key socio-legal skills – cultivating a mentality of problem-identifying, norm-querying, and evidence-gathering.

There is certainly scope for significantly experimental module structures, for instance, tethering to a single learning activity subject to longitudinal review during the year, or adopting wholescale simulation projects, or even structuring the course round a few core case studies. However, given institutional and logistical constraints, it makes sense to think about less challenging ways to capture some of that spirit – through activities that serve big-picture objectives and that encourage the hunting and probing of constructs and concepts, rather than the consumption of 'facts' on a plate.

Cases cited

Case C-303/06 Coleman [2008] ECR I-5603
Case C-428/07 Horvath [2009] ECR I-06355
Case C-36/02 Omega [2004] ECR I-09609

References

Aggestam, L (2008) 'Ethical power Europe?' 84 *International Affairs* 1
Ball, R and C Dadomo (2010) 'UKCLE law subject survey: European Union law', http://eprints.uwe.ac.uk/14747/ (last accessed 30 August 2011)
Beger, N (2009) 'Queer readings of Europe: gender identity, sexual orientation and the (im)potency of rights politics at the European Court of Justice' 9 *Social and Legal Studies* 249
Besselink, L (2008) 'The notion and nature of the European Constitution after the Reform Treaty' Social Science Research Network paper, http://papers.ssrn.com/sol3/papers.cfm?abstract_id=1086189 (last accessed 10 December 2011)

Biggs, J (1996) 'Enhancing teaching through constructive alignment' 32 *Higher Education* 347

Bourdieu, P (1994) 'Rethinking the state, genesis and structure of the bureaucratic field' 12 *Sociological Theory* 1

Cardwell, M and J Hunt (2010) 'Public rights of way and level playing fields' 12(4) *Environmental Law Review* 291–300

Citizens Advice (2005) *Home from Home? Experiences of Migrant Workers in Rural Parts of the UK, and the Impact on Local Service Providers*, CAB Evidence Briefing (London: Citizens Advice)

Citizens Advice (2008) *No One Written Off: Reforming Welfare to Reward Responsibility*, Response to the Welfare Reform Green Paper (London: Citizens Advice)

Cohen, A (2008) 'Scarlet robes, dark suits: the social recruitment of the European Court of Justice' EUI Working Papers RACAS 2008/35

Department for Communities and Local Government (2008) *Rough Sleeping 10 Years On: From the Streets to Independent Living and Opportunity* (London: Communities and Local Government Publications)

Durkheim, E (1984) *The Division of Labour in Society* (London: Macmillan)

EU Network of Independent Experts on Disability Discrimination (2004) 'Baseline study: disability discrimination law in the EU Member States', www.pedz.uni-mannheim.de/daten/edz-ath/gdem/04/synfinquinn.pdf (last accessed 10 December 2011)

European Commission *Public Opinion: Eurobarometer surveys*, http://ec.europa.eu/public_opinion/index_en.htm (last accessed 21 December 2011)

European Commission (2011) Eurobarometer 75 'Public opinion in the European Union', http://ec.europa.eu/public_opinion/archives/eb/eb75/eb75_en.pdf (last accessed 21 December 2011)

European Commission (2004) Eurobarometer 62 'Public opinion in the European Union', http://ec.europa.eu/public_opinion/archives/eb/eb62/eb62_en.htm (last accessed 21 December 2011)

European Parliament debate, 2009 A6–0149/2009; 1 April 2009, Brussels

Gellner, E (1983) *Nations and Nationalism* (New York: Cornell University Press)

Fitzpatrick, B and C Hunter (2011) 'Problem-based learning in a new law school' 22 *UKLCLE Newsletter*

Fitzpatrick, S (2000) *Young Homeless People* (Basingstoke: Macmillan)

Hegel, G W F (1991) 'Elements of the philosophy of right' (Cambridge: Cambridge University Press)

Hobbes, T (2008) *Leviathan* (Oxford: Oxford University Press)

Hunter, R, C McGlynn and E Rackley (eds) (2010) *Feminist Judgments: From Theory to Practice* (Oxford: Hart Publishing)

Kenney, S (2002) 'Breaking the silence: gender mainstreaming and the composition of the European Court of Justice' 10 *Feminist Legal Studies* 257

Law Society and General Council of the Bar (1999) *A Joint Statement Issued by the Law Society and the General Council of the Bar on the Completion of the Initial or Academic Stage of Training by Obtaining an Undergraduate Degree* (London: Law Society)

Legal Week (2011) 'Law Student Report 2010' (London: Incisive Media)

Majone, G (1993) 'The EC between social policy and social regulation' 31 *Journal of Common Market Studies* 153

Meyers, N and D Nulty (2009) 'How to use (five) curriculum design principles to align authentic learning environments, assessment, students' approaches to thinking and learning outcomes' 34 *Assessment and Evaluation in Higher Education* 565

Nic Shuibhne, N (2009) 'Margins of appreciation: national values, fundamental rights and EC free movement law' 34 *European Law Review* 230

Obradovic, D (1996) 'Policy legitimacy and the European Union' 34 *Journal of Common Market Studies* 191

Oliver, M (2002) 'Creativity and the curriculum design process: a case study' Higher Education Academy Paper (York: Higher Education Academy)

Peebles, G (1997) ' "A very Eden of the innate rights of man"? A Marxist look at the European Union treaties and case law' 22 *Law and Social Inquiry* 581

Pernice, I (1999) 'Multilevel constitutionalism and the Treaty of Amsterdam: European constitution making revisited?' 36 *Common Market Law Review* 703

Poiares Maduro, M (1999) 'We still have not found what we have been looking for. The balance between economic freedom and social rights in the European Union' Working Paper 4/99 (Lisbon: Faculdade de Direito, Universidade Nova de Lisboa)

Refugee Action (2006) *The Destitution Trap: Asylum's Unsold Story*, findings from 125 interviews (London: Refugee Action)

Schepel, H and R Wesseling (1997) 'The legal community: judges, lawyers, officials and clerks in the writing of Europe' 3 *European Law Journal* 165

Shelter (2011) *The Impact of Welfare Reform Bill measures on affordability for low income private renting families*, Research Report (London: Shelter)

Snyder, F (1989) 'Ideologies of competition in European Community law' 52 *Modern Law Review* 149

Stalford, H (2010) 'EU law and children's rights: a case study of EU family law' 10 *Contemporary Issues in Law* 1

Trades Union Congress (2008) *Hard Work, Hidden Lives*, Full Report of the Commission on Vulnerable Employment (London: Trades Union Congress)

Zeff, E (2003) 'Negotiating in the European Council: a model European Union format for individual classes' 4 *International Studies Perspectives* 265

Index

The manufacturer's authorised representative in the EU is Springer
Nature Customer Service Centre GmbH, Europaplatz 3, 69115 Heidelberg,
Germany. If you have any concerns regarding our products, please
contact ProductSafety@springernature.com

Printed and bound by CPI Group (UK) Ltd, Croydon, CR0 4YY
29/04/2026
02099450-0016